Building and Sustaining
Learning Communities

Building and Sustaining Learning Communities

The Syracuse University Experience

Sandra N. Hurd
Syracuse University

Ruth Federman Stein
Syracuse University

Foreword by Vincent Tinto

ANKER PUBLISHING COMPANY, INC.
Bolton, Massachusetts

BUILDING AND SUSTAINING LEARNING COMMUNITIES
The Syracuse University Experience

ISBN 1-882982-68-1

Composition by Lyn Rodger, Deerfoot Studios
Cover design by Christina Williams, Aurora Design Studio

Anker Publishing Company, Inc.
176 Ballville Road
P. O. Box 249
Bolton, MA 01740-0249 USA

www.ankerpub.com

About the Authors

Sandra N. Hurd, professor of law and public policy, currently serves as interim dean of the Martin J. Whitman School of Management at Syracuse University (SU). She participated in the development of the School of Management's freshman course in 1991 and served as its director from 1996–2002. Professor Hurd was the first coordinator of the Management Learning Community and now serves as SU's director of learning communities for academic affairs. Her primary area of research is international product liability and safety. Professor Hurd's publications appear in such journals as the *American Business Law Journal,* the *Journal of Product Liability,* the *Journal of Legislation,* the *International Journal of Technology Management,* the *Maryland Journal of International Law and Trade,* and the *University of Pennsylvania Journal of International Economic Law.* She is coauthor, with Ruth Federman Stein, of *Using Student Teams in the Classroom* (2000). Professor Hurd was named a master teacher by the Academy of Legal Studies in Business and is a member of the Syracuse University Gateway Fellowship. Recent awards include the School of Management Award for Excellence in Teaching (2000), the Tankersley Leadership Award (2001), and the Chancellor's Citation for Outstanding Contributions to the University's Academic Programs (2001).

Ruth Federman Stein is a teaching consultant at the Center for Support of Teaching and Learning at Syracuse University. Her work includes organizing Focus on Teaching sessions for faculty, helping to coordinate Syracuse University's Vision Fund program, conducting teaching workshops, and teaching consultation. She also serves as a visiting faculty consultant for Syracuse University's Project Advance program. Dr. Stein coauthored *Using Student Teams in the Classroom* (2000) and is a past president of the Board of Education in Syracuse, New York. She currently is serving as the Mayor's Education Advocate.

Contents

Part II: Learning Community Profiles

Foreword

Research has more than amply demonstrated that involvement is a key to student success in higher education. Simply put, the more students are involved with faculty, staff, and peers, the more likely they are to learn and persist. But while colleges and universities have paid a good deal of attention to student social involvement (e.g., clubs, extracurricular activities), they have done less to engage students academically, even within the classroom. It is still the case that too many students, especially first-year students, encounter learning as isolated learners whose learning is separated from one another. As importantly, they typically sit passively in classrooms unable to engage actively with others in the construction of knowledge. Fortunately that is beginning to change. Syracuse University is among a still small but growing number of universities that have taken on the challenge of student involvement in learning by initiating a number of endeavors that involve faculty, administrators, and student affairs professionals across the campus. One such endeavor is captured by the university's use of learning communities. This book provides a case study of how learning communities evolved at Syracuse University. It is a significant contribution to the learning community literature because it not only gives candid portrayals of how a variety of learning communities evolved but also discusses much of the scaffolding that is essential for creating learning communities within a large university.

Profiles of individual learning communities reveal how Syracuse University has adapted learning communities to serve a wide range of students and academic themes. These range from discipline-based linked course learning communities open only to first-year students enrolled in the school, such as the Management Learning Community, to themed learning communities open to undergraduates from throughout the university as well as the SUNY College of Environmental Science and Forestry, such as Arts Adventure. As we proceed to further enrich the learning experiences of our students, one thing is clear, namely that we all learn better when we learn together. Syracuse

University's efforts to expand learning communities are one important way in which we seek to build a wide variety of educational communities in which all students become actively involved in learning.

Vincent Tinto
Distinguished University Professor
Chair, Higher Education Program
Syracuse University

Preface

Developing learning communities involves considerable collaboration between the academic and student affairs divisions of a university at multiple levels, and one cannot underestimate the importance of these partnerships. This book attempts to give a candid description of how faculty and staff in one large research university have worked and struggled together to build a variety of learning communities.

ORGANIZATION OF THE BOOK

The chapters in Part I of this book first provide an introduction to the history and theory underlying learning communities and the research that has been conducted to understand the impact they have on student success. They also describe the institutional impetus for learning communities at Syracuse University and how the program evolved. Part I additionally discusses the importance of and specific strategies for relationship building in creating a learning community program and examines the importance of forging genuine academic affairs–student affairs partnerships to promote integrated learning experiences. Other chapters address critical issues imbedded in structuring learning communities that include a writing course, illustrate a successful method for developing an integrated linked-course learning community curriculum, and describe the complexity of assessing a large, diverse learning community program. The final chapter in Part I examines several of the institutional challenges Syracuse University must face as the learning community program grows.

Part II consists of individual profiles of a cross-section of learning communities at Syracuse University. These particular communities represent the variety of structures and pedagogies developed by faculty and staff to meet the particular needs of their discipline or intellectual interest as well as students' needs and interests. In these profiles, the authors share their successes and failures in designing, implementing, and evaluating their learning community. A final chapter, "Lessons Learned," summarizes some general observations and key lessons learned as learning communities were established at Syracuse University.

The bibliography is more than a listing of works cited: It is an extensive learning community bibliography that is a comprehensive resource for those interested in learning communities.

Sandra N. Hurd
Ruth Federman Stein

Acknowledgments

Only a few weeks after our book *Using Student Teams in the Classroom: A Faculty Guide* (2000) was published, Susan Anker contacted us to inquire if we would be interested in writing a book on learning communities. Since Sandra N. Hurd is Syracuse University's director of learning communities for academic affairs, how could we resist writing about our learning community experiences and sharing what we've learned with others? Syracuse's learning communities are the culmination of hard work, dedication, and commitment by many, many faculty, staff, administrators, and students. This book is a tribute to all of them. We are also deeply indebted to the staff and faculty who took time out of their already very busy lives to share their experiences and perspectives in the chapters they contributed.

PART I

Learning Community Research, Theory, and Practice

1

Learning Communities: An Overview

Ruth Federman Stein

INTRODUCTION

During the transition to the college environment, entering students confront significant challenges. Students face academic hurdles as they adjust to the expectations of their professors, demands of college assignments, heavier study requirements, and midterm academic pressures. While tackling these new academic challenges, on-campus students are simultaneously learning to share a room or suite with roommates and trying to balance their social and academic lives. Other adjustments may include meeting more diverse groups of students, large classes, spread out campuses, and becoming aware of and learning to use a large assortment of resources. Many students live at a distance from their familiar home environments or commute to a very different setting. Community college students generally live off-campus and work part-time or full-time jobs, often juggling families as well. Learning communities are one strategy to create a more integrated college experience that has proved successful in alleviating the sense of fragmentation and lack of cohesiveness that students in two-year or four-year schools may experience as they adjust to college life.

WHAT IS A LEARNING COMMUNITY?

Even though there is no single accepted definition of a learning community, learning communities do share certain characteristics and intentions, including creation of an environment in which more intellectual interaction will occur among students and with the faculty and staff with whom students interact.

Residential Learning Communities

Residential learning communities are designed to arrange student time and space to form a community. Students live together, generally on one or two floors of a residence hall, and they also take one or more courses together. Residence life and student affairs staff coordinate residence hall activities in relation to the course or courses that the students are taking and the theme of the learning community, thus making connections for the students between in-class and out-of-class experiences. For example, in the Arts Adventure Learning Community, students take two classes together and attend various cultural programs as a group. In the residence hall, programming is related to the arts, for example, a speaker on the "Three P's" (see Chapter 15).

Non-Residential Learning Communities

Non-residential learning communities make connections for students in various ways through courses. Small groups of students may be linked together in several classes or recitation sections of larger classes. This type of group may be led by a peer instructor. Sometimes courses are paired, and faculty coordinate the syllabi and assignments of the paired courses, or students may participate in a team-taught learning community in which courses are tied together by a common theme. Because students are linked together in these classes or groups, they evolve naturally into learning communities as they interact with each other and have shared experiences.

HISTORY: THE BEGINNINGS OF LEARNING COMMUNITIES

John Dewey (1916) wrote:

> *The development within the young of the attitudes and dispositions necessary to the continuous and progressive life of a society cannot take place by direct conveyance of beliefs, emotions, and knowledge. It takes place through the intermediary of the environment (p. 26).*

Recent research still supports the ideas that Dewey advanced many years ago. Colleges and universities do try to develop environments that foster student learning, but too often learning is fragmented, and student lives outside the classroom are disconnected from the learning environment. Students take many individual, self-contained courses to meet basic requirements, but they do not see how the courses may be related, especially if they are not connected with their majors. Tussman (1969) described the dilemma of students taking three, four, or five courses during a semester with "no attempt at horizontal integration." Each professor has a certain percentage of a student's time, but "no teacher is in a position to be responsible for...the student's total educational situation (p. 6)."

To address these concerns, Tussman developed the Experimental Program at Berkeley based on concepts from Alexander Meiklejohn's Experimental College at the University of Wisconsin (1927–1932). The Experimental College was a college within a college that enrolled up to 155 male students. Faculty and students shared living quarters, and the college had its own rules. Instead of semesters, there were six-week modules, and there were no conventional grades. The two-year program was organized around "civilization," to address Meiklejohn's concern with the lack of a philosophical focus in a curriculum filled with elective courses. During the first year, it focused on Greek civilization and, for the second year, on the United States (Education, 2000). The Experimental College was closed in 1932, ostensibly because of the Depression. However, equally responsible for its demise was its lack of popularity on campus: Allowing a group of students to have its own policies upset campus politics. The program was reinstituted in 1948 and has existed since then in various forms; it still stresses a broad yet integrated education (Board of Regents, 2003).

The Experimental Program at Berkeley, which lasted for four years (1965–1969), was designed for lower division students by Tussman, a former student of Meiklejohn. The curriculum was not organized into discrete courses or disciplines; rather, it incorporated reading, writing, and discussion in the social sciences and humanities. The core of the program focused on readings from certain periods in Western civilization, and a few broad questions framed each semester's studies. The program had its own house, which was used for faculty offices and seminars, as well as for informal student activities. Because Tussman saw education as a social enterprise, the program tried to create a learning community to engage in a common intellectual life.

Tussman's work inspired faculty in Washington state, who, in 1970, were planning a new state school: The Evergreen State College (Gabelnick et al., 1990). Evergreen's curriculum is built around "coordinated studies" programs that may last anywhere from a quarter to a full year, taught by faculty teams and organized around interdisciplinary themes (p. 14). Barbara Leigh Smith (1991) describes how Evergreen faculty redesigned the entire curriculum with their colleagues and cites two examples: "Matter and Motion"—a full year integrated program in physics, chemistry, mathematics, and laboratory computing—and "The Paradox of Progress"—a program that probes Western civilization, emphasizing great books in the sciences, social sciences, and the humanities.

At the same time, the idea of learning communities was also developing in the eastern part of the country. Patrick Hill adapted the learning community concept to a research institution, SUNY Stony Brook, and Roberta Matthews began a learning community program at La Guardia Community College. East and west merged in 1983 when Patrick Hill became provost at Evergreen, and in 1985 the movement expanded further when the Washington Center for Undergraduate Education at Evergreen was established.

Based on the initial work of these people and institutions, enthusiasm for establishing learning communities has grown, and learning communities have been expanding. For example, beginning in the 1980s, Seattle Central Community College developed a large number of team taught interdisciplinary learning community programs, and courses from all disciplines have been integrated into them (Bystrom, 1999), and in the 1990s, Temple University in Philadelphia began developing its learning communities program, to mention just two examples.

Residential learning communities that are linked to academic programs or courses have also been evolving. As large research universities developed, the practice of faculty living in the residence halls declined. Student affairs divisions replaced the faculty in the residence hall, unintentionally creating a divide between students' academic and cocurricular lives. Residential learning communities are one way to meet the need to support student development in a holistic way.

RESEARCH AND THEORY

In an address at the Inaugural Conference on Learning Communities, Patrick Hill (1985) stated that learning communities respond to and help to alleviate a number of educational problems. He argues that learning communities increase the intellectual interaction between faculty and students, as well as among students, and reduce the number of seemingly isolated courses that students take, especially outside their majors. Learning communities help students grasp not only the complexity of today's problems but also help them understand how various disciplines overlap to solve complex problems. Because students become more connected through their studies and interactions in learning communities, college retention rates increase.

Research supports Hill's assertions that learning communities address many of higher education's problems. Astin (1985) developed his theory of involvement, that "students learn by becoming involved," (p. 133) based on his assessment of practices in higher education in an effort to determine the most effective methods for educating students. The term *student involvement* refers to the "amount of physical and psychological energy that the student devotes to the academic experience" (p. 134). Astin's theory of involvement is based on his findings from a longitudinal study of college dropouts published in 1985. He concluded that every factor that affected student persistence in college could be related to the involvement concept (p. 144). Students who lived in a campus residence, students who joined social fraternities or sororities, students who participated in extracurricular activities of almost any type, and students who held part-time jobs on campus were more likely to stay in college.

Subsequent learning community research builds on Astin's theory of involvement. Through learning communities, students are formed into cohorts that may take two or more classes together, thus creating natural student groups that build student academic involvement. Additionally, residential learning communities try to increase student involvement by creating residential experiences that connect to the classroom.

Boyer's study, *College: The Undergraduate Experience in America* (1987), found a number of areas of "tension," including "a great separation, sometimes to the point of isolation, between academic and social life on campus. Colleges like to speak of the campus as community, and yet what is being learned in most residence halls today has little connection to the classrooms" (p. 5). Based on the research of Arthur Chickering, Boyer recommends that educational programs "should be developed in the residence halls not only to foster a sense of community, but also to provide an enriching influence" (p. 207). Many learning communities try to build residence hall activities that enhance the classroom experience to provide a more focused and intellectual experience for students. One technique that many learning communities use to promote intellectual engagement is to hold certain classes late in the afternoon, just before dinner, to allow students the opportunity to continue class discussion as they walk together to the dining hall and eat dinner.

Tinto's research into the college classroom as the focus of the educational experience for students also relates to the concerns that Hill raised. In a major study of the Coordinated Studies Programs at Seattle Central Community College, Tinto (1997) asked two questions: "Does the program make a difference?" And, "If it does, how does it do so?" First-year students in the traditional curriculum and in the Coordinated Studies program were sampled at the beginning and end of a fall quarter. Then a qualitative study was done to determine "how participation in a collaborative learning program influenced students' learning experiences and how those learning experiences fit in with their broader experiences as first-year students" (p. 605).

The study's results support basic learning community theory in four ways. First, the study found that students in a learning group were better able to connect their academic and social needs because class groups often met informally for meetings and study groups after class. Students' social and academic lives thus became naturally connected. Second, the collaborative nature of the curriculum enriched the student experience because students learned from more diverse voices, rather than the perspective of one faculty member. Students had class activities that not only tied their own experiences to the course, but also helped them become aware of other viewpoints. Third, students in learning communities had higher GPA's. More importantly, students felt that they gained more intellectually and that the quality of their learning was more profound in the learning community setting. Fourth, the studies found that even in nonresidential schools, such as a community college, students became more involved and had higher GPA's when they were in a collaborative learning situation.

WHY ESTABLISH LEARNING COMMUNITIES?

Learning communities address important educational concerns. Obviously, small informal learning communities, perhaps best described by the term *student teams*, can be established within the classroom (Stein & Hurd, 2000). But the scope of learning communities goes far beyond the classroom team that may be established by faculty in a particular course. Learning communities in the context of this book are established within the institutional setting by intentionally redesigning curricula and frequently the residential life component to build a community of learners among students and faculty. On campuses, both large and small, learning communities are one way of responding to a number of concerns.

To Promote Intellectual Communication Between Faculty and Students

The lack of intellectual communication between faculty and students as well as among students is a basic concern. In many classes, faculty see students only during lectures, particularly if students never come in during office hours. Additionally, students often have no opportunity to interact with other students in the class because the class is set up with no time for discussion or the exchange of ideas.

To Make Connections Among Courses

Another concern that is voiced by students is the lack of a relationship or connection among courses, especially courses that are outside students' majors. For example, at a Gateway Student Forum at Syracuse University, a group of students expressed their view that the curriculum had too many requirements and that many students take courses simply to fulfill core requirements. "Courses should be geared toward stimulating critical thinking among students who are taking the course," not just fulfilling a requirement (Stein, 1999). This problem is exacerbated when students do not think about looking for courses that connect when selecting courses, and faculty do not help the students make connections among the courses that they are taking.

To Bridge Students' Academic and Social Worlds

Another issue, especially for first-year students, is bridging their academic and social worlds. In another Gateway Student Forum held in 2000, students reported that "they were searching for people to help bring the two worlds together....Having a network of people (friends and professors) makes it easier for students to build bridges between their academic and social worlds" (Stein, 2000).

To Increase Student Retention

Student retention is another serious issue that learning communities address. Cuseo (1991) cites several studies that show that more than half of the students who leave college do so during their first year. Research cited by Gabelnick, MacGregor, Matthews, and Smith (1992) points out that "students enrolling in learning community programs generally exhibit higher retention: it is not atypical for a learning community group to exhibit a 90–100 percent rate of completion in the program" (p. 117). These students also continue to persist in college "to a higher extent than students not enrolling in learning communities" (p. 117).

To Enrich Residential Life for Staff

One benefit of learning communities that may be overlooked is the effect on residence life staff. Learning communities offer residence life staff different kinds of experiences in working with students that round out their skills and improve their marketability in the residence life field.

To Give Faculty New Perspectives

Faculty, too, gain benefits from teaching in learning communities. If they teach in linked courses, the planning with other faculty gives them new perspectives on their discipline and how they present it to students. Traditionally faculty work and teach in isolation, sharing their work—generally research—at conferences or through publication. Learning communities with linked courses encourage collaboration in terms of teaching. Faculty meet on a regular basis to plan their courses and to discuss where their courses have commonality. They work together to build connections among their courses, so that each class supports and enhances the other classes in the learning community (see Chapter 5). Teaching in learning communities also provides opportunities for faculty to carry out research and develop presentations and publications. Evenbeck, Jackson, and McGrew (1999) describe the labor involved as well as the benefits of teaching in learning communities and conclude that the difficulty of finding time to work and plan is offset by the benefits. According to Evenbeck et al., collaboration involved in developing learning communities "creates a new sense of collegiality among faculty." As faculty rethink their courses, they approach their work from a different perspective. Their focus changes to "student learning rather than subject-matter teaching" (p. 55). Instead of lecturing to students, for example, faculty may design activities that actively engage the students with course concepts. The learning environment thus becomes learning- or student-centered, and faculty begin to approach teaching quite differently.

To Promote Greater Interaction and Its Attendant Benefits

Finally, integrating students' academic and social lives in a residential learning community allows greater interaction between students as well as among students, faculty, and staff. The benefits that result include enhanced intellectual and social development; improved GPA, involvement, and satisfaction; and increased persistence to graduation. Tinto (1997) suggests that enhanced intellectual and social development may continue over the course of the first year in college, and possibly the entire student career. Learning communities that do not include a residential component are also beneficial for students because their connected courses enable them to feel attached to a group of students.

CHALLENGES

If the benefits of establishing learning communities are so clear and obvious, what are the challenges in establishing them?

Philosophical Issues

First, there are some philosophical issues to confront. In some disciplines at Syracuse University, for example drama or architecture, faculty believe that their students automatically form learning communities because they spend so much time working together in their first-year classes. Rather than formalizing this arrangement in a residential learning community, these faculty prefer to have their students mix with a range of students from different majors in their residence halls. Another related concern is raised by those who think learning communities may insulate students from the broader community, exposing students to less diversity by clustering them based on interests or academic disciplines. This issue is of special concern to some in disciplines that are gender imbalanced, such as education and information management and technology.

Practical Issues
One must deal also with the practical issues—the nuts and bolts of organizing learning communities. Establishing a learning community requires careful planning and work. Whether the impetus for establishing learning communities comes from a school's administrators, from faculty, or from residence life, the work involved in creating learning communities entails much communication and negotiation among various campus entities. It requires designing the particular learning community model that is going to be used, recruiting faculty to create the courses and teach in the learning community, developing the residence life component if it is a residential learning community, recruiting students for the learning community, and assessing the learning community. After the first iteration of the learning community, its design needs to be reviewed and revised based on the results of the assessment. These summary steps are merely a hint of what goes into planning a learning community, but no matter what type of learning community one wants to plan, these philosophical and logistical issues must be confronted.

ORGANIZING LEARNING COMMUNITIES

Because so much depends on the context, there is no single way to organize learning communities and no simple formula for creating successful learning communities. Each campus that organizes learning communities establishes communities that are unique to its campus culture. Each campus must develop its own vision of what a successful learning community is like. Even within one campus, each learning community may function quite differently. Just as there is no single set of criteria for establishing successful learning communities, neither is there agreement on a single, clear-cut definition of learning communities. Some define learning communities by course/academic structure. Some define them as linked courses (Gabelnick et al, 1990, p. 5). Others define them more broadly as communities that may be organized along "curricular lines, common career interests, avocational interests, residential living areas, and so on" (Astin, 1985, p. 161).

Syracuse University, for example, has learning communities that are variations on the models that Gabelnick (1990) and Goodsell Love and Tokuno (1999) describe. Residential learning communities are "partnerships between Academic Affairs and Student Affairs that intentionally integrate academic components and cocurricular experiences to promote, enhance, and support students' academic, personal, and professional growth and success" (Office of Learning Communities, 2000). Non-residential learning communities are "partnerships between/among faculty that intentionally integrate academic courses and experiences to promote, enhance, and support students' academic, personal, and professional growth and success" (Office of Learning Communities, 2000).

LEARNING COMMUNITY MODELS

In 1990, Gabelnick, MacGregor, Matthews, and Smith described five learning community models. Since then, they and others have simplified the number of models (Goodsell Love & Tokuno, 1999; Shapiro & Levine, 1999). Each model is quite flexible and may have various configurations. Indeed, each institution that initiates learning communities tends to put its own particular imprint on the model, based on its own structure, curricula, and student profiles. The traditional learning community models are described in a general way here.

Students in Large Classes

Curricular Design
Small groups of students can be linked together in several courses as subsets of larger classes. Often known as a Freshman Interest Group (FIG), this model gives freshmen a support system for large classes. Each FIG typically has a one-credit seminar led by an upperclass student attached to it.

Faculty Responsibilities
This model does not contemplate faculty having to change the way they do their work. Faculty do not have to coordinate their syllabi or do any co-planning with the faculty from the other linked courses although some faculty choose to do so. They may meet with the subset(s) of students at the begin-

ning of the semester to welcome the students and introduce themselves and their courses.

Peer Leadership Possibilities
A peer advisor meets with the group at the beginning of the semester and then continues to meet with the group on a weekly basis to discuss adjustment issues, campus resources, study groups, or just to talk about student concerns and issues. The peer advisor also draws the intellectual connections among the academic courses in the FIG.

Curricular Possibilities
Activities are organized by the peer leader and could involve having dinner together, attending a cultural event, or having an informal get-together.

Paired or Clustered Courses
Curricular Design
Two courses are paired, and the same group of students takes both classes. In a clustered model, three or four courses are linked together, and the same group of students takes the entire cluster. Often the courses have a common theme.

Faculty Responsibilities
In paired classes, faculty may coordinate their syllabi and some assignments though they teach individually. The amount of coordination varies, often depending upon faculty commitment. In clustered courses faculty plan together on a regular basis to build intellectual connections and to reinforce common expectations.

Peer Leadership Possibilities
Usually paired courses do not include peer leaders, but they can be used for advising, tutoring, or as undergraduate teaching assistants. In clustered courses, peers may assist with or help teach weekly discussion groups.

Curricular Possibilities
If classes are scheduled in a block, faculty can plan common activities such as field trips, speakers, or experiential learning activities.

Team-Taught Learning Communities
Curricular Design
Courses may have various configurations, but faculty generally develop a common theme that fits the disciplines involved in the community.

Faculty Responsibilities
Faculty work together to select the theme, plan the curriculum, and teach the courses.

Peer Leadership Possibilities
Team-taught learning communities have opportunities for peer leadership, ranging from weekly discussions about various aspects of the interdisciplinary programming to planning committees that work along with the faculty.

Curricular Possibilities
Because these learning communities are often full-time, many different kinds of experiences can be incorporated into the block of time, ranging from community building activities, to field trips, to book discussions, to service learning. Sometimes a seminar is included that relates all the courses in the learning community.

Residence Hall Based Learning Communities
Curricular Design
The curriculum design varies from a single course, paired or clustered courses, or team-taught courses. Residence halls can also be used for classes.

Faculty Responsibilities
This type of learning community requires coordination with residence life and student affairs staff. Faculty may visit the residence hall to participate in various programs, may eat in the dining hall with groups of students, may hold classes or have offices in the residence hall, or may even live in the residence hall.

Peer Leadership Possibilities
Students have many options for leadership in this environment as they may participate in learning community committees within the residence hall. Upper-division students and RAs have multiple opportunities for becoming involved with the learning community.

Curricular Possibilities
Numerous opportunities exist for connecting the intellectual life of the classroom to life in the residence hall: discussion groups, speakers, service projects, transition to college life, community building, or academic support.

ESTABLISHING A CLIMATE FOR SUPPORTING LEARNING COMMUNITIES

When trying to effect change in higher education, one typically runs into some kind of resistance. People will be dissatisfied with the status quo and will want improvement, but, at the same time, change must be handled carefully. Research (Ely, 1990; Stein, 1997) has shown that certain conditions must be met to establish a positive climate for change. That is not likely to happen successfully if faculty and staff are told to establish learning communities. Effective change cannot be dictated from above. Rather, dissatisfaction with the status quo, commitment, and leadership are the most important priorities for creating change. The morale of the individuals who are expected to implement the innovation will also be negatively affected if they have not participated in designing the innovation and if they have not had adequate time for planning and training. Several chapters in this book focus on these concerns. For example, Chapter 3 discusses strategies for developing effective relationships among learning community faculty and staff, and Chapter 8 examines some significant institutional challenges that occur when institutions have to change to accommodate learning communities.

ASSESSING LEARNING COMMUNITIES

As learning communities are planned and outcomes are developed, an assessment plan should also be designed. The plan should be developed to measure the outcomes that are drawn up for the learning community and to assess the impact of the learning community on its stakeholders: students, faculty, staff, and the college or university. Some of the information that is needed for assessment may already be collected by the college or university, for example, retention statistics and GPAs, so the evaluation planners should be cognizant of what information is already available and link up with those efforts, rather than duplicating them.

To develop an accurate picture of the impact of learning communities, baseline information should be collected at the beginning of the program. Both quantitative and qualitative methods should be incorporated into the assessment plan. Some early formative assessment is also necessary to obtain feedback on how the community is working and whether some early changes are necessary. More detailed information on assessment is discussed in Chapter 7.

CONCLUSION

The concept of learning communities is becoming a popular approach for creating a campus environment that fosters significant intellectual interaction among students, faculty, and residence life staff. Learning communities are an ideal solution to major campus concerns: creation of a more stimulating academic environment, new student adjustment to the college environment, and increasing retention. But creating learning communities is not a task that should be undertaken without extensive forethought and planning, even though some models are easier than others to implement. Learning communities should not be created without adequate discussion, planning, and resources. Despite all the work involved in planning an effective learning community, student satisfaction makes it all worthwhile.

Ruth Federman Stein is a teaching consultant at the Center for Support of Teaching and Learning, Syracuse University.

REFERENCES

Astin, A. (1985). *Achieving educational excellence: A critical assessment of priorities and practices in higher education.* San Francisco, CA: Jossey-Bass.

Board of Regents. (2003). *History of ILS and the Meiklejohn house.* Madison, WI: University of Wisconsin. Retrieved February 26, 2003, from http://www.wisc.edu/ils/history.html

Boyer, E. (1987). *College: The undergraduate experience in America.* New York, NY: Harper & Row.

Bystrom, V. A. (1999). Learning communities in the community college. In J. H. Levine (Ed.), *Learning communities: New structures, new partnerships for learning* (pp. 87–95). Columbia, SC: University of South Carolina, National Resource Center for the First-Year Experience and Students in Transition.

Cuseo, J. S. (1991). *The freshman orientation seminar: A research-based rationale for its value, delivery, and content* (The First-Year Experience Monograph Series No. 4). Columbia, SC: University of South Carolina, National Resource Center for the First-Year Experience and Students in Transition.

Dewey, J. (1916). *Democracy and education.* New York, NY: Macmillan.

Ely, D. (1990, Winter). Conditions that facilitate the implementation of education technology innovations. *Journal of Research on Computing in Education, 23*(2), 298–305.

Education. (2000, November/December). *Brown Alumni Magazine, 101.* Retrieved December 12, 2002, from http://www.brown.edu/Administration/Brown_Alumni_Magazine/01/11-00/features/education.html

Evenbeck, S. E., Jackson, B., & McGrew, J. (1999). Faculty development in learning communities: The role of reflection and reframing. In J. H. Levine (Ed.), *Learning communities: New structures, new partnerships for learning* (pp. 51–58). Columbia, SC: University of South Carolina, National Resource Center for the First-Year Experience and Students in Transition.

Gabelnick, F., MacGregor, J., Matthews, R. S., & Smith, B. L. (1990). *New directions for teaching and learning: No. 41. Learning communities: Creating connections among students, faculty, and disciplines.* San Francisco, CA: Jossey-Bass.

Gabelnick, F., MacGregor, J., Matthews, R. S., & Smith, B. L. (1992). Learning communities and general education. *Perspectives, 22*(1), 104–121.

Goodsell Love, A., & Tokuno, K. A. (1999). Learning community models. In J. H. Levine (Ed.), *Learning communities: New structures, new partnerships for learning* (pp. 9–17). Columbia, SC: University of South Carolina, National Resource Center for the First-Year Experience and Students in Transition.

Hill, P. J. (1985). *The rationale for learning communities.* Paper presented at the Inaugural Conference of the Washington Center for Improving the Quality of Undergraduate Education, Olympia, WA.

Meiklejohn, A. (1923). *Freedom and the college.* New York, NY: The Century Company.

Office of Learning Communities. (2000). *Mission statement.* Syracuse, NY: Syracuse University.

Shapiro, N. S., & Levine, J. H. (1999). *Creating learning communities: A practical guide to winning support, organizing for change, and implementing programs.* San Francisco, CA: Jossey-Bass.

Smith, B. L. (1991). Taking structure seriously: The learning community model. *Liberal Education, 77*(2), 42–48.

Smith, B. L. (2001). *The challenge of learning communities as a growing national movement.* Prepared for the Association of American Colleges and Universities Conference on Learning Communities, Providence, RI. Retrieved December 12, 2002, from http://www.cgc.maricopa.edu/learning/communities/pdf/lc_conf_2001.pdf

Stein, R. F. (1997). *Conditions that facilitate the implementation of innovative freshman experience courses: A comparative analysis of three courses.* Unpublished doctoral dissertation, Syracuse University.

Stein, R. F. (1999). *Gateway student forum report.* Syracuse, NY: Syracuse University, Center for Support of Teaching and Learning.

Stein, R. F. (2000). *Gateway student forum report.* Syracuse, NY: Syracuse University, Center for Support of Teaching and Learning.

Stein, R. F., & Hurd, S. N. (2000). *Using student teams in the classroom: A faculty guide.* Bolton, MA: Anker.

Tinto, V. (1997, November/December). Classrooms as communities: Exploring the educational character of student persistence. *Journal of Higher Education, 68*(6), 599–623.

Tussman, J. (1969). *Experiment at Berkeley.* London, England: Oxford University Press.

2

Learning Communities at Syracuse University: A Strategy for Collaboration and Joint Responsibility

Michele Jachim

An interview with Ronald R. Cavanagh, Vice President for Undergraduate Studies, and Barry L. Wells, Senior Vice President for Student Affairs

Syracuse University (SU) intentionally embraced the strategy of learning communities in the late 1990's. Committed to promoting learning and the academic, professional, and personal growth of our students through the responsible collaboration of all campus constituencies, SU read the available national data to indicate that learning communities could promote holistic student success.

Any institution that deliberately characterizes itself as student-centered should certainly be judged on its capacity to facilitate student success. For a private institution of higher education like SU, graduation rates and the attractiveness of graduates to the marketplace or programs of professional or graduate education are important benchmarks of institutional success. So when the question, "Could the learning community strategy contribute to Syracuse University's institutional success by promoting student success?" was raised, the answer was a resounding "Yes," and the learning community campaign began.

The Division of Undergraduate Studies and the Division of Student Affairs jointly sponsored the process of developing and implementing the learning communities strategy at SU. Developing learning communities provided a distinct opportunity for the university community to engage the institutional core values of quality, caring, diversity, innovation, and service and to demonstrate the tenets of the SU Compact, which include the support of scholarly learning and adherence to the highest ideals of personal and academic honesty. In implementing learning communities, faculty, students, and professional staff were encouraged to collaborate within and across classrooms and residence halls.

The vice presidents of undergraduate studies and student affairs who were charged with supporting the creation of a seamless learning environment across the campus concluded that the anti-silo strategy of learning communities was essential. Far too many students experience the environment of American higher education as disconnected, atomized, inconsistent, or lacking wholeness. Far too few students experience a clear and vital link between and among their classes, let alone between classes and life in the residence hall, or between themselves as students and the faculty and professional staff of their university. The learning communities strategy at SU was to be offered as an experiment in coherence.

Like any experiment, it is preferred that the conditions under which it is conducted are conducive to a reasonably successful outcome. In the case of learning communities at SU, the operating conditions for this experiment were groomed for a number of years by two gentlemen who began their working relationship on opposite sides of an issue.

In 1980, Ronald R. Cavanagh was associate dean for student services in the College of Arts and Sciences. Barry L. Wells was associate director of admissions and financial aid. The two participated in an administrative hearing board deciding the fate of a student appealing the loss of a scholarship.

"I was most impressed with the thoroughness of his preparation for the hearing, the articulateness of his arguments, and the passion and concern he expressed for the well-being of the students," said Cavanagh. "He was concerned with the holistic development of the student and believed that the institution must be as well. Since this has long been my philosophy of education, I was quite intrigued by this individual."

Wells's accounting of the early days of his collaboration with Cavanagh was similar, and he noted, "although Ron and I couldn't convince one another to change positions, we both respected the points that the other person made and the manner in which they were made." He added, "Ron was intelligent, candid, ambitious, and committed to making a difference at Syracuse."

He still is, and these traits are energizing for people working with him, for him, or around him."

Shortly after this initial meeting, Cavanagh contacted Wells about a position that he had available in the dean's office of the College of Arts and Sciences. Wells agreed to talk to Cavanagh about the position as a professional courtesy even though he wasn't interested in making a change. Cavanagh convinced Wells that this was an outstanding opportunity to join his new team in the Arts and Sciences dean's office.

And so it was.

"We established a mutual trust in our relationship and respect for one another's perspective. We know that we can count on one another and that we will see things through to the end when we work on projects together. The students, therefore, will reap the benefits of our long-term commitment to Syracuse University and the fortitude that we both bring to the table when dealing with institutional priorities," said Wells.

Their collaborative efforts are many. They have worked together on a number of projects such as the improvement of academic advising, the reduction of student attrition, the successful implementation of supplemental instruction, the joint development of the minor in management program between the School of Management and the College of Arts and Sciences, and the advocacy and implementation of the mid-semester progress reporting system at SU. Wells and Cavanagh are also jointly responsible for promoting assessment of student experiences at SU, such as administration of the National Survey of Student Engagement (NSSE) and preparation of related retention and assessment reports, as well as the development of a formal new student orientation program.

"Ron is a good talker, and I'm a good listener," said Wells. "He has a strength for the theoretical while I have a strength for the practical. We both believe in taking the initiative, acting decisively, and establishing priorities whenever we are convinced that such actions are in the best interest of our institution. We both believe in hiring the right people for the jobs that must be done, and we are enthusiastic about the challenges that confront us on a daily basis. We are partners even though we are different, and we are productive because we believe in the value of collaboration."

"Throughout the years, we have shared the same focus, prioritizing the quality of the undergraduate student experience and whatever could be done to improve it," said Cavanagh.

Their partnership repeatedly sends the message that the Office of Student Affairs is a full partner with the Office of Academic Affairs in planning the learning communities initiative. One of the reasons that Cavanagh and Wells initially emphasized residential learning communities is that they provided an excellent opportunity for maximum interaction and involvement between academic affairs and student affairs. They hoped that the residential learning communities strategy would be recognized as a unifying institutional philosophy, integrating the aspirations of academic affairs and student affairs and providing an ideal way to collectively walk-the-walk and talk-the-talk of this student-centered research university. "I think that the particular working relationship that Barry and I share is effectively communicated with other faculty and professional staff colleagues around the university," said Cavanagh. "Barry and I enjoy one another, we respect each other, and we never forget that the reason we have been given this opportunity to work together is to model the university's vision of 'working together and sharing responsibility to promote academic, professional, and personal growth.' I think that such a working relationship has benefited the students in the learning communities," explained Cavanagh.

The Focus: Residential Linked-Course Learning Communities for First-Year Students

Step one in the learning community campaign was deciding what learning communities would or should look like, recognizing that they came in many shapes and sizes. The vice presidents assembled a small group of faculty, administrators, and professional staff to take a first cut at identifying model(s) that would accomplish institutional goals and at the same time satisfy incoming and continuing students, their parents, the faculty, student affairs professionals, and a budget-conscious vice chancellor.

The priority was residential linked-course learning communities for first-year students. This focus created the opportunity not only for students to have regular interaction with course faculty, but also for faculty and the professional staff of the Office of Residential Life in the residence halls to have regular interaction. The learning communities strategy had the dual purpose of facilitating interaction, collaboration, and a sense of shared responsibility among academic affairs and student affairs personnel as well as promoting affiliation, bonding, and increased persistence to graduation among incoming students.

Starting with residential learning communities had the additional benefit of making it clear to students that the separation between what goes on inside and outside of the classroom is not absolute and that there are important connections between in-class and out-of-class learning. Finally, focusing on residential learning communities allowed faculty to see the kind of learning that takes place outside their classrooms. For example, students working in city soup kitchens learn to appreciate social circumstances different from their own, and student government leaders learn the sheer energy needed to move tasks to a successful conclusion. Faculty can use this knowledge to become better overall educators.

Learning communities are all about relationships, the skills of interactive inquiry, and other human building blocks of success. Wells and Cavanagh hoped that learning communities would encourage the emergence of self-confidence and a sense of belonging among entering students who might otherwise feel anxious, disconnected, and alone in a large university. They hoped that by recognizing, empowering, and appropriately challenging students within a communal experience, the students would learn early in their collegiate lives to take risks and to make the personal effort needed for genuine learning.

The Integrated Learning Seminar

The initial pilot of learning communities at SU included a one-credit integrated learning seminar. It was hoped that this seminar, which focused on the dynamics of learning, would become a signature for SU learning communities and symbolic of the project as a whole. Certainly not every learning community needs to have such a seminar and subsequently not all have. However, the original learning seminar, developed collaboratively by academic and student affairs, involves students' learning about four basic elements from both faculty and residence hall staff. Those elements are 1) the individual student learning audit; 2) the pedagogical assumptions for linked courses; 3) student survival strategies; and 4) the developmental philosophy of student affairs.

Individual student learning audit. Each student is asked to reflect on his or her strengths and weaknesses, idiosyncrasies, and proclivities as a learner. The students are asked to identify the times they find most effective for studying (e.g., morning, night, afternoon); the places they find most effective (e.g., residence hall room, library, empty classroom); and the range of sound, intensity of light, etc., that characterize the most effective study environments. Each student is asked to assess the conditions under which it is most effective for him or her to study (e.g., alone, with another person, or in a specific study group); and to what extent he or she takes responsibility for creating those conditions. Finally, each student is asked to assess his or her relationship with professors, TAs, and laboratory or studio assistants, etc., and how he or she is using office hours or cultivating a relationship with those individuals.

The pedagogical assumptions for linked courses. Professors of the linked courses meet in the residence hall setting and discuss with learning community students and student affairs professionals their own pedagogical assumptions for linked courses. This discussion makes public the assumptions about learning that went into the creation of a particular linked course. The participants discuss why the particular texts were selected and presented in a specific order; why particular tests, quizzes, or exams are being used; or the purpose of specific kinds of homework assignments, service learning options, and tutorial help sessions that are built into the course. The session gives students a regular opportunity to ask professors "why," "how," "what," and "when" they think that students are learning in their courses. Faculty receive invaluable feedback on the assumptions they make when designing curriculum, and students understand the underlying logic of courses. This pedagogical conversation is critical to the effectiveness of the learning communities strategy.

Student survival strategies. These are the critical skills and dispositions students need to learn in various university environments. Skills include everything from notetaking, to time management, to participating in study teams, to test preparation. Dispositions include accepting primary responsibility for their own learning and accepting responsibility for the quality of the learning experience for others in the learning community. Student success remains a matter of providing opportunity and support and eliciting a commitment from students to invest their personal energy in the pursuit of learning.

The developmental philosophy of student affairs. Students and professional staff together examine the assumptions of the developmental philosophy of student affairs programming. Residentially based learning communities are well positioned to support the expectation that students will grow not only intellectually, but also personally and professionally during their undergraduate years. To this end, the institution establishes programs, uses media, and provides incentives and disincentives to shape the maturation of student behavior. It is important that students in learning communities understand and discuss this institutional decision-making and how it impacts their lives. In the end, unless student behavior supports such institutional goals, administrative initiatives will prove to be ineffective.

National data on learning communities indicate that students learn more, learn faster, and retain information longer when they work collaboratively with other students, faculty, and staff in a responsibly challenging but supportive environment with clear goals, appropriate skill development, and timely feedback. Students who have participated in learning communities are said to be more satisfied with their institutions, to perform better academically, and to involve themselves with other activities on campus.

Faculty and staff derive a significant sense of pride and professional satisfaction from their collaborative participation in the creation and implementation of learning communities. There is little question that the learning communities strategy adds value to all participants. SU remains committed to the ongoing quantitative and qualitative assessment of the effects of learning communities, not only for students but also for faculty and staff. Only time will tell if the inclusion of this learning community strategy as a specific early response arrow in the SU quiver has in some way affected the student retention and graduation rate profile that is vital to a student-centered research university. However, the prima facie anecdotal evidence is that it will do so positively.

Michele Jachim is coordinator of communications and events, Division of Student Affairs; Ronald R. Cavanagh is vice president for undergraduate studies, and Barry L. Wells is senior vice president for student affairs, all of Syracuse University.

3

Strategies for Building Learning Community Relationships

Sandra N. Hurd

INTRODUCTION

Shortly after I agreed to serve as the faculty coordinator for learning communities at Syracuse University (SU), I attended a learning community conference where I listened and talked to faculty in like positions discuss how they do their work. The theme that ran through all the presentations and conversations was that the key to the successful development of a learning community program was building relationships. One faculty director likened himself to Pearl Mesta: His key to success was putting together committed, creative, caring faculty; creating an environment that allowed them to do their work; and then getting out of their way. He was right. It is both that simple and that difficult.

In this chapter I want to share with you some of the strategies I have found useful in building relationships that support the development, implementation, and assessment of learning communities at SU. Let me set the stage by providing some background about the university and our Learning Community Program.

SU is comprised of 13 separate schools and colleges, nine enrolling both undergraduate and graduate populations, three enrolling only graduate students, and one continuing education, which enrolls both undergraduate and graduate students. We have over 10,000 undergraduate students and slightly less than 4,000 graduate students. These students are served by over 800 full-time and close to 600 part-time and adjunct faculty, as well as over 3,000 staff and administrators. There is no general education requirement at SU, and freshmen are admitted directly into the various schools and colleges.

The Learning Community Program at SU began with a small pre-pilot project conducted by the School of Management and the Office of Residence Life in 1998, involving 27 students who lived together and took three required management courses and a learning community seminar together. (See Chapter 9 for details on the evolution of the Management Learning Community.) Management was asked to participate because several years earlier we had created management floors in a residence hall as part of our freshman gateway course. When we created the floors, our goals were to build community among our freshmen and enhance the academic environment in the residence hall. Imagine our surprise when we discovered learning communities!

The program grew rapidly with institutional support. (See Chapter 2 on institutional perspective.) In fall 2001, there were 13 residential communities serving 456 students, primarily freshmen, and three non-residential learning communities serving 395 students, primarily upper-class and graduate students. Twenty-four residential and five non-residential communities, serving approximately 1,700 students are in place for the 2003–2004 academic year. Plans are already in the works for additional learning communities for 2004–2005.

Residential learning communities at SU are partnerships between academic affairs and student affairs that intentionally integrate in-class and out-of-class learning experiences. Non-residential learning communities are partnerships between/among faculty from different academic disciplines that offer integrated courses and experiences. I serve as director of learning communities for academic affairs (part-time). There is a director of learning communities for student affairs (full-time), who is also an associate director of residence life. We are supported in our work by an administrative assistant (full-time), a graduate assistant (communications), and the Center for Support of Teaching and Learning (assessment). We work with faculty, administrators, staff, admissions, housing, the registrar's office, and each of the university's nine undergraduate schools and colleges on a regular basis, and we rely on student, faculty, staff, and administrator expertise throughout the university. It is no wonder, then, that building relationships is of paramount importance.

What are the key elements to building relationships? We have identified a number of them in our strategic plan, and we keep them in mind in all of our dealings with our many constituents throughout the university.

Build Trust

The faculty, staff, students, and administrators with whom we work must feel confident that we are completely honest in our dealings with them and that we don't make promises we can't keep. Being honest is not difficult, but making sure that we can live up to our word is not always easy in an environment where policies and personnel change, resources shift, and perspectives undergo constant reevaluation. Occasionally, we have found ourselves in the difficult position of following close on the heels of a program or initiative that had made promises that weren't kept, which raised natural suspicion about our own claims. In these situations, we have taken care to stay in constant communication about what we were doing and why, under-promise, and over-deliver. If there has been even a chance that our plans weren't going to work out, we have honestly communicated that possibility and partnered to develop a contingency plan. Building trust is time consuming, but it is among the most important things that we do.

Listen Carefully to the Concerns and Needs of Others and Respond

People need to know that their concerns have been heard. Too often people weigh in on an issue and then never get any feedback that their perspective has been taken into account in the decision-making process. It's not necessarily as important that they get the result they advocated as it is that they know that their contributions to the discussion were paid attention to and valued. When we make a decision, we communicate that decision to all interested parties, detailing the concerns that were raised and our response to each of those concerns. We can't please everyone, but we can at least let them know that their concerns were given a full and fair hearing.

Understand That Yours is not the Only Difficult and Complex Job and Respect the Environment in Which Others Work

It is often too easy to think that everyone else's job has got to be less difficult than yours. It is important to remind yourself constantly that everyone you deal with has equally although perhaps differently complex and difficult jobs to do. It may not seem to you that asking a department secretary to take on managing enrollment in a learning community course is a burdensome request, but without understanding the demands of her or his job, you don't know what impact your request has. It is important to try to understand others' jobs and how they work.

Understanding the work environment is especially critical when you are trying to promote partnerships between faculty and student affairs staff. Their work lives are vastly different (see Chapter 6) and any attempt to partner them must recognize and account for those differences.

Wherever Possible, Align Your Interests With the Interests of Others

When I first started working on the learning communities project, I was focused primarily on student learning and how I could help create the best environment in which students could grow and develop both academically and personally. Although I considered myself more aware than many faculty members about the programs and initiatives at the university, I discovered that, in fact, I was not tuned in to many of the big picture concerns that administrators dealt with on a day-to-day basis.

I was invited to sit on a number of committees by virtue of my position and discovered whole new worlds I had never been exposed to, retention and persistence to graduation among them. I found that it was easy to align my interest in students with larger concerns. The ethical imperative of student success was a good fit with the financial imperative of retention. Understanding these dynamics allowed the learning communities program to take a huge step forward. We could think about our work in ways that created natural fits with existing programs and specifically advanced the goals of the university. Retention is an excellent example. Studies by our Division of Student Support and Retention revealed that we were losing a worrisome number of high achieving students who reported that they didn't feel sufficiently challenged by their academic work and couldn't find ways to connect with other students who shared their interest in learning. Armed with that information, we starting thinking about how we might create a learning community to address those students' concerns. It was a short step to proposing a residential college that would bring our best students and faculty together to share learning experiences that would satisfy the students' thirst for knowledge and connect them with like-minded peers. At the same time, it would give faculty the opportunity to interact with our most promising learners. Aligning our interests with those of the university has provided support and revenue streams to which we would otherwise not have access.

Share Information With People Who Need—or Just Want—to Know

It is extremely important to keep the community informed about what you are doing. It not only heightens awareness, but also meets people's very real need to know what is going on, especially when what is happening has an impact, even if only tangential, on their area of responsibility or interest. Nobody likes to be surprised, especially publicly, by the unexpected. We ask to be put on the agenda of a number of groups and committees each semester to give them an update about the learning community program. Making these presentations serves multiple purposes. It not only keeps everyone in the information loop, but also surfaces issues and concerns that we might not otherwise be aware of. It is time-consuming, to be sure, but, in the long run, it is time very well spent.

Involve all Stakeholders in Decisions That Affect Them

As important as it is to communicate effectively with the entire SU community, it is even more important to make every effort to involve all stakeholders in the decisions that affect them. With a university of the size and complexity of SU, it is not always easy to identify stakeholders, let alone find a time to bring them all together. Yet, failing to identify or include a significant stakeholder can undo untold hours of work. For example, when we set to work the first year developing a comprehensive marketing strategy for learning communities, we didn't include the publications office in putting together our plan. Weeks were wasted when we discovered that publications simply couldn't meet the deadlines we had set for our plan.

There are three key groups that we work most closely with that allow us to reach many of our stakeholders. The first is the Learning Community Council, a group created in fall 2000 to help and advise us. The council's membership includes senior administrators in academic and student affairs, directors of key programs, our graduate assistant, and undergraduate students. It is the responsibility of the council to provide coordination and communication among the various areas that have a stake in learning communities and to identify and work toward resolving institution-wide issues arising out of the Learning Community Program. The second group is the Academic Coordinating Council (ACC). The ACC is comprised of representatives from virtually all the academic affairs and student affairs units as well as, for example, admissions, housing, registrar, and computing. They constituted themselves many years ago to make order out of what had become a chaotic new student orientation as schools and colleges unilaterally added new programming to the schedule, unaware of the other demands that were being made on students' time. Despite its large size (close to 50 members), it is a high-functioning group that has the knowledge and expertise to understand what impact new programs or policies will have on the institution. Their help in understanding the issues and solving the problems has been essential to the growth of learning communities. The final group is the student Learning Community Advisory Board. Made up of representatives of all the learning communities, the board organizes learning community events, participates in recruiting, and provides us with student feedback on a whole host of issues.

Support People in Their Work

The learning communities program asks much of faculty, staff, students, and administrators who already have plenty to do. Like many workplaces, the university frequently adds to people's responsibilities without at the same time expressly relieving them of something else to make room. In order for that to work at all, let alone without resentment, it is critical to provide help and support to make the added responsibilities as easy as possible to manage. We have developed a number of support systems. One important support system is DocuShare, a web-based information management application. We have created an extensive DocuShare site for the Learning Community Program. It contains public areas for general information and private areas for each learning community. In the public areas, we post sample documents such as learning objectives and assessment plans, timelines, deadlines, contact lists, course information, and anything else we believe will be helpful or of general interest. The private area for each learning community allows participants to exchange information, work on documents together, and post documents that everyone can read (for example, student papers) without ever leaving their offices.

We have also developed a series of workshops that we will conduct on demand for groups or even an individual. Topics for these workshops include an overview of learning communities, how to use DocuShare, developing learning objectives, marketing your learning community, creating assessment plans, understanding student affairs and academic affairs, and learning community curriculum development. In addition to faculty and staff workshops, special training is provided to the resident advisors on learning community floors.

Each May we hold a learning community retreat. Learning community teams are invited to spend a half or full day away from campus working together. The learning community staff as well as consultants from the Writing Program and the Center for Support of Teaching and Learning are available to work with individuals or teams throughout the day.

Providing support for those who give so generously of their time to make learning communities work is critical to our success. Our goal is never to ask someone to do something without providing the tools with which to do it.

Be Patient

Institutions, offices, and people have their own rhythms and cycles. Those may or may not match your own. When they don't, it's important to be patient. Sometimes when you just wait patiently and curb the impulse to push, things come to pass. Several years ago, I approached our Department of Languages, Literatures, and Linguistics about a language learning community. I had in my own mind settled on Spanish because it is the largest of the language majors, and we have a popular program abroad in Spain. I thought there would be tremendous student interest in living in a Spanish-speaking learning community to learn more about the country and hone language skills, and I knew that language learning communities were popular at other institutions. After a preliminary conversation with the department chair, a representative from our Division of International Programs Abroad and I made a presentation at a faculty meeting about the learning community program. Nothing happened, but I wasn't particularly surprised. It was clear from the questions and comments at the faculty meeting that the department was operating with limited resources and there was some resentment that they were being asked to take on yet another significant project. For a year, I checked in with the department chair every once in a while to see if anyone was interested. After that I stopped checking. Almost a year after that, a faculty member from the French department contacted me, wanting to talk about a French learning community. It had taken that long for the faculty to think about resources, how a learning community might serve their own interests, and how it all might work. It all came together quickly after that, and we now have our first language learning community. The evolution of the French learning community taught me the importance of just letting some things happen in their own time. I should note, however, that a strategy of patience is sometimes at odds with an administrative mandate to make things move quickly and a matter that must be negotiated.

Let go of Things That Aren't Important

When you are passionate about something, the distinction between what is really important and what would just be nice to have happen can sometimes be lost. It is important to check in with yourself frequently and decide what battles really need to be fought, what's worth going to the mat for. With a limited amount of time and energy, it's important to spend it wisely. A related, but equally important, issue is the tricky one of deciding when the relationship is more important than the issue, no matter how strongly you feel about it, especially as it affects the long-term success of the program. The answers to these questions will be, of course, very situation specific, but they are good questions to ask yourself as you decide what's really important and what's not.

Recognize and Reward Everyone Who Helps You

Resource constraints are a fact of life at SU, which is heavily dependent on tuition revenues. Academic affairs and student affairs both provide financial support for the learning communities program, but there is never enough to compensate learning community participants adequately for their work. There are also significant equity issues raised by the disparate salary structures in the various schools and colleges. Because we can't pay people what they are worth, we have had to devise multiple other ways in which to provide recognition and rewards.

We try to make people throughout the university aware of the contributions of those involved in learning communities. In our learning community newsletter, which is published twice each semester and distributed to all faculty, staff, administrators, and learning community students, we highlight the accomplishments of learning community participants. We also include those accomplishments in regular reports that are made to academic affairs, student affairs, and the chancellor. In addition, we send thank you notes to participants, with copies to chairs, supervisors, deans, or whoever is in a position to reward them through salary increments or other forms of compensation. We also host an annual dinner for everyone at the university who worked with learning communities during the year. At that dinner, we give awards and certificates of recognition in a variety of categories.

Finally, we provide travel support for participants to attend learning community conferences or participate in other professional development activities related to learning communities. Fall 2002, for example, we took 18 professional staff from residence life to the learning community conference at The Ohio State University.

There is, however, one important group of learning community participants who do receive additional compensation. Contingent faculty in the Writing Program are given a stipend to work the extra hours necessary to develop linked courses, attend meetings, and engage in assessment activities.

CONCLUSION

Building partnerships to support learning communities at SU has not only been a rewarding personal experience—I have had the opportunity to meet and work closely with extraordinary people—but has in many ways changed the way the university does its work. Bridges have been built between areas that previously had little interaction. For example, although the Housing Office and the Registrar's Office share a building, many of them had never even met anyone who works in the other office. Now that we have had to link where students live with what courses they take, representatives from those offices work together on common issues. Bridges are also built to the larger Syracuse community, as learning communities take advantage of the opportunity to tap the expertise of community leaders in designing and implementing the learning community curricula.

Learning communities have also promoted and enhanced the academic affairs-student affairs partnership, not only at the administrative level, which has long enjoyed a successful working relationship (see Chapter 2), but also among individual faculty and staff. The Native American Studies Learning Community, for example, partners faculty from anthropology, religion, and sociology with staff from the Office of Multicultural Affairs, a graduate student in the Higher Education Program, and professional and paraprofessional staff from residence life. These kinds of partnerships blur the boundaries between students' in- and out-of-class experiences, enhancing the students' academic and personal development and success.

Even our information systems are affected. In the first years of the learning community program, when we needed data from a variety of offices at the university, we spent hours converting it to a common format so we could work with it. Now, most of our databases have been redesigned so that information can be shared efficiently and effectively.

Learning community advocates have long argued that learning communities have the power to transform our institutions of higher education into places that can provide a significantly better environment for student learning and development. That process is certainly happening at Syracuse.

Sandra N. Hurd is professor of law and public policy in the Whitman School of Management and director of learning communities for academic affairs at Syracuse University.

4

Roles of and Structures for Writing Courses in Learning Communities

Rebecca Moore Howard and Vivian Rice

Becky's Introduction

After 20 years of teaching writing and administering writing programs, I marvel that any writing program offers any instruction to first-year students that is not part of a learning community. My own writing program, I should hasten to note, teaches quite a bit of first-year writing that has no connection to any learning community. But I regard freestanding writing instruction as the less effective instruction that we offer. From my position as writing program director, the best conditions for teaching that I can offer instructors are the sections that are part of learning communities. In every year that I have been its director, the Syracuse Writing Program has offered an increasing number of sections of its introductory course, Writing 105, in learning communities. I hope that trend will continue. Every year, an increasing number of writing instructors expresses interest in teaching in learning communities, because every year, they continue to hear the positive reports from those who are already teaching in learning communities.

Mine is not, however, a utopian vision of the role of writing courses in learning communities. My experience has demonstrated that these arrangements can go very, very wrong. The composition instructor can become an assistant to—rather than a colleague of—the instructor of the other course(s). The composition course in the learning community can lose all sense of its autonomous goals and instead pursue only the goals with which the other learning community instructors charge the writing instructor. Not surprisingly, the composition instructor can feel belittled and deprofessionalized by the experience.

35

After 15 years' experience in administering linked-course instruction and now the writing links in learning communities, I have compiled a set of guidelines that promote a successful, productive integration of composition courses in learning communities. Now, however, I am not the sole administrator of the writing links in learning communities; I work with Vivian Rice, who is responsible for the implementation and oversight of the linked writing courses offered by our department. "My" guidelines have therefore undergone field-testing by another administrator and have been substantially revised and improved through her work. What is presented in this essay, then, are "our" guidelines.

VIVIAN'S INTRODUCTION

The learning community initiative at Syracuse University is fairly young; the first official learning community was launched in the fall of 1998 as a collaboration between the School of Management and the Office of Residence Life. Twenty-seven students were involved that first year. One of the four courses in that pre-pilot project was WRT 105, the required freshman composition course. The number of writing classes taught as linked sections of learning communities has increased each year since then. In the fall of 2001, there were seven sections in three different learning communities. Even then the style and level of involvement with the links varied. In the management link, for example, faculty and residence life staff teaching three of the required classes met weekly to plan together. They continue to experiment with overlapping assignments as part of their collaboration and frequently attend each other's large group activities, both academic and social. For a quite different mix, the nonresidential Newhouse learning community forms a looser link. In this learning community, only some of the students from the large required communications lecture are clustered into the small sections of the required writing studio classes, so the ties are somewhat relaxed and the involvement of the teachers less intense.

From the seven WRT 105 sections that were a part of learning communities in 2001, the number increased to 13 sections in 2002 and continues to grow. The variety has increased also: We have added the learning community for Women in Science and Engineering (WISE), a select group of women from many different scientific majors with the unifying interest of being women in predominantly male fields. Two of the new learning communities we are adding are similarly focused interest groups. One, Light Work, will include an upper-division writing elective as a required component. This academic course will link with Light Work/Community Darkrooms, a public access photography facility and gallery, and will offer students a variety of experiences working back and forth between their writing and photography, both their own and that of visiting artists.

A commitment to the concept of learning communities, we've discovered, requires flexibility. No one definition, no one approach will fit the differing opportunities provided. In this paper, we share some of what we are learning about these variations as they have played out in Syracuse's Writing Program and as they connect to published accounts of teaching writing in linked-course arrangements at other institutions.

BLUEPRINT

Our essay begins by describing the structural possibilities of linked-course instruction; explains ways in which composition courses can, through linked-course instruction, contribute to the goals of learning communities; explains the dangers posed to the composition courses and their instructors by virtue of their participation in learning communities; and concludes by offering guidelines for integrating composition courses into learning communities.

STRUCTURAL OPTIONS FOR THE COMPOSITION COURSE IN LEARNING COMMUNITIES

Writing courses can be integrated into learning communities in a variety of ways, each suited to particular institutional conditions. While Zawacki and Williams (2001) define learning communities as "curriculum change initiatives that link, cluster, or integrate two or more courses during a given term, often around an interdisciplinary theme, and involve a common cohort of students," (p. 109) much of the variation between types is connected to the arrangements for writing assignments in the various courses in the learning community.

Double-Graded Assignments

In 1985, when the writing-across-the-curriculum movement was in its heyday in American higher education, C.W. Griffith's authoritative review of the various manifestations of writing-across-the-curriculum singled out linked-course instruction for praise: "Probably the most dramatic effect of writing-across-the-curriculum on the freshman level is the recent phenomenon of the 'linked' or 'coregistered' course . . ." (p. 401). Griffith went on to offer what at that time must have seemed a supportable generalization: "In these programs, students typically receive instruction in writing in one course, write about the content of the other, and are graded by both instructors" (p. 402).

Coenrollment

Since that time, however, a variety of linked-course arrangements have proliferated. Terry Myers Zawacki and Ashley Taliaferro Williams (2001), the authors of the most comprehensive source currently available on the potentials for writing courses in learning communities, assert their ideal for learning communities: two separate classes with "a one-to-one correspondence in class size, making it possible for all of the instructors in the link to assign, talk about, and be responsible for writing" (p. 114). This arrangement enables "fully linked sections of two or more courses in which students are coenrolled, and it is the most typical arrangement. Instructors of these fully linked courses are well positioned to "help their students 'process' writing" (p. 117). Teachers in this type of link might use work from the linked courses to enrich their own classes. All three linked classes in SU's Management learning community use writing in important ways; all four teachers begin their classes talking about writing. The students in the learning community hand in a one-page paper about their expectations for the learning community the day before classes start. Copies of each paper are given to all the teachers in the learning community. During the first session of each class, the teachers talk about patterns they have observed about the writing, focusing the students' attention on that skill and giving the students their four different perspectives (Hanlon, C., personal communication, January 8, 2003).

Hybrid Assignments

Zawacki and Williams point to a further benefit of fully linked sections: Some of the assignments that instructors create in fully linked courses, they say, are "hybrid assignments" that mix or transcend disciplinary expectations (p. 118). Pamela Gay (1991) describes a variant on this experience. When she taught a class fully linked with a biology course, the biology instructor responded to students' drafts-in-progress for an assignment in the composition course (p. 192). Interestingly, though the classes were closely linked, each teacher gave separate assignments; the writing teacher asked the students to write about themselves and their history as writers, and the biology teacher asked the students to write about themselves as science learners (p. 184). These sorts of collaborations are well-documented in fully linked course arrangements: Intellectual and pedagogical excitement happens in ways not available to freestanding or partially linked courses.

Separate Goals, One Assignment

Writing more than a quarter-century ago, Marilyn Sutton (1978) calls her linked course an "adjunct" course—a significant word choice. She says that the purpose of the writing adjunct course is to teach writing, not to teach the companion subject matter (p. 106). "It is clear from the beginning that the writing adjunct carries a distinct course content in composition and that the writing adjunct instructor will be responsible for determining the syllabus in composition and evaluating each student's progress as a writer" (p. 104). The writing instructors in her linked-course system work with their students to set sensible goals for the semester's work and have their own course content. But they work with their students on papers assigned not in the writing course but in the companion course, which (again significantly) Sutton calls the "sub-ject-matter course." In the arrangement that Sutton describes, students receive responses from two readers, both of whom are attached to the adjunct course (p. 106). Although Sutton herself does not say so, the students in such an arrangement would surely have a clear understanding that what they are learning in their writing class matters someplace besides that writing class, though at the same time the writing course is subordinated ("adjunct") to the other ("subject-matter") course.

Partial Links

Nancy H. Kerr and Madeleine Picciotto (1992) describe yet another possi-bility for linked-course instruction: partial links. Oglethorpe University links writing courses to liberal arts survey courses such as sociology and biology. "All students in the composition class were also enrolled in a section of the base course, but not all students in the base course concurrently took the composition class" (p. 107). This structure almost predetermines that the link will be a loose one since not all the students in the lecture class will ben-efit from any overlapping of coursework. The Arts Adventure Learning Community at Syracuse has only some of its students enrolled in linked sec-tions of freshman writing (see Chapter 15). Those students have the advan-tage of a second environment that incorporates the same vocabulary and stresses the same priorities. Many of the students in the linked sections show the benefit they have received by their deeper understanding of course con-tent and higher GPA.

Large Lecture Course Links

In another learning community arrangement, sections of the writing course are linked to a large lecture course:

> *While this is not an ideal WAC [writing-across-the-curriculum] situation, students are writing in the context of a discipline, and there is an exchange of ideas and methods between the two teachers (one reason it is especially important to employ experienced writing teachers). In this exchange, then, both teachers stand to gain. The noncomposition teacher engages in discussions about writing and writing assignments. At the same time, the FYC [first-year composition] instructor gains valuable WAC experience, something that is not generally a feature of traditional programs, in which FYC is disconnected from WAC (Zawacki & Williams, 2001, p. 115).*

Even when the lecture course instructors have little pedagogical flexibility, say Zawacki and Williams, they at least see ways to incorporate write-to-learn principles into their course design (p. 115). Joyce Magnotto (1990) discusses ways teachers in the fields of psychology, philosophy, business math, and statistics accomplished this without adding to their grading work load. The teachers noted benefits that reached beyond the specific assignment, whether freewriting, journal writing, peer review. As might be expected, the writing affected the students' depth of understanding and retainment of the subject matter of the lecture class. It also changed students' perceptions of the material: Students petrified of mathematics or statistics lost their fear after writing about their fears and about how the subject relates to the real world (pp. 74–76).

ASSETS OF WRITING COURSES IN LEARNING COMMUNITIES

As many institutions are discovering, composition courses play integral roles in the structure and success of the learning communities. The reason is easy to find: Composition scholarship has long explored and endorsed principles that also inform learning communities—principles such as active learning, community-building, collaboration, intensified interdisciplinary learning, and diversity training.

Active Learning

With their writing-across-the-curriculum ideals, writing courses are invaluable to the goals of learning communities. Zawacki and Williams (2001) note that throughout its history, the learning community movement has recognized writing as integral to its endeavors (p. 110). At most universities, first-year composition is a small-enrollment course, and small-enrollment courses lend themselves very nicely to the active learning sought in learning communities. "Although LC [learning community] structures are quite variable, they all have the common goal of fostering greater academic coherence and more explicit intellectual connections among students, between students and their faculty, and among disciplines" (p. 109). In small classes, students more easily engage in active learning. Vince Tinto, Anne Goodsell Love, and Pat Russo (1993) saw this at Seattle Central Community College, encouraged "by a high level of social, emotional, and academic peer support that emerged from classroom activities" (p. 19). Active learning was encouraged by the set-up of the learning communities, in part, because they increased the students' comfort levels (p. 19). They claim that students in this learning community program "often spoke of their desire to continue in college as a direct result of their CSP [learning community] experience" (p. 20).

Community Building

Small-enrollment courses lend themselves, too, to the learning community objective of student retention (Zawacki & Williams, 2001, p. 115). Tinto, Goodsell Love, and Russo (1993) explain this function of learning communities: Students "feel comfortable in those [common, shared] classes" and are enabled "to build a network of peers. That network then functions as both an academic and social support system . . ." (p. 18). Learning communities provide the conditions in which this sense of community grows and in which retention therefore increases. In small classes, students are more likely to form bonds with their fellow students, their teachers, and the intellectual enterprise and are thus more likely to continue their college education. As the classes that the university has customarily designated for limited enrollment, composition classes make a ready contribution to the retention goal of learning communities.

Collaboration

Since the pioneering work of Kenneth A. Bruffee in the early 1980's, composition professionals have accepted student collaboration as a valuable tactic in pedagogy. Bruffee (1984) describes collaborative learning as "as a way of engaging students more deeply with the text and also as an aspect of professors' engagement with the professional community" (p. 635). With professionals the collaboration often extends to both assignments and pedagogy, an additional though often unstated goal of most learning communities. Subsequent theorists (such as Howard and Lunsford & Ede) have taken the principle further, asserting that all writing is collaborative and that composition instruction should acknowledge and work with this fact.

Whether in the strong or weak version of the principle, student collaboration is valued in learning community theory, too. Tinto, Goodsell Love, and Russo (1993) observe that students attend and participate in class more readily when they feel a sense of community; their "academic performance and persistence" is "greater" (p. 20). In collaborative settings, they say, students are more likely to learn than merely to memorize (p. 21). Indeed, Paul Baker (1999) describes learning communities as having this fundamental feature: "The group is organized to learn as a whole system" (p. 99) rather than as a collection of individuals. Tinto, Goodsell Love, and Russo (1993) even found the effect of collaboration changed students' basic perceptions of learning, giving them "a new model of learning that encouraged students to embrace an expanded picture of the learning process" (p. 20). At Syracuse University, we have found the value of collaboration to be especially enhanced with our residential learning communities, since students living on the same floor and attending the same classes will naturally work together. Several of our learning communities capitalize on this feature, with the instructors holding office hours and classes in teaching spaces in the residence halls.

Intensified Interdisciplinary Learning

Significantly, writing courses further the goals of learning communities through the writing-across-the-curriculum principle, "to write is to learn": Students better understand course material when they are writing about it. The idea that writing is connected to thinking is deeply embedded in composition theory, resulting in the assertion that writing not only expresses what one knows and has learned but that the act of writing is itself a means of learning. Early in the 1980s, C.H. Knoblauch and Lil Brannon (1983) articulated this principle for generations of compositionists to come:

> *The concern is to create intellectual dialogue as a way of stimulating more learning, to use writing as a means of personal discovery but also as a means of communicating the honest extent of the writer's understanding, including difficulties, inadequacies of insight, imperfect or unproductive connections among ideas and information, so that a more experienced learner can provide, through reinforcing commentary, some new directions for exploration. (p. 471)*

Joyce Magnotto's (1990) description of her linked-course program's goals indicates the importance of the writing-to-learn principle in the field of composition studies: "Writing to learn has been the main focus at Prince George's because it offers practical ways to increase and improve student writing without unduly burdening faculty who must teach five classes per semester" (p. 77). While Magnotto is recommending writing to learn from the perspective of limiting the quantity of grading an overloaded teacher might have, this writing also inherently benefits the students, enhancing the amount they remember and their understanding of the material. Ashley Williams clearly recognizes the increased depth writing to learn can add to a student's understanding when she comments on "the degree to which writing to learn, speculation, and integration is crucial to meaning making." She goes on to comment on how "In the changing social and power dynamics created by collaborative and experiential learning and by 'wired' writing, our students' work occupies a different space" (Zawacki & Williams, 2001, p. 123). Gesa Kirsch (1988) describes Susan Peck MacDonald's survey of students, which used self-assessment to evaluate the linked-writing course: "While some students were disappointed not to receive instructions in such matters as sentence structure and grammar, almost all students say they better understand the course material because they frequently write about it" (p. 52).

Diversity Training

As these aforementioned principles are put into action in writing classes, they become particularly well-chosen sites for training in issues of diversity. William Koolsbergen (2001), writing an article specifically on this topic, has said that "because learning communities are designed by faculty from different disciplines who come together to find a way to approach teaching and learning through the different perspectives of the disciplines, they are the ideal structure for dealing with diversity" (p. 26). While the diversity of the faculty and their collaboration in the learning community serves as a model for students, it is not the only way that learning communities are ideal sites for training in diversity. Tinto, Goodsell Love, and Russo (1993) also claim that the learning community setting, because of its multidisciplinary approach, "also provides a model of learning that encourages students to express the diversity of their experiences and world views" (p. 19). Within the specific classroom, Koolsbergen (2001) discusses using many of the principles commonly practiced as a part of composition pedagogy as the students work together to design a list of "ground rules for discussion" of diversity (p. 26).

PERILS OF INTEGRATING WRITING COURSES INTO LEARNING COMMUNITIES

Two important problems are raised by the entry of writing courses into learning communities. First, the writing course may devote itself exclusively to a skills orientation to instruction: Everyone involved, including the writing instructor, may easily lose sight of other goals for writing instruction. The second problem is closely related: The composition instructor may find herself in a subordinate position to the other instructors in the learning community.

Exclusive Focus on Traditional Rhetoric

The outcomes statement developed by the Council of Writing Program Administrators (1999) for first-year composition clusters course outcomes in four categories: rhetorical knowledge; critical thinking, reading, and writing; processes; and knowledge of conventions. Though the balance and emphasis may shift from one learning community to another, the goals listed in these four clusters will probably fare reasonably well in the writing courses in learning communities; none of these threatens or disrupts the orderly transmission of knowledge in the academic disciplines.

Not included in the necessarily conservative WPA outcomes, however, are goals widely shared by compositionists nationwide. These widely shared goals reach beyond the confines of what John Clifford (1991) calls "traditional rhetoric," to help students "to read and write and think in ways that both resist domination and exploitation and encourage self-consciousness about who they are and can be in the social world" (p. 51). We would not want to guess at the exact percentage of compositionists who endorse this revisionary agenda, but the position is certainly well articulated in the scholarly literature (Clifford, 1991; Crowley, 1998; Horner, 2001; Malinowitz, 1998; Russell, 1995). Composition historian James Berlin (1996) explains revisionary rhetoric in terms of the 20th century "linguistic turn" of structuralism and poststructuralism, which "can be seen as an effort to recover the tools of rhetoric in discussing the material effects of language in the conduct of human affairs" (p. xvii). In composition studies, Berlin (1996) offers "social-epistemic" rhetoric as his own label for the linguistic turn: "Social-epistemic rhetoric is the study and critique of signifying practices in their relation to subject formation within the framework of economic, social, and political conditions" (p. 77). The revisionary rhetoric that Berlin and others endorse is evident in two of the learning outcomes for Writing 105, the introductory composition course at Syracuse University: Outcome #13 says, "Students will develop a working understanding of contemporary theories of authorship," and #14 says, "Students will develop a working understanding of the potentials and problems of academic literacy" (Syracuse University, 2002).

How will these less conservative goals for writing instruction fare in learning communities? The answer will vary from one instructor to another, one community to another. But certainly the scope of possibility for writing instruction in learning communities will be limited by the degree of structural power accorded to the writing instructor. If that writing instructor is adjunct to the other courses in the learning community, if the writing instructor is a "teacher" while the others are "professors," if the writing instructor must attend the lectures of her colleagues in order to teach her writing class—the scope of the writing course is likely to be restricted to very traditional expectations and goals. David Young points to this dynamic when he says that in his learning community he was sometimes seen as the grammar cop by his colleagues, who wanted him to take sole responsibility for technical correctness (Zawacki & Williams, 2001, p. 118).

Subordination of the Writing Instructor

The figure of the writing teacher subordinated to colleagues in the disciplines appears in a variety of sources on linked-course instruction, and nowhere in this literature is it interrogated. In the linked arrangement at Oglethorpe University, for example, the composition instructors became students in the companion course (although Kerr and Picciotto don't describe the arrangement in those terms); they often attended class sessions of the "base course" in order "to focus writing assignments on current content in the base course and to aid the base course instructor in using writing effectively to enhance classroom learning." Kerr and Piccioto (1992) say nothing about the companion course instructors' attending the composition class in order to learn how to help students improve their writing. "Further assignments in the composition class were related—sometimes closely, sometimes not so explicitly—to the base course materials" (p. 108). Though a few writing instructors might welcome the new perspectives gained from such an arrangement, few would willingly continue in such an arrangement, surrendering the autonomy of their own classes to become tutors for (and students in) their colleagues' classes. The collegial politics of such arrangements are signaled in Robert J. Cullen's language as he describes writing instructors and base course professors. The fact that many writing programs are significantly staffed by teaching assistants and adjunct instructors too easily makes such arrangements seem natural, erasing the ways in which they subordinate the work of an entire academic discipline—the discipline of composition and rhetoric. If one partner in a learning community is a TA or part-timer, shouldn't that person's course be subordinated to the one taught by the tenured professor? When the two instructors disagree, how can the instructor hired as contingent faculty possibly hold her own against the professor in whom the institution has invested as much as two million dollars? In the presence of institutionally uneven power relations, Baker's (1999) principle for learning communities, "All members of the group are learners" (p. 99), can too easily become "The writing teacher is the student of the other teachers."

GUIDELINES FOR INTEGRATING WRITING COURSES INTO LEARNING COMMUNITIES

To assure the success of writing courses in learning communities so that they realize their potential for promoting active learning, community, collaboration, and intensified interdisciplinary learning, we offer the following suggestions:

Write the Contract Before Beginning the Job

Before the writing instructor commits to a learning community, she should be assured that she is entering an arrangement of collegial reciprocity and not becoming the tutor or teaching assistant to the instructors of the other courses in the community. What will be the roles of the other instructors in writing activities and writing instruction?

Articulate the Goals for Writing in the Learning Community

How compatible is the revisionary rhetoric that may inform the writing program with the goals and expectations of the learning community? Alternatively, how ready is the writing instructor to limit her instruction to traditional rhetoric?

Plan the Number of Extra Meetings or Workshops That Will be Part of the Learning Community

Some of our learning communities meet weekly, some bi-monthly, some monthly. The difference in time commitment is significant. Meeting frequency is also closely linked to the kinds of goals set by the learning community: how closely the teachers want to discuss student learning and progress, for instance, as well as how much time they have available to commit. Determining these limits ahead of time will assure that the teachers feel their work is truly collaborative. In the description of one of the learning communities at George Mason, Terry Zawacki (2001) claims: "In the most successful versions of fully linked courses, the faculty members meet often to plan, rethink, and revise their assignments in the light of students' learning needs" (p. 117). While this is a model several of our learning communities follow, others set their own quite different priorities and define their success in alternate ways.

Determine How the Success of the Learning Community and of the Linked Writing Course Will be Measured

Student evaluations will tend to assess the writing course according to how well students performed on writing assignments in the other courses. If they fared poorly on the writing assignments in their other classes, they will assert that the composition class was a failure. By what less reductive, less instrumentalist means will the success of the composition course be measured?

Consider the Labor Issues

If the writing instructor is contingent faculty, how will she be compensated for the extra work that is inevitably involved in learning communities? Although many part-timers are dedicated instructors who will enter learning community work uncompensated, social justice demands that already low-paid adjuncts are not asked or allowed to do pro bono work for the institution. Higher course rates or additional stipends are in order.

Assure Strong, Continuing Administrative Support

Even if the writing instructors in learning communities are full-time, tenured faculty, they are likely to be regarded by their colleagues in other disciplines as non-scholars or sub-scholars. Since the inception of composition instruction in the late 19th century, the teaching of composition has been regarded as something that any literate person can do and that none but the unfortunate would want to. So for teaching assistants, adjuncts, and even full-time, tenured composition faculty, a strong support structure needs to be in place, staffed by knowledgeable administrators willing to intervene in difficult negotiations. If teaching assistants are involved in learning communities, they must be carefully and constantly mentored. Teaching writing is a difficult job, made more complex by interactions with other courses in the disciplines.

Barbara Leigh Smith's (1993) vision for learning communities explains why writing courses are a natural fit: "Learning communities are a purposeful attempt to create rich, challenging, and nurturing academic communities where they might not otherwise exist" (p. 32). Smith continues, "The learning community approach fundamentally restructures the curriculum and the time and space of students" (pp. 32–33). Her statements echo in the more politically charged language of John Clifford (1991): "Writing, when studied and practiced in a rich sociopolitical context, can open spaces for the kind of informed resistance that can actually affect hegemonic structures" (p. 47). Both learning communities and writing instruction provide outstanding means of teaching traditional materials for traditional purposes, and both also provide ways of interrogating and re-imagining those materials and purposes. The benefits of including writing courses in learning communities surely warrants the measures that must be taken to assure an environment in which both traditional and revisionary rhetoric may be taught by writing instructors who enjoy full collegial parity with the other instructors in the learning community.

Rebecca Moore Howard is former chair of the writing program and Vivian Rice is outreach coordinator of the writing program, both of Syracuse University.

REFERENCES

Baker, P. (1999). Creating learning communities: The unfinished agenda. In B. A. Pescosolido & R. Aminzade (Eds.), *The social worlds of higher education* (pp. 95–109). Thousand Oaks, CA: Pine Forge Press.

Berlin, J. (1996). *Rhetorics, poetics, and cultures: Refiguring college English studies.* Urbana, IL: National Council of Teachers of English.

Bruffee, K. A. (1984). Collaborative learning and the "Conversation of Mankind." *College English, 46*(7), 635–652.

Clifford, J. (1991). The subject in discourse. In P. Harkin & J. Schilb (Eds.), *Contending with words: Composition and rhetoric in a postmodern age* (pp. 38–51). New York, NY: Modern Language Association.

Council of Writing Program Administrators. (1999). The WPA outcomes statement for first-year composition. *WPA: Writing Program Administration, 23*(1/2), 59–66. Retrieved December 24, 2003, from http://www.english.ilstu.edu/Hesse/outcomes.html

Crowley, S. (1998). *Composition in the university: Historical and polemical essays.* Pittsburgh, PA: University of Pittsburgh Press.

Cullen, R. J. (1985, Spring). Writing across the curriculum: Adjunct courses. *ADE Bulletin, 80,* 15–17.

Gay, P. (1991). A portfolio approach to teaching a biology-linked basic writing course. In P. Belanoff & M. Dickson (Eds.), *Portfolios: Process and product* (pp. 182–193). Portsmouth, NH: Boynton/Cook.

Griffith, C. W. (1985). Programs for writing across the curriculum: A report. *College Composition and Communication, 36*(4), 398–403.

Horner, B. (2001). "Students' right," English only, and re-imagining the politics of language. *College English, 63*(6), 741–758.

Howard, R. M. (2001). Collaborative pedagogy. In G. Tate, A. Rupiper, & K. Schick (Eds.), *A guide to composition pedagogies* (pp. 54–71). New York, NY: Oxford University Press.

Kerr, N. H., & Picciotto, M. (1992). Linked composition courses: Effects on student performance. *Journal of Teaching Writing, 11*(1), 105–118.

Kirsch, G. (1988). Writing across the curriculum: The program at Third College, University of California, San Diego. *WPA: Writing Program Administration, 12*(1/2), 47–55.

Knoblauch, C. H., & Brannon, L. (1983). Writing as learning through the curriculum. *College English, 45*(5), 465–474.

Koolsbergen, W. (2001, Summer/Fall). Approaching diversity: Some classroom strategies for learning communities. *Peer Review,* 25–27.

Lunsford, A. A., & Ede, L. (1990). *Singular texts/plural authors: Perspectives on collaborative writing.* Carbondale, IL: Southern Illinois University Press.

Magnotto, J. (1990). Prince George's Community College. In T. Fulwiler & A. Young (Eds.), *Programs that work: Models and methods for writing across the curriculum* (pp. 65–82). Portsmouth, NH: Boynton/Cook.

Malinowitz, H. (1998). A feminist critique of writing in the disciplines. In S. C. Jarratt & L. Worsham (Eds.), *Feminism and composition studies: In other words* (pp. 291–312). New York, NY: Modern Language Association.

McCarthy, L. P. (1987). A stranger in strange lands: A college student writing across the curriculum. *Research in the Teaching of English, 21*(3), 233–265.

Russell, D. (1995). Activity theory and its implications for writing instruction. In J. Petraglia (Ed.), *Reconceiving writing, rethinking writing instruction* (pp. 51–78). Mahwah, NJ: Lawrence Erlbaum.

Smith, B. L. (1993). Creating learning communities. *Liberal Education, 79*(4), 32–39.

Sutton, M. (1978). The writing adjunct program at the Small College of California State College. In J. P. Neel (Ed.), *Options for the teaching of English: Freshman composition* (pp. 104–109). New York, NY: Modern Language Association.

Syracuse University. (2002, July 16). *Learning outcomes for WRT 105: Academic writing.* Retrieved December 24, 2003, from http://wrt.syr.edu/pub/handbook/105outcomes.html

Tinto, V., Goodsell Love, A., & Russo, P. (1993). Building community among new college students. *Liberal Education, 79*(4), 16–21.

Zawacki, T. M., & Williams, A. T. (2001). Is it still WAC? Writing within interdisciplinary learning communities. In S. H. McLeod, E. Miraglia, M. Soven, & C. Thaiss (Eds.), *WAC for the new millennium: Strategies for continuing writing-across the-curriculum-programs* (pp. 109–140). Urbana, IL: National Council of Teachers of English.

5

Using Grids to Develop a Learning Community Curriculum

Nance Hahn

*L*ike most human endeavors, residential learning communities grow unevenly. Many take off with a burst of energy, cohering neatly around a common vision, then slow down to navigate conceptual and administrative roadblocks, only to stretch forward again, sometimes awkwardly, toward the next milestone. One rough patch sometimes occurs when new learning communities begin blending curricula. When key players are convinced of the project's merit, they propel their fledgling communities with a mix of faculty commitment, administrative flexibility, and the unflagging good will of residence life staff. But once the thrill of the founding moment subsides, learning community planners are left to grapple with the reality of competing course goals and course calendars vaguely to markedly out of sync. If planners are to work effectively as a team, they need to become acquainted with one another. If they are to craft an overarching curriculum, they must first understand each course in its own right. The challenge is further compounded by the fact that administrators and residence life staff and faculty members from one discipline to another have differing perspectives, different social styles, and even different terms for the concepts, practices, and activities of their daily lives. Those charged with orchestrating early planning meetings must find ways to help participants to bridge gaps. At Syracuse University, the planners of one early residential learning community used timelines and grids to analyze the community components and then to structure and document curriculum development.

Beginnings of the Management
Learning Community at Syracuse University

In the new community at Syracuse, first-year School of Management students would live together on two floors of a residence hall and enroll in the same sections of four courses: the introductory management course, a course in college writing, a mathematics course, and a one-credit course in college learning strategies. Faculty members for all but the mathematics course, residence life staff, and the faculty member coordinator of the learning community were to work together to design and develop the curriculum that would become the new community's academic foundation. Duties such as publicizing the community, enrolling prospective participants, and scheduling classes fell to the coordinator. So the team that would support the community throughout the semester formed around the issue of curriculum and could luxuriate— although it felt far from luxurious at times—in curriculum design.

The faculty coordinator, along with the instructor managing the writing segment of the curriculum, agreed to serve as curriculum discussion facilitators. Having teaching responsibility themselves, both facilitators well understood the faculty members' disciplinary commitment to the fields in which they had invested their intellectual lives. They understood the college teacher's view of the fifteen-week semester as almost always "too short." And they recognized that some faculty members have a limited tolerance for icebreakers, the simple social games that encourage a group to get to know one another. The residence life staffers, on the other hand, would not only understand the social utility of icebreakers, but would want to honor the clear social need for them by according them time and engaged effort at the very outset of the curriculum writing process. This difference in styles and preferences would be accentuated when participants talked about their work in specialized terms that might amount, under pressure, to speaking different languages.

Before the group came together for the first time, the facilitators agreed that it would be useful to have a grid displaying group members' various activities and responsibilities, perhaps week by week, over the first semester. Such a grid would allow them to see each endeavor—courses or residence hall floor activity—as a formerly freestanding component of the community. It would also be the framework into which new components, such as a workshop to support writing the major project in the management course, would be placed. As days passed and the initial curriculum-planning meeting loomed, the facilitators' original intent to collect syllabi and construct the grid themselves gave way to the realization that the group would need to create the grid ad hoc at the first meeting. As they considered this plan, the facilitators realized that they had stumbled on a method for meeting many of the group's needs with a single activity.

TRACING TIMELINES TO TELL THE STORIES OF THEIR COURSES

The curriculum group's first task was to begin to know each other and each other's courses; then they could plan next steps in curriculum construction. Confident that everyone present was feeling the pressure of time and would value an organized, analytic approach, the facilitators drew on narrative theory as well as their own experience as writers and storytellers to devise an opening activity calculated to serve as both an icebreaker and a way to move the group toward constructing a grid of activities and responsibilities. As the group gathered, they announced the goal of constructing a grid in stages. The "grand grid," facilitators said, would serve to organize and document their work. It would line up courses and hall activities next to each other so participants could see what everyone else is doing. It would make visible the areas of commonality and overlap. It might even be used to document the learning community's workings for other administrators and faculty members, and for prospective students and their families. Next, confident of the human appeal and leveling power of narrative, the facilitators invited each participant in turn to tell the story of his or her course or semester. Later the facilitators would learn to relax beginners with phrases like, "Just think of it as the comic strip character Charlie Brown's novel. 'A man was born. He lived and died.'" But this first time they simply coached speakers by encouraging them to begin with the semester's opening day, work toward familiar milestones (such as midterm examinations) and end with exams, final office hours, or whatever constituted closure at semester's end. As each faculty or staff member spoke in turn, as each separate semester soon-to-be-intertwined unfolded, a facilitator sketched a rough timeline on the whiteboard, stacking one above the other.

This way of working was new for most of the group, an effect that in itself was positive because it meant they shared the experience of moving into unfamiliar territory together. Participants talked freely, in part because they had complete authority over the content of their story; it was their personal experience and their professional expertise. Because the accounts were understood to be retrospective and conversational, no one in the group felt called upon to critique. Everyone warmed to the task of telling about the work they loved, and facilitators had to enforce the five-minute time limit.

Not surprisingly, participants focused on a range of aspects of their semester experience. Management faculty chose a mix of content areas and student project due dates. Writing instructors saw the semester in terms of research, drafts and revisions, and skills they expected students to have acquired in relation to various assignments. The education faculty member who would co-teach college learning strategies with a member of the residence life staff described modules that she felt could be interchanged rather easily. The group's attention was for the most part focused on each speaker in turn and briefly on the facilitators' occasionally comic efforts to capture the gist of the talk on the whiteboard. But a glance around the table at the listeners revealed that even at this early stage, the task preceding grid construction was accomplishing analytic and contrastive work.

As each speaker talked through the outline of his or her semester, listeners were tacitly invited to consider their own courses or activities in relation to the course being described. The summer mail contact with students and the welcome party that preceded the beginning of the semester in the School of Management intrigued the writing instructors who later mentioned that they wished they had pre-course contact with their students. Likewise, the in-class reflective essay and self-prescription for continued writing growth that came at the end of writing classes caught the attention of management faculty. And both subgroups were curious about time management techniques their students would gain from the college learning strategies course.

In between accounts, group members asked for clarification of routines and definition of terms. Everyone was interested in how other instructors set up student teams or small groups, whether students received specific instruction regarding how to work together (management faculty said they always provided it, while writing instructors sometimes did), and how long a team or small group stayed together. They toyed with the idea of preserving student team integrity from course to course. The pace of courses also became a conversation topic as the group checked to see where demands on students were particularly heavy. They were relieved to discover that the writing course was front loaded, with research, planning, and extensive drafting during the first six weeks, while the management course became progressively more demanding as the semester went on. But by this point in the exercise, participants were beginning to invest in the workings of the new community enough to consider moving some of their own course elements if it made for a more smoothly working whole. Concerns about due dates prompted the facilitators to begin trying to align the sketched timelines more accurately. The group was clearly ready to move to a more elaborated calendar grid—a week-by-week account of the community's life.

But before a new panel of whiteboard was pulled into place, the residence life staff responsible for community building and weekly floor activities confessed discomfort with describing their work along a timeline. On the one hand, they believed their contribution was essential to the operation of the community, a sentiment fully supported by everyone around the table. At the same time, they conceived their usual floor activities, after an opening effort at building community, as episodic and completely interchangeable. And because they had just listened to faculty accounts of courses in which each component intentionally laid the ground for the next, their confidence was shaken by what looked to them like their own lack of planning or scaffolding. "I guess our activities could go any old way," one staffer said, shaking her head. Faculty members, however, were quick to disagree. They remarked that resident advisers choose activities based on their reading of residents' needs, and that analysis of any semester's array would almost certainly reveal a sound developmental progression. With encouragement from all stakeholders— "We want to come up with a way to do this so we all support each other"— the facilitators prepared to move to a first grid.

FROM TIMELINES TO GRID

With an hour and a half of hard work behind them, the group was restless and beginning to bond in good-natured opposition to their facilitator taskmasters. One last push, facilitators assured them, would get them to a grid each subgroup could work on (sigh) in preparation for the next meeting. The facilitators drew vertical lines through the stacked timelines and asked clarifying questions to make sure the entries would make sense to everyone working on the grid after the meeting adjourned. The most developed four-week section of their grid, fleshed out by facilitators' questions, looked like Table 5.1.

Facilitators transcribed, reproduced, and distributed the grid to the planners, a task that SmartBoard technology has greatly simplified since this group first convened. Planners in turn came to the next meeting with their own courses more fully committed to the grid and eager to work on problem areas that remained difficult to mesh. The college learning strategies course, writing workshops, and floor activities gained direction from the grid, while the writing and management courses worked on making their potential and implicit connections more dynamic and explicit. Not surprisingly, some sections of the grid—to say nothing of the courses they represented—never

Table 5.1

	Week 4	Week 5	Week 6	Week 7
Residence hall floor activity	?	Line Up and Power Inversion (game-like activity examining power relationships)	Learning community faculty visit to talk about students as learners	Upper class management students visit to talk about how they became learners
Management course	Writing assignment 2 posted; research notes for industry analysis; team building	Conflict management essay; faculty feedback on research notes	Continue research notes; writing assignment 2 returned	Interview Day (Autumn Break)
Writing course	1st portfolios due; intro unit 2—team approach to first-person research	Reading, lecture, and discussion on how who you are affects what you (can) see	Fieldwork and field research notes; interview techniques and practice	From writing it down to writing it up—drafting from field research notes
College learning strategies	Collaboration; teamwork; managing team time	Notetaking techniques	Learning styles?	
Writing workshops	Research notes; building a working bibliography		Using individualized faculty input and feedback	

quite connected. Others, like the weeks on research and interviewing shown above, flowed into each other seamlessly. Planners found themselves intrigued with each other's courses and willing to make adjustments to make stronger connections. They began to develop common terminology—"team" to refer to an ongoing small group of students, "feedback" to refer to faculty commentary on students' written work—and realized they needed to distinguish between library or Internet research and field research, of which interviewing was a subcategory.

Excited by the possibilities of the grid exercise, the group played with separate grids for content and skills, teaching strategies, and assessment and evaluation. They also developed a step-by-step guide for beginning learning communities interested in using the grid process.

How to Use a Grid to Discover and Enhance Connections Among Courses

1. **Take time for each instructor to tell the story of her or his course.**

   Don't skip this step, no matter how tempted you are. You may believe you already know each other's courses. Or you may think jumping to #2 will save time. The story can be brief; two or three minutes are often enough. A few minutes spent on this first step will focus the work session, set a context for the project, and function as a social icebreaker.

2. **Sketch a rough timeline for each story.**

   Use a paper flipchart, blackboard or whiteboard. Don't attempt integration at first.

3. **Work from familiar anchors such as course introductions or final examinations toward more detail.**

   Coach the hesitant or confused with examples. Press anyone who says, "I just cover the material" with requests for content topics.

4. **Decide when and how to combine the timelines into a rudimentary grid. Use weeks or sections—whatever seems to work in common.**

   Be prepared to change the units as you continue working together. "Beginning," "middle," and "end" may seem enough at first. Later you may find yourselves gridding by weeks or even days.

5. **Reproduce and share grids with all participants.**

   Make copies with generous white space to encourage notes between meetings. Update grids frequently.

6. **Give early grid(s) time to incubate. Return to them at each get together.**

   A good grid is a work in progress. Tinker with it. Use it to stimulate mid-semester discussion and adjustments. A good grid can also be a useful product as well as a process. Administrators, faculty members curious about learning communities, and prospective students and their families can all profit from grids. Adjust content and complexity to intended audience.

7. **Remember that course content is only one plane along which to grid. Once you have a basic grid, consider adding skills students acquire,**

kinds of assessment and evaluation you routinely build in, modes of teaching and learning, and so on.

Some examples of skills students acquire include evaluating sources; integrating information from several sources; drafting, revising, and editing; finding everyday examples of principles; applying theory.

Some examples of teaching/learning modes inlcude lecture; small group discussion; recitation; laboratory experiments and observations; field observation; individual presentations.

Nance Hahn formerly taught writing and administered pre-college programs at Syracuse University.

6

The Power of Faculty–Student Affairs for Promoting Integrative Learning Experiences in Learning Communities

Cathy McHugh Engstrom

INTRODUCTION

I must admit that for over 15 years, beginning with my work with theme-based residential living-learning communities at three different institutions, I considered myself rather skilled at promoting academically based learning environments in residence halls. However, it was not until I began working directly with learning communities (those initiatives that involved an intentional restructuring of the curriculum to foster intellectual and social connections) that I realized how naïve I had been about understanding and experiencing student engagement in genuine integrated learning experiences. Two particular experiences helped me to this realization and taught me much.

First, over five or so years, I have been invited to participate in various learning community processes, from initial planning meetings, through semester-long meetings, and various assessment activities. I have been fortunate to see the process unfold at several institutions.

Second, I have developed a first-semester course for our master's students, Laboratory in Learning Communities (LLC), in which they are immersed in various interdisciplinary learning communities at three nearby campuses. In this course, I hope to foster their passion for promoting integrated learning experiences that intentionally link the academic, social, and affective domains of students' lives and to observe and hear from students what these experiences mean to them. My hope is that this course teaches them the qualities, skills, and competencies required to foster partnerships across disciplinary and functional units on college campuses. In other words, I am trying to foster students' appreciation for and expertise in bridge-building and their understanding of the courage and risk-taking required to foster educational reform.

The LLC class often includes debunking students' myths about faculty work and faculty attitudes toward students. Invariably, after students attend their first planning meeting and hear a faculty member share his or her concerns about a student, they come back awestruck that faculty 1) know the names of their students, 2) know what is going on in the lives of their students, and 3) actually care! It's always fun to watch my students' enthusiasm develop when they listen to botany, writing, and residence life instructors talk about their "Three Sisters" plant experiment. (Corn, squash, and beans are stronger, healthier, and more vibrant when grown together than when they grow independently.) The students have written a paper reporting on the experiment as well as a journal entry reflecting on it. The writing instructor talks about using the assignment to review with the students the proper way to write up an experiment "like a scientist" and compare it to the writing style used in their journal entry. The residence life staff member talks about the journal assignment, in which the students examine how the lab findings relate to developing a sense of community on their floor and the recent floor activity where the floor prepared and served food at the local homeless shelter.

By the end of the LLC course, many of my students, sadly indeed, wish they could do their undergraduate experience all over again. Meiklejohn, the founder of the first learning community in the early 1900's, would be appalled at their descriptions of their undergraduate years—the fragmentation and disconnection between their social and academic lives, and their failure to find relevance in many of the courses they took, particularly in solving concrete problems that matter to them. Most disturbing to me are my students' reports that their undergraduate experiences did not foster any intellectual curiosity; in fact quite the opposite occurred.

These attitudes, however, typically get challenged in my course as the students listen to undergraduates share their experiences in learning communities. They are convinced that learning communities can be a powerful mechanism on a residential floor culture to make it okay both to study and help one other academically. They are amazed at how accountable students feel to each other to do their group work in a timely, responsible manner, and how students will give their peers the third degree if they missed or were late for class. They watch students move toward the front of the classroom to engage fully in the course, rather than move progressively to the back.

It is important to push educators to implement learning community models that engage in curriculum integration, pedagogical change, and partnerships dedicated to learning. Based on current trends and societal conditions, the situation at many colleges and universities is ripe for promoting the kind of integrated learning experiences espoused by Meiklejohn, his colleagues, and students 75 years ago in the Experimental College at the University of Wisconsin, Madison, particularly if we approach our educational reform efforts with faculty and student affairs working in close collaboration.

Higher education is in the midst of a major transformation. Educators have identified a critical need to refocus on the primary purpose of higher education, namely to increase the relevance and importance of the undergraduate experience and student learning (Boyer Commission on Educating Undergraduates in the Research University [Boyer Commission], 1998; Wingspread Group, 1993). Legislators, governing boards, families, and community groups have pushed for universities and colleges to develop socially responsible and responsive knowledge. Higher education is being challenged to prepare students to deal with major societal challenges such as violence, poverty, illiteracy, and now central on many minds, terrorism. However, for the most part, our current curricula and organizational structures are filled with individualized, isolated, disconnected experiences for students where their cocurricular lives are separate and distinct from their experiences in the classroom.

Barr and Tagg (1995) have advocated that institutions move from a teaching to a learning paradigm. A student learning paradigm requires a new way of thinking and acting at both institutional and individual levels. Terenzini and Pascarella (1994) stressed that "... faculty members, joined by academic and student affairs administrators, must devise ways to deliver undergraduate education that are as comprehensive and integrated as the ways students actually learn" (p. 32). Deep learning is facilitated when the academic and social domains of the college experience are merged or become seamless. A student learning paradigm suggests a "whole new mindset" (Terenzini & Pascarella, 1994, p. 32); different roles and responsibilities for faculty, student affairs, and college and university structures (Engstrom & Tinto, 2000; Kuh, 1996; Love & Goodsell Love, 1995); and ultimately a new set of roles, responsibilities, and levels of accountability for students.

In this chapter, I begin with a brief historical context for why student affairs and faculty typically do not work together. Second, I share a few trends and forces affecting higher education that create significant promise for reconceptualizing these relationships so we might be more successful in making the cocurricular and curricular lines obsolete as we intentionally encourage students to capitalize on the interrelatedness of the in- and out-of-class learning experiences (Terenzini & Pascarella, 1994). Third, I propose a partnership framework for carefully examining how faculty and student affairs professionals work together. I describe and offer a continuum of relationships, demonstrating varying levels of engagement, shared learning, and institutional reform. Finally, I leave you with some strategies to consider in helping student affairs and academic affairs work toward developing partnerships that minimally challenge—and optimally begin to dismantle—organizational barriers hindering the widespread use of integrated learning experiences.

SETTING THE CONTEXT FOR STUDENT AFFAIRS–ACADEMIC AFFAIRS PARTNERSHIPS

Barriers to Partnerships

Strong forces in the history of American higher education have acted as barriers to developing integrated learning experiences. Our system of higher education over the past 100 years has been built upon the research model introduced in the states in the mid-1800s. The primary focus of faculty at many institutions became research and the production of knowledge. The model was also an impetus for the emergence of the system of elective courses and the growth of professional schools. Faculty were rewarded for their research and expertise in their academic disciplines; they handed over advising, discipline, and administrative responsibilities to a new group of professionals on college campuses, the student affairs professionals. These individuals were viewed, and often still are, as solely responsible for the psychosocial, ethical, and emotional well-being of students.

Throughout most of the 20th century, student affairs units and academic departments became increasingly autonomous, specialized, and complex. As student affairs functions and academic departments became more specialized and discrete over the years, each developed its own culture, including unique value systems, ways of knowing, norms of behavior, roles and responsibilities, customs, language, and work habits. These different cultures translated into diverse organizational structures, professional preparation, goals, priorities, and reward systems. Using descriptors on the extreme, faculty often have been described as introverted, isolated, reflective, cautious, likely to move at their own pace, creative, and innovative. They value nonconformity and prefer organizational structures based on shared governance and peer leadership. Their loyalties are often primarily to their discipline rather than their institution. Faculty rewards, particularly at research institutions, are based more on scholarly contributions to an academic discipline than on teaching and student or institutional success. Faculty members consider it their right and responsibility to challenge structures that are threats to academic freedom. They take pride in challenging the status quo.

On the other hand, student affairs administrators are often depicted as extroverted, action-oriented, focused on products or results without engaging in any critical intellectual analysis of issues, and skilled at securing resources, managing crises, and solving problems. Student affairs professionals often seek student involvement in decision-making and serve as student advocates, particularly for students whose experiences are marginalized. Their reward system benefits those who demonstrate loyal behavior to supervisors and conscientious adherence to institutional policies and norms of behavior. Student affairs organizational structures tend to be characterized by hierarchical structures (residence life typically having more layers of bureaucracy than many Fortune 500 companies), centralized decision-making, and defined responsibilities and lines of authority. Student affairs organizational structures are set to maintain the status quo, which surfaces contradictions and tensions when student affairs professionals try to promote student engagement and involvement in decision-making.

The strength and sustainability of these cultures have resulted in our inability to change quickly in response to changing needs of students (Love & Goodsell Love, 1995) and have led to relationships often characterized by misunderstanding, disrespect, conflict, and antagonism (Blake, 1979; Schroeder, 1998). As Blake (1979) shared, "It is hardly surprising that different human personalities tend to end up as professors or administrators of student affairs. In caricature, the professorial extreme is almost the mirror image of the student personnel administrator extreme" (p. 284). Many faculty and student affairs professionals speak different languages literally and metaphorically (Knefelkamp, 1991), and members of each group tend to be suspicious of those who cross borders (Brown, 1997).

Opportunities

Although the obstacles just described are real and formidable, recent trends and forces affecting higher education hold significant promise and hope for a re-conceptualization of faculty and student affairs partnerships that might allow us to create integrated learning experiences across a seamless curriculum (Kuh, 1996). Paradigm shifts about knowledge and the teaching/learning process are occurring in education, the humanities, and the social sciences. Educators are challenging the objective and cognitive assumptions about knowledge and are advocating that the individualist, independent, and competitive climate of our institutions be complemented with inclusive, caring elements of community (Belenky, Clinchy, Goldberger, & Tarule, 1986; Palmer, 1987). Increasing numbers of scholars in the social sciences, humanities, and education *and* professionals in student affairs are advancing perspectives that are more inclusive, collaborative, egalitarian, and less hierarchical (Rhoads & Black, 1987). In addition, the academy is beginning to embrace a broader notion of scholarship that recognizes innovative applications of research and the integration of research, teaching, and service as important scholarly activities (Boyer, 1987; Angelo & Cross, 1993). Faculty reward structures that support this view of scholarship open up new, exciting possibilities for how faculty construct their work and the type of partnerships that might now be meaningful.

Leaders in student affairs have called for professionals to work with faculty to consider seriously how to design integrated learning experiences and to confront the seemingly insurmountable divide between classroom and out-of-class learning (AAHE, ACPA, NASPA, 1998; ACPA, 1994; Kuh, 1996; Love & Goodsell Love, 1995). Kezar and Rhoads (2001) recommend that faculty and student affairs focus on freeing themselves from "the philosophical boxes" (p. 162) that have hindered each group's capacity to learn new ways to think about how institutions might be organized to promote more holistic learning approaches for our students.

A FRAMEWORK FOR ANALYZING FACULTY–STUDENT AFFAIRS PARTNERSHIPS

Over the past decade, academic affairs and student affairs have come together to offer learning activities in a multitude of ways. How might these various faculty–student affairs partnerships be characterized? How would we describe how they work together? What dimensions are critical to the sustainability and power of learning communities for promoting shared learning experiences among students, student affairs personnel, and faculty? I propose that we closely examine the nuances, unspoken assumptions, and behaviors embedded in these relationships to understand better how collaboratively we all in fact work.

I have identified the following interrelated questions that I hope are useful for examining the levels of involvement and collaboration of student affairs personnel and faculty in learning community initiatives. To what degree do faculty and student affairs colleagues working on learning community initiatives experience the following outcomes? How might faculty and student affairs staff respond to the following questions?

- Have you developed shared, mutually agreed-upon vision and goals to ground learning community initiatives or, as Smith (2002) put it, "to come to a common understanding about why you are doing this learning community?"

- Do you team-teach?

- Do you develop one integrated, joint syllabus in which interdisciplinary themes for the learning experience are shared, understood, and regularly communicated by all parties?

- Do you link assignments and connect them to students' daily lives and experiences on a regular basis?

- Do you invest the time and energy necessary to engage in ongoing, regular communication? Do you know one another?

- Do you visit your colleagues' classes to get a better appreciation of how to link the material across the curriculum?

- Do student affairs and faculty members working on this initiative have a heightened understanding and appreciation for one another's work?

- Do you continually challenge your mental maps and consider cross-divisional and interdisciplinary perspectives based on shared learning goals?

- Do you value, solicit, and learn from the diverse expertise, perspectives, and knowledge of individual partners? Is this experience a learning experience for you? Do you find yourself continuously shifting back and forth from being the teacher to being the learner, depending upon the particular expertise and experiences in the group?

- Do you aggressively find ways to make intentional connections between what is happening in students' lives and the formal curriculum so that these distinctions are permeable and flexible? Do you work to dismantle policies and procedures that may get in the way of fostering such connections (e.g., space policies)?

- Do you create and implement shared, inclusive, facilitative decision-making structures that promote work related to the shared vision? How have you included students in these decision-making mechanisms? Have you given students meaningful ways to take responsibility to learn and live?

- Do you feel increasingly comfortable with and value the increasing ambiguity and fluidity in each other's roles and responsibilities? As soon as we begin to push toward making ongoing connections between students' lives and the coursework, the traditional roles of faculty and student affairs begin to break down. Are you ready for this messiness, lack of certainty?

- Do you care about one another and work to provide learning experiences for all partners? Are you working together for the long haul rather than for a one-shot experience?

- Are you investing energy into building relationships based on respect, trust, and mutual understanding?

- Do you recognize conflict as a source of learning and resolve difficult issues through conversations based on candor, honesty, and empathy?

- In what ways have you worked together to create a safe environment to take risks, make mistakes, and share vulnerabilities?

- Have you developed a belief that each participant's involvement makes a significant, positive difference in the lives of students, the institution, and the community?

- In what ways do your partners and you stimulate creativity and an entrepreneurial spirit in each other's work?

- Do you share and distribute resources (e.g., staff, funds, facilities) equitably?

- Do you engage in joint scholarship, assessment, and evaluation regarding your learning community program?

- Do you celebrate shared accomplishments together?

- Do you demonstrate courageous leadership by consistently advocating for one another and communicating publicly about the contributions each partner makes to student learning?

- In what ways do you and your partners identify and challenge organizational structures and systems that hinder efforts between faculty and student affairs to work towards designing innovative, seamless learning experiences?

Responses to these questions can provide substantial insight into the degree to which partnerships are and can be built upon a foundation of mutual learning and trust and predict the success faculty and student affairs will enjoy in promoting meaningful, connected, and sustainable student learning experiences.

MOVING FROM CLEARINGHOUSE TO COLLABORATION: A PARTNERSHIP DEVELOPMENT SCHEME

Clearly, there is a continuum of low to high collaborative relationships. Those more low-level collaborations that I observe on college campuses I tend to call forums, where student affairs personnel provide clearinghouse or resource support functions to faculty who are involved in the real meat of learning community work. For example, residence life staff might give faculty information on how to secure a dining hall pass, how to reserve lounge spaces for classroom use, and how to obtain the number of desired residence hall floors or spaces. Student affairs staff may address requests to secure programming funds to support the academic programming of the faculty member (e.g., a trip to the theatre). At this low end of the collaboration continuum, relationship building between individual student affairs professionals and faculty members is not essential. The interactions between faculty and student affairs staff are likely to be one-dimensional, superficial, one-time, and a means to an end. Certainly, at this end of the partnership continuum, faculty and student affairs professionals would not reflect upon their work in significantly different ways. The organizational structures remain status quo.

Cooperative partnerships require more engagement by faculty and student affairs staff in developing and implementing learning community initiatives. These types of partnerships probably characterize how most faculty and student affairs currently work together on learning community initiatives. The FIG model and linked learning communities that include a freshman seminar are good examples of a more cooperative endeavor between faculty and student affairs staff. In both of these models, faculty and student affairs staff can do their work rather independently, but both parties are essential to the initiative's success. The functions assumed by each individual are well defined and tend to tap what is typically and traditionally considered to be each partner's strengths and area of responsibility. For example, student affairs professionals exercise their skills in orienting students to campus, laying out expectations for student behavior, building community, and attending to transitional and academic support needs of students. Faculty members often are sought out for their expertise in the content areas and positive teaching reputation. Both faculty and student affairs professionals may be actively engaged in the student learning process, but not in learning from one another. Their roles and responsibilities remain unexamined and intact. Students assume the primary responsibility for making connections across the curriculum and sorting out the relevance of their coursework to their lives as college/university citizens. These initiatives provide invaluable learning opportunities for students, particularly in helping students make the transition to college; however, the impact of these programs for fostering curricular coherence, connections, and educational reform is limited.

At the highest end of the collaborative partnership continuum—authentic collaboration—faculty and student affairs create and share common understandings about the purpose and goals of the learning community program. The focus of this level of collaboration is not on producing a final product but rather on mutually constructing the vision, goals, and processes for developing integrated student learning experiences (Engstrom & Tinto, 2000). All participants seek to develop a democracy that values the inclusion of many voices, many ideas, many perspectives focused on student learning and community responsibility. Each partner is perceived and recognized as holding important knowledge and experiences that can contribute to the group and students' learning. The responsibilities and roles of participation are in constant negotiation; authority is shared and continually shifts based on the expertise in the group. Conflicts and difficult dialogues are essential to promoting trusting relationships (Bruffee, 1987; Matthews, Cooper, Davidson, & Hawkes, 1995), community, and different ways of knowing (Palmer, 1987).

In this process, faculty and student affairs staff (and hopefully students) will recognize and confront their biases and presuppositions about one another. This reflection initiates what Bruffee (1987) referred to as a "re-acculturation process." Each partner must renegotiate membership in groups or cultures with which they have affiliated as they learn to become members of another group or culture. The educational process of this re-acculturation can be extremely difficult and painful, and often incomplete. Boundaries become permeable and even reconstructed. Consequently, members in these partnerships must be open to cultural change, exercising new levels of ingenuity and innovention (Bruffee, 1987). Because the driving principles and pedagogies that undergird learning communities are consistent with working collaboratively, we should work towards the higher end of this collaboration partnership model with passion and vigor. A discussion about this vision of collaboration requires some imagination. Faculty and student affairs personnel are heading down unknown, uncharted paths in which the roles and responsibilities of those involved are in constant renegotiation.

However, progress up the collaborative continuum is evident when faculty and student affairs staff are working together to develop shared goals and a joint curriculum or when students refer to all faculty and student affairs staff as teachers and advisors (educators). A learning community coordinator who reports jointly to a provost and a vice president for student affairs symbolizes the need to integrate in a structural way the two sides of the house. Involvement of learning community faculty in the selection of their learning community residence director and resident advisers demonstrates the fluidity of roles and valuation of diverse perspectives. Examples of dynamic roles and responsibilities are evident when we hear faculty insight into roommate problems or gender dynamics on the floor, and a residence director shares ideas on how to integrate the community conflicts into the upcoming book assigned in a writing course. I think we are making progress toward authentic collaboration on my own campus when learning community programs have openly embraced my students into their classrooms and meetings. Faculty and student affairs professionals are willing to expose their vulnerabilities, their tensions, and struggles so critical in the development of strong partnerships. I think this vivid understanding of the journey of developing powerful learning community experiences is missing in the higher education literature. Finally, when an ethos of learning (Kuh, 1996) starts to permeate a campus culture, we can feel confident that interdisciplinary and cross-departmental connections are being made. On my own campus, we are convinced that the only way to change our campus student culture from one in which too many students value partying and basketball games to one in which the predominant student values are learning and the pursuit of intellectual interests is for partnerships between student affairs personnel and faculty to be at the center of our learning community initiatives. I was optimistic that we were making progress when I interviewed a woman management student at the end of her yearlong experience in a clustered learning community. When I asked her to reflect upon the benefits of participation in this learning community, she shared that it made her feel smart for the first time in her life. She always got good grades but she never felt smart until she found herself on a residential floor being sought after by her peers for help. In high school, she tended to do her homework in isolation, away from her peers. To learn with and teach her peers was at the center of her residential learning community experience and motivated her to apply for several leadership experiences that also allowed her to bridge the academic-social divide (peer facilitator for the School of Management freshmen gateway class and resident adviser). I am doubtful that this woman would have had the same experience on a non learning community floor at my institution. We are hopeful that in a few years, these types of experiences will dominate the campus landscape, rather than be the exception.

From a national perspective, there are a few institutions that stand out in terms of engaging in authentic partnerships with students, faculty, student affairs professionals, and the community. Syracuse University began its learning community initiative based on the premise that student affairs, specifically residence life, and academic affairs had to work side-by-side to develop the program goals, themes, and processes. The residence life associate director and the faculty member who are jointly responsible for SU's learning communities program share business cards (one name on one side, the other name on the other side) to symbolize the collaborative nature of their work. Wagner College has adopted the "Wagner Plan for Practical Liberal Arts," a four-year comprehensive undergraduate curriculum. All students are required to complete three learning communities, two reflective tutorials with community-based learning, a liberal arts core requirement, a major, and other components. Organizationally at Wagner College, the dean of the college oversees both the student affairs and academic support dimensions of the institution. The dean of the college provides the linkages among students, faculty, student affairs professionals, and the community.

Conclusion

What can be learned from institutions that promote and sustain collaborative partnerships that encourage, or require, faculty and student affairs professionals to work together across cultural differences and forces of specialization and fragmentation? What recommendations can be shared to promote learning-centered and civic-minded, engaged campuses that recognize the inter-relatedness of in- and out-of-class educational experiences?

I would recommend a few concrete steps to consider. First, in any learning community initiative, at the most basic level, faculty and student affairs personnel need to get to know each other and meet on a regular basis. This suggestion seems so simple yet is so easily ignored amidst our endless competing priorities. Collaborative relationships are built on trust. We must know each other well before we can enter into any type of trusting relationships. Send your learning community teams away to conferences or curriculum retreats. A key turning point in the School of Management faculty–student affairs partnership on my campus was the informal time spent over daiquiris at a learning community conference, away from the distractions of our campus and our lives.

In addition, we must take the time to truly understand each others' work. I am constantly amazed at how ignorant my student affairs colleagues are about the demands and realities of faculty life. For example, I hear them complain in the summer about the absence of faculty members and their seeming resistance to attend summer planning meetings or meetings over vacations. Typically, faculty members are on a nine-month contract (they are not paid in the summer) and are using summer time to catch up on their research. They accrue no vacation time but often are buried in papers or exams to read. Likewise, most faculty members have no idea about the kinds of crisis management responsibilities assumed by student affairs staff.

We also have to find ways to tap the unexpected knowledge and expertise that we each can bring to better understanding and supporting students. I am convinced that writing instructors know more about the issues and challenges facing college students than any staff or faculty on campus. How often do we seek out these folks for their knowledge and insights? Learning communities really open up these opportunities for shared knowledge.

I also encourage campuses to create strong, visible, active leadership or advisory teams comprised of faculty and student affairs professionals from diverse disciplines and student affairs functional areas (not just residential life). These teams must be encouraged to develop a shared vision and purpose for their learning community initiatives and work side-by-side to develop and implement processes critical to the quality and sustainability of their programs. They must publicize and reward the hard work of successful partnerships.

Authentic collaborative relationships have the potential to develop when senior administrators' agendas focus visibly on student learning, community engagement, and the development of student citizenship. Senior-level administrators should support collaborative initiatives by celebrating those relationships that require the most time, risk, and innovation. The inclusion of involvement in learning communities as a factor in promotion and tenure decisions is also critical. Institutional leaders must adopt a more inclusive view of scholarship that values interdisciplinary, integrated approaches to teaching and broaden the definition of research to include the development of knowledge that addresses preparing our students to think critically and engage in solving complex community issues. Without these paradigm shifts in how scholarship is viewed, it is not likely that partnerships between student affairs and faculty will reflect anything more than fragmented efforts at the periphery of campus life. And our graduate programs (including our graduate teaching programs) must include training on innovative pedagogies, curriculum coherence, and educational reform. Finally, it cannot be forgotten that innovations in teaching and learning can be expensive (Barr, 1998). Administrators must provide adequate resources in the areas of staffing, facilities, program development, and assessment in order for faculty–student affairs initiatives in the learning community arena to be created and sustained. Clearly, such partnerships are very powerful vehicles for transforming our institutions into learning-centered organizations (Engstrom & Tinto, 2000) that promote individual and institutional civic responsibility and enrich our students, our institutions, and our society.

In closing, let me leave you with a few thoughts shared in focus groups with learning community students who participated in residentially based linked learning communities. I think their voices reinforce our need to work tirelessly to create the inclusive, dynamic, intellectually and socially vibrant communities in which faculty and student affairs work in partnership.

> **Suzie:** *When I am in class, I am more comfortable sharing my own opinions. If you have any questions, you know your peers already. So you're okay, let me just ask the question. Anything you want to say, you are willing to say it. Because the people around you understand you and your personality. And I think I learn better.*

> **Bob:** *And another big benefit is hanging out and just talking. Or playing foosball. And the other good thing is that there always are people studying. So you can always have the opportunity to get help. Just knock on anyone's door. Just knock and walk in. It's a nice place.*

> **Dana:** *One amazing thing for me was our relationships with our teachers. Immediately, they are like, "You can call me John. You can call me Suzy. This is Ann. This is David." They used their first names, and that's such a huge barrier right there. I really feel they see us as equals, and I think they care more about me than just on the academic level. That is what they give off. Because you know, like John [the instructor]. I had my academic advising meeting with him and his first questions were "How do you like the learning community? Are you adjusting to being away from home okay? How was your weekend?" As opposed to "Okay, get out your textbook and take notes." They ask me things like that which makes me feel like they really care. My*

relationships with the learning community teachers are much stronger than in other classes.

This chapter offers opportunities and models for establishing collaborative partnerships between faculty and student affairs professionals. Learning community initiatives are ideal locations for these relationships to develop and thrive. These partnerships are very powerful vehicles for transforming our institutions into learning-centered organizations (Engstrom & Tinto, 2000) that promote student responsibility for their learning and provide the social and academic supports critical for students to flourish.

Cathy McHugh Engstrom is associate professor of higher education at Syracuse University.

REFERENCES

American College Personnel Association (ACPA). (1994). *The student learning imperative: Implications for student affairs.* Washington, DC: Author. Retrieved February 25, 2003, from http://www.acpa.nche.edu/sli/sli.htm

American Association for Higher Education (AAHE), American College Personnel Association (ACPA), & National Association of Student Personnel Administrators (NASPA). (1998). *Powerful partnerships: A shared responsibility for learning.* Washington, DC: Author.

Angelo, T. A., & Cross, K. P. (1993). *Classroom assessment techniques: A handbook for college teachers* (2nd ed.). San Francisco, CA: Jossey-Bass.

Barr, R. B. (1998). Obstacles to implementing the learning paradigm: What it takes to overcome them. *About Campus, 2*(3), 18–25.

Barr, R. B., & Tagg, J. (1995). From teaching to learning: A new paradigm for undergraduate education. *Change, 27*(6), 12–25.

Belenky, M., Clinchy, B., Goldberger, N., & Tarule, J. (1986). *Women's ways of knowing: The development of self, voice, and mind.* New York, NY: Basic Books.

Blake, E. S. (1979). Classroom and context: An educational dialectic. *Academe,* 280–292.

Boyer Commission on Educating Undergraduates in the Research University. (1998). *Reinventing undergraduate education: A blueprint for America's research universities.* Stanford, CA: Carnegie Foundation for the Advancement of Teaching.

Boyer, E. L. (1987). *College: The undergraduate experience in America.* New York, NY: Harper & Row.

Brown, J. (1997). On becoming learning organizations. *About Campus, 1*(6), 5–13.

Bruffee, K. A. (1987). The art of collaborative learning. *Change, 3,* 42–47.

Engstrom, C. M., & Tinto, V. (1997). Working together for service learning. *About Campus, 2*(3), 101–105.

Engstrom, C. M., & Tinto, V. (2000). Developing partnerships with academic affairs to enhance student learning. In M. J. Barr & M. K. Desler (Eds.), *The handbook of student affairs administration* (2nd ed., pp. 425–452). San Francisco, CA: Jossey-Bass.

Gabelnick, F. (1997). Educating a committed citizenry. *Change, 29*(1), 30–35.

Kezar, A., & Rhoads, R. (2001). The dynamic tensions of service-learning in higher education: A philosophical perspective. *The Journal of Higher Education, 72,* 148–171.

Knefelkamp, L. L. (1991). *The seamless curriculum. CIC Deans Institute: Is this good for our students?* Washington, DC: Council for Independent Colleges. ED 356 720.

Kuh, G. D. (1996). Guiding principles for creating seamless learning environments for undergraduates. *Journal of College Student Development, 37,* 135–148.

Love, P. G., & Goodsell Love, A. (1995). *Enhancing student learning: Intellectual, social, and emotional integration* (ASHE-ERIC Higher Education Report No. 4). Washington, DC: George Washington University.

Matthews, R. S., Cooper, J. L., Davidson, N., & Hawkes, P. (1995). Building bridges between cooperative and collaborative learning. *Change, 27*(4), 34–40.

Nelson, A. R. (2002). *Education and democracy.* Madison, WI: University of Wisconsin Press.

Palmer, P. (1987). Community, conflict, and ways of knowing. *Change, 19*(5), 20–25.

Rhoads, R. A., & Black, M. A. (1995). Student affairs practitioners as transformative educators. Advancing a critical cultural perspective. *Journal of College Student Development, 36,* 413–421.

Schroeder, C. C. (1998). *Developing collaborative partnerships that enhance student learning and educational attainment.* Washington, DC: American College Personnel Association. Retrieved December 24, 2003, from http://www.acpa.nche.edu/srsch/charles_schroeder.html

Senge, P. M. (1990). *The fifth discipline: The art and practice of the learning organization.* New York, NY: Doubleday.

Smith, B. L. (2002, October 10). *The challenges of learning communities as a growing national movement.* Paper presented at the Making of Learning Communities on the Occasion of the 75th Anniversary of Alexander Meiklejohn's Experimental College, Madison, WI.

Terenzini, P. T., & Pascarella, E. T. (1994, January/February). Living with myths: Undergraduate education in America. *Change, 26*(1), 28–32.

Wingspread Group on Higher Education. (1993). *An American imperative: Higher expectations for higher education.* Racine, WI: Johnson Foundation.

7

The Challenge of Assessing Learning Communities in a Collaborative Environment

Barbara A. Yonai

*T*he diversity of schools and colleges at Syracuse University and the tradition of decentralizing services has always been a challenge for assessment planning. Balancing the necessity of university-wide data collection with local interests continues to be critical to the success of any assessment effort. The assessment of learning communities is no exception. In fact, the diversity of models, topics, and structures at Syracuse, while providing wonderful opportunities for students, adds to the complexity of the assessment process. In addition, because this was one of the first major collaborations between student affairs and academic affairs that occurred at the faculty and staff level rather than at the administrative level, the differences in the two cultures had not been previously negotiated.

From the beginning of the learning communities program at Syracuse, it was clear that various participants (faculty, staff, and students) were interested in different questions, methodologies, and reporting techniques. It was also clear that there was a need for gathering information within each learning community so that faculty and staff could monitor student learning and make improvements to their community. However, it was also critical to provide information across learning communities to administrators.

This chapter describes how Syracuse University developed a plan that addresses both these local, formative needs and the university-wide, summative needs. First, an overview of how the different cultures of student affairs and academic affairs influence the assessment process is provided. Second, our approach to developing an assessment plan is described, including the formation of a committee to design and oversee the plan. Third is a discussion of the implementation of the assessment plan. An overview of lessons learned is provided in the concluding section.

STUDENT AFFAIRS–ACADEMIC AFFAIRS
CULTURAL DIFFERENCES IN APPROACHING ASSESSMENT

The learning communities initiative at Syracuse University has been, from the beginning, a collaboration between student affairs and academic affairs personnel. Therefore, it was also a requirement that the assessment process represent the perspectives of these two dimensions of the university. However, just as the development of learning communities must account for the cultural differences and similarities of these two groups, so must the assessment process.

Table 7.1 outlines some of the key cultural characteristics of student affairs and academic affairs personnel that influence assessment issues. An earlier version of this table was developed by Hurd, Peckskamp, and Yonai (2002), based on the work of Engstrom and Tinto (2000).

The key to developing an assessment plan is not only to understand these differences, but to use these differences to strengthen the work that is being done. This does require negotiation and opportunities for multiple perspectives to be considered. For example, student affairs personnel focus their assessment questions on personal growth, student characteristics, and team building while academic affairs personnel focus their questions on the classroom experiences. Together these perspectives provide a comprehensive view of the activities of learning communities.

Academic affairs will most likely view assessment or research on learning communities as part of their scholarly work, which values individual work rather than teamwork. Publications and presentations often are future-oriented, and timelines are imposed by the faculty member rather than others. However, student affairs personnel operate in a hierarchal environment that rewards collaboration and cooperation. This approach requires answers to specific assessment questions, uses data to make decisions, and requires data quickly. Faculty are accustomed to questioning and challenging authority and structures whereas student affairs personnel are expected to be loyal to the institution and provide the requested information in a timely manner. These cultural differences are more obvious when there is pressure from administrators for data to be collected using either specific methods or within a timeline that not all groups agree is appropriate.

Table 7.1

Assessment Issues: Differences between Academic Affairs and Student Affairs

Dimension	Academic Affairs	Student Affairs	Impact on Assessment
Student learning	Emphasis on critical thinking, acquisition of knowledge; belief that intellectual/academic activities in the classroom are superior to out-of-class activities	Emphasis on personal growth—social and affective; believe AA and SA have the shared purpose of educating the whole student	Different interests in types of questions asked; different focus of the evaluation; combined efforts lead to developing a comprehensive assessment plan
Work environment	Structures emphasize collegiality through shared governance; peer leadership; loyalty to the academic discipline	Hierarchical structures; centralized decision-making; interest in moving up the administrative ladder; loyalty to department and institution	Pressure by administrators to assess student affairs feels necessity to respond; academic affairs faculty can ignore the pressure
Ways of working	Engage in solitary, autonomous, independent work; thinking and reflecting; focus on the future	Work collaboratively to solve problems with immediate deadlines; action-oriented; little reflection time	Academic affairs wants to think and discuss assessment; student affairs are more anxious to set tasks
Personality type	Introverted; reflective; independent; skeptical	Interpersonally adept; extroverted; problem solvers	Different levels of comfort with collaboration and meetings
Areas of expertise	Academic discipline; teaching content related to academic discipline; research skills; writing skills; creative activity	Student characteristics; interpersonal dynamics, team building, managing conflict; institutional processes	Different focus; different levels of comfort with research expertise and methodology; potential to develop more comprehensive approach
Important norms/values	Ambiguity, autonomy, flexibility, innovation, critical analysis; nonconformity; responsibility to challenge structures that are threats to academic freedom	Goal and task completion; accountability; cooperation; public loyalty to institutional policy	Potentially conflicting norms requires understanding, listening, and collaboration; potential to provide multiple perspectives on same program
Reward system	Normally based primarily on scholarly/creative productivity	Based on loyal behavior to supervisors, adherence to current administrative norms	Impacts timelines; conflict about who is driving the assessment—internal versus external pressures and needs
Assessment goals	Some use classroom assessment techniques; most would like assessment to go away	Generate quantitative data; need to use assessment to demonstrate effectiveness, fiscal responsibility	Potential conflict between accountability and scholarly work; timelines, methodology impacted

We recognized many of these issues prior to working on the assessment plan, but we were not prepared for some of the effects these cultural differences would have on our planning. In the following section we describe our method for developing an environment where assessment issues could be discussed and addressed.

DEVELOPING AN ASSESSMENT PLAN

The number of people from academic affairs and student affairs from a variety of offices and programs within those units who were involved with learning communities brought different perspectives and needs to the table. This meant that one of several things could happen:

- Either too much or too little assessment could occur (e.g., multiple requests for the same data or everyone thinking it is someone else's responsibility).

- The focus of the assessment could be formative only (for improvement purposes) or summative only (for making decisions about the future of the program).

- The questions being asked would be too narrow (e.g., How did students like the ropes course?) or too broad (e.g., What is the impact of learning communities on retention?)

We recognized that in order to design and implement a comprehensive assessment plan it was critical to form a committee that would combine the perspectives of academic affairs and student affairs personnel in a comprehensive assessment approach. This committee would be responsible for developing and overseeing the assessment process and for establishing an environment where assessment issues would be addressed. Because the Center for Support of Teaching and Learning (CSTL) at Syracuse University has a 30-year history of working with faculty and staff to develop and assess new and existing programs, we were asked to facilitate the assessment process and to form an assessment steering committee. In addition to the director of learning communities for academic affairs and director of learning communities for student affairs, staff and faculty from several departments were asked to participate on the committee. We wanted to ensure that the academic affairs and student affairs perspectives were addressed, but in addition we wanted representatives from several key programs that worked with multiple learning communities. These offices included the Division of Student Affairs (director of assessment), the Office of Residence Life (director and coordinator of assessment), the Writing Program (faculty member working with several learning communities and coordinating the learning communities writing faculty), the School of Education's Department of Higher Education (a faculty member who was leading a graduate program on learning communities), the Center for Community and Public Service, and the State University of New York School of Environmental Science and Forestry. In addition, there were graduate student observers from the higher education program.

The first meetings were spent learning about the different perspectives and needs of the members of the group. It became clear that a first step was to identify and make public the purpose and role of the Assessment Steering Committee in order for the committee and the rest of the university community to understand how the committee planned to operate and to support the assessment of learning communities. The committee was clear that its role was to provide guidance and support, but it was not responsible for conducting the assessment. The responsibility of conducting the assessment would be within the individual learning communities, with CSTL supporting the individual learning communities (LCs) and providing the institutional perspective.

The following roles for the committee were identified:

- To develop a community of learners, including staff, faculty, and students, that focuses on assessing LCs at Syracuse University

- To coordinate the development of a coordinated institutional assessment plan for LCs at SU

- To assist the coordinators of individual LCs in the development of learning outcomes and assessment plans

- To provide campus-wide opportunities for faculty and staff conversations about the assessment of LCs

- To assist in the development of institutional recommendations about LCs

- To review and disseminate institutional assessment findings

- To share data with other internal and external institutional research efforts as appropriate

Once the roles were clearly defined, we could begin to develop the assessment plan. The committee recognized that it was important to distinguish between the assessment of individual learning communities and the assessment across learning communities. While the committee was focusing on the institution-wide assessment, their role was also to provide a framework for personnel to assess their individual learning communities. Since academic affairs and student affairs faculty worked together on the learning community, it was important to provide a framework that would support academic affairs' needs for scholarly work and faculty's reluctance to assess while supporting student affairs' needs for data to make decisions. The committee adopted the following model for assessing individual learning communities.

Purpose: To improve individual learning communities

Learning Outcomes: Incorporate both student affairs and academic affairs outcomes

Model: Assessing student learning outcomes (described below)

Assessment Plan: Linked to learning outcomes; includes methods, data sources, and analysis procedures; includes necessary resources and how assessment plan will be managed

Report: Includes overview of plan, what worked, what is being changed, summary, and recommendations

We adopted the assessment model generally employed at Syracuse University for the individual learning communities to provide consistency with other assessment work being conducted. This model is one commonly accepted within the field (see Figure 7.1). As part of the model, a team would develop goals, provide experiences, collect assessment data, and then make changes to goals, experiences, or assessment techniques as warranted.

Figure 7.1

Assessment Model

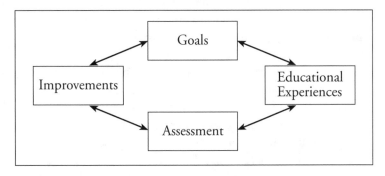

It is important to note, however, that one can enter the model at several different points. For example, the team may have some idea of its goals and from that can develop educational experiences and assessment techniques. On the other hand, the team may be more confident about what they want

students to do (i.e., educational experiences) and from that can develop goals and assessment techniques. This is not a linear process, but rather a cyclical one that allows for constant revision and rethinking based on what is learned. It is not unusual for the mission and goals to be developed as the program evolves and, in fact, it is critical that they be revisited and updated.

The second component of the learning communities assessment plan addressed the university-wide assessment needs. The purpose of this aspect of the assessment plan was different: determining under what conditions learning communities are working and what can be done to improve the program overall. This required a different focus than was described above. The committee agreed on the following model for assessing across all learning communities.

Purpose: To determine under what conditions learning communities are successful, what we can learn about best practices, and how we can improve learning communities overall

Outcomes: Based on the goals for learning communities at Syracuse University

Model: Program evaluation (determine purpose, audience, questions, data collection methods, analysis procedures, interpretation, and reporting)

Assessment Plan: Linked to goals; descriptive data about learning communities (e.g., number, student demographics, application numbers, participation numbers)

Report: Combination of meta-analysis of individual learning community reports and institution-wide data

In implementing this model, the first activity for the committee was to examine the goals for learning communities at Syracuse University. The committee determined that the goals developed by the original learning communities planning group during the pilot were too broad and did not have enough clarity to develop assessment techniques. Therefore, the Assessment Steering Committee addressed the issue of clarifying the mission and goals of learning communities at Syracuse University. The inclusion of representatives from different offices strengthened these statements and again provided a more global perspective. The student affairs–academic affairs partnership provided an opportunity to develop goals that addressed both the in- and out-of-class experiences. It was agreed that the mission for learning communities at Syracuse University is "to promote, enhance, and support students' academic, personal, and professional growth and success through the development of residential and non-residential learning communities at Syracuse University."

The goals for learning communities at Syracuse University as articulated by the Assessment Steering Committee and approved by the Learning Community Council are:

- Building partnerships among faculty, staff, and students to increase interaction, involvement, and learning inside and outside the classroom

- Connecting the curricular and cocurricular experiences of students to create a seamless learning experience

- Facilitating college transitions by fostering smaller communities of students, faculty, and staff

- Promoting opportunities for individual students to make more meaningful connections with members of the Syracuse University community

- Supporting students' successful completion of their academic programs

- Contributing to the continuous enrichment of the intellectual climate of the university

- Fostering students' active commitment to the Syracuse University community as students and alumns

After the goals were developed, the committee turned its attention to developing research questions for each of the outcomes. We found that we had many research questions, but we tried to focus on the questions that related to the outcomes. There may be additional research questions that arise as the project progresses, but it was important to start with those that matched the program goals. We then identified assessment tools that would allow us to monitor our progress on each of these goals. This step proved more challenging in negotiating the differences between student affairs and academic affairs. The interest in scholarly work had to be balanced with the need for quick data to provide administrators. Through a gradual process supported by all members of the team, we were able to examine our current efforts and add additional methods that would address both the short-term and long-term needs of the participants.

We started with identifying tools and methods currently employed at the university that matched our assessment questions. Some tools that were being used at the time were part of an ongoing longitudinal study that some administrators were advocating be continued. However, the assessment committee felt these methods could be improved in order to address our current learning community program needs. Because we did not have a replacement methodology at that time, it was difficult to convince stakeholders to discontinue a long-term effort. As a committee, we were able to form a response to the stakeholders and convinced the administration that continuation of these instruments would not provide us with the information to improve our learning communities program. There were also pressures from student affairs staff who were being asked to provide data quickly and from faculty who had to design experiences for their students. The timeline for faculty and staff work did not always coincide with the needs of the program. Staff needs were immediate, and there was not always time to think about the methodology. Faculty also had immediate needs, but the methodology was more lengthy and, because it was linked to a course, not always timely. We continue to negotiate these different needs and through the development of new methodologies are able to address the needs of both groups.

The next step was to determine where new tools and methods were necessary. We developed a matrix to help us with this next step. (See Table 7.2.) The matrix in Table 7–2 provides a sample of the goals, research questions, and methods we identified; it is not intended to be comprehensive. Using a matrix helped us understand the relationship among the outcomes, the research questions, and the methodologies. As part of this process, we also had to determine who was conducting each assessment and when the data would be collected.

IMPLEMENTING THE ASSESSMENT PLAN

The assessment plan is currently being implemented and data are being collected, analyzed, and reported to the learning community faculty, staff, students, and administrators. This is done through written documents and oral presentations to various interested groups on campus, including the Learning Community Council, the Office of Residence Life staff, and several all-university committees.

There are three areas that required additional attention that the committee had not expected. The first area was the development of a database in order to identify the learning communities' population at various points in time. The second was redesigning the yearly reporting format for the individual learning communities. The third area was the need to clarify further the role of the committee in overseeing the collection and dissemination of learning community data.

Accurately tracking student interest in and subsequent enrollment in learning communities is critical to a longitudinal assessment effort. In our program, we actually have to track two different groups of students—first-

Table 7.2

Matrix of Sample Outcomes, Questions, and Methods

Outcomes	Research Questions	Methods
Building partnerships among faculty, staff, and students to increase interaction, involvement, and learning inside and outside the classroom	Do faculty who teach in LC and non-LC settings report a difference in student engagement? Do faculty and staff report differences in their interaction with students?	End of year report including questions directly related to these research questions
Promoting opportunities for individual students to make more meaningful connections with members of the Syracuse University community	Are students meeting more often with faculty members outside of class? Are students engaged in other educational experiences such as study abroad and internships?	Questions from the National Survey of Student Engagement or locally developed survey instruments Student records data regarding participation in other organizations and activities
Supporting students' successful completion of their academic programs	What is the retention rate for 1st, 2nd, 3rd, and 4th year? Do LC students continue and graduate at a higher rate than non-LC students? Are LC students who drop out more likely to return than non-LC students?	Comparative retention studies based on current institutional research reporting practices Data collected from the student records system

year students and returning students. For these two groups, the application and subsequent enrollment processes occur at different times of the academic year using different procedures. In addition, students may participate in several learning communities during their Syracuse University experience.

There are several key points at which we want to track our learning community students—when they apply; when they are placed into one or more learning communities; when they choose a learning community from those placements (returning students only); at the official enrollment date (October 1 for all official federal and state reporting); and at the end of the first semester and subsequent semesters. Our learning communities database includes fields for students' learning community choices, the learning communities placements, and the community in which they subsequently enroll for every year they participate in learning communities. This file is used to gather data from our student records system for fields such as gender, ethnicity, GPA, courses, school/college, and retention. The database is used to generate acceptance letters to students prior to their placement but is also used for mailings of newsletters as well as assessment instruments. All learning community faculty and staff are included in the database as well.

We redesigned the yearly report from the individual learning communities and asked that the learning community team complete this report at the end of the academic year. The purpose of the report was twofold. One purpose was to provide an opportunity for the team to reflect on the previous year's experience and to continue the dialogue on what worked well during the learning community and how they could improve the experience in subsequent offerings. The questions we developed for the yearly report were designed to allow both student affairs and academic affairs personnel the opportunity to contribute to the assessment of the learning community. The second purpose was to gather assessment information across learning communities to better understand what worked and under what conditions. The faculty coordinators were asked to address the following questions in the yearly report:

- What were the student learning outcomes for your learning community?

- How did you assess these outcomes?

- How did your learning outcomes or your assessment plan change during the year?

- What did your assessment teach you about the students? Did they achieve the learning outcomes?

- For next year, what would you do the same as this year? Why?

- What might you do differently next year? Why?

- Describe the following program components, indicating what worked well and what you would change: faculty/staff interactions, living arrangements, academic and community space, the enrollment process, publicity and recruiting, and facilities.

- What benefits do students, faculty, and staff enjoy by participating in learning communities?

In addition, there were five questions that each faculty and staff member was asked to respond to individually. The faculty coordinator could either summarize these responses or provide them verbatim. These questions were:

- How has your involvement in learning communities influenced your teaching and interaction with learning community students? Students in general?

- How does your learning community experience compare to other non-learning community interactions with students?

- Describe the level of interaction you have had with students (frequency, duration, etc.).

  - On average, did you interact with learning community students—outside of class—more often, less often, or just as often as non-learning community students?

  - On average, was the length of interaction with learning community students longer, shorter, or equal to the length of interaction with non-learning community students?

  - Was there a difference in depth or substance of conversation?

- Do you think students developed a good understanding of course material as a result of participation in learning communities?

- How would you compare the performance of students in your learning community courses with that of students you have taught in non-learning community courses?

The third area requiring our attention was the necessity for further clarifying the role of the Learning Community Assessment Committee. This developed as a result of the clash between the student affairs and academic affairs cultures. While both cultures are working for the good of the program, their needs often create a tension. Faculty and student affairs personnel gather data about learning communities for their own use. For example, faculty may be conducting research as part of their larger research agenda (e.g., students' attitudes toward diversity) and student affairs administrators may be asking for data to demonstrate that learning communities are effective. While the overall plan calls for gathering and reporting these data, there is nothing to preclude individuals or groups from gathering and disseminating data about their own part of the program. This multiple perspective approach provides a richness of data, but without a coordinated response these different viewpoints may confuse the various constituent groups. Due to variations in methodology, sampling, and analysis, data may be distributed that are in direct conflict with the official results reported by the committee. Therefore, in April of 2002, the committee drafted the following statement entitled "Supporting, Facilitating, and Coordinating LC Institutional Assessment" to clarify how these efforts would be coordinated, the expectations for those conducting research, and the committee's role in responding to different research reports.

Issue. Distinguishing between official institutional assessment of learning communities versus other research being conducted by departments or individual faculty

Description of the Learning Community Assessment Committee (LCAC) role. One goal of the LCAC is to encourage individual- and departmental-initiated assessment projects on SU learning communities. The LCAC's responsibilities to all these projects are those of facilitation, coordination, and dissemination. To these ends, the LCAC offers its support in the following ways:

> *Facilitation. The LCAC encourages individuals beginning LC assessment projects to share their study goals and methods. The LCAC can provide an overview of LC assessment done at SU to date that relates to the new project.*

> *Coordination. The LCAC maintains an assessment database on which institutional assessment is based. Individuals wishing to use these data should contact the LCAC for assistance.*

> *Dissemination. The LCAC maintains a centralized location for recording and disseminating information about the coordinated institutional assessment plan for learning communities. To this end, the LCAC will review all assessment projects to prepare a description of their fit to the overall LC assessment plan. These reviews and copies of the assessment projects themselves will be part of the LCAC documentation of the comprehensive LC assessment plan.*

What We Have Learned

As a result of our learning communities assessment work, we have learned much about the process of assessing a project that includes staff from different backgrounds and with different interests. The most important thing we have learned is that the development, implementation, and reporting of assessment efforts requires detailed conversation and time in order to build collaboration and consensus. Obviously, assessment would be easier if methods and outcomes were dictated from higher administrative officials, but the results would not be as useful nor as complete. The combined perspectives of academic affairs and student affairs personnel provide a comprehensive approach that can be embraced by a larger group of university faculty and staff.

This collaboration requires that all participants be patient and be willing to listen. A facilitator who provides opportunities for the necessary conversations is critical. We found that it was particularly useful to have assessment representatives from student affairs and academic affairs who were able to discuss the process with their respective leaders and to obtain their support for the collaborative efforts being developed.

The actual collection of data is also a slow and time-consuming process. Ongoing support and follow-up with each of the learning communities is necessary to ensure that there is an assessment plan, data are being collected, and the report is completed. In addition, some institutional data require several semesters to collect and analyze. For example, the results from the National Survey of Student Engagement are available in August following the administration of the survey. Retention data are not available until after a year or more has passed.

We have been successful in actively encouraging research partnerships with graduate students, faculty, and staff. Graduate students have participated in our meetings, gathered data, and reported their results to individual learning communities. Initially, the data gathered by the graduate students were shared only with the individual learning communities until procedures (including informed consent) were developed that allowed for the sharing of these data with the Center for Support of Teaching and Learning so that the results could be incorporated into the larger institutional assessment effort.

Our assessment efforts have provided information about what is working in the learning communities program and under what conditions different models are successful. We have started to develop an understanding of how learning communities can be effective on our campus. We have also used what we have learned to refine our assessment efforts and have used the information we gathered to assist new learning communities. But equally important, we have learned more about student affairs–academic affairs collaboration and what impact this has on assessment.

Barbara A. Yonai is director of the Center for Support of Teaching and Learning and assessment coordinator for Syracuse University's learning communities.

REFERENCES

Engstrom, C. M., & Tinto, V. (2000). Developing partnerships with academic affairs to enhance student learning. In M. J. Barr & M. K. Desler (Eds.), *The handbook of student affairs administration* (2nd ed., pp. 425–452). San Francisco, CA: Jossey-Bass.

Hurd, S. N., Peckskamp, T. L., & Yonai, B. A. (2002). *Assessing learning communities: Student affairs/academic affairs collaboration.* Paper presented at The Ohio State University Conference on Living-Learning Programs, Columbus, OH.

8

Institutional Challenges

Sandra N. Hurd

*T*he learning community profiles in the next part of this book provide insight into the kinds of challenges that individual learning communities have faced and, in most cases, overcome. There are, however, a number of challenges that arise at the institutional level and affect all learning communities in one way or another, visibly or behind the scenes. This chapter highlights three issues (although there are certainly more) that are particularly difficult to resolve: the location of residential learning communities, housing selection by returning students, and advising and course registration for first-year students.

LEARNING COMMUNITY LOCATION

Where to locate learning communities is a continuing challenge. One challenge is matching the academic and programmatic needs of the community with the spaces that are the right size and configuration. Another challenge is locating the learning communities appropriately with respect to Office of Residence Life staffing patterns and needs.

Our housing is divided into north and south campuses. North campus has 15 residence halls ranging in size from 46 to 586. These halls are coed by alternating floors, wings, and/or rooms. Floors range in capacity from seven to 81 with just about everything in between. Room types include singles, open doubles, split doubles, and suites. South campus, available only to upper-class students, has three 60-person residence halls, coed by alternating rooms, and two- and three-bedroom apartments that house 1,900 students.

Different learning communities have vastly different space needs on a variety of dimensions. These needs may simply be a function of how large the community is—our learning communities are currently as small as 20 and as large as 80, although planning has begun for a 250-student learning community. These needs may be academic and programmatic—particular classroom or seminar space (e.g., management, which holds all three linked classes in the residence hall), community space (e.g., multicultural has a significant number of activities in the residence hall that involve all its residents), technology requirements (e.g., international relations needs international video capabilities), or special fitness (wellness) or cooking (French) facilities. Sometimes these needs relate to the gender make-up of the community (e.g., women in science and engineering). Learning communities currently occupy about 25% of the bed space at the university. As new learning communities have come online, it has become increasingly difficult to find appropriate space in which to house them. As the program continues to grow, it will be even more of a challenge.

The difficulty of finding appropriate space is compounded as we try to work within residence life staffing patterns and needs. As is the case with most residence life units in institutions across the country, there is likely to be significant turnover each year as residence directors (RDs) move up the career ladder in residence life (either here or elsewhere) or shift to other student affairs positions or move on to graduate programs. It is not unusual for as many as a third of our RD positions to be filled anew each year. Because our residential learning communities are partnerships between academic affairs and student affairs, it is important that the RDs work closely with the learning communities in their buildings. But how is that best accomplished?

The first year that we had a significant number of learning communities, we decided to spread them out among the residence halls so that (most) RDs would have only one community for which they were responsible. This was much less successful than we anticipated. Several veteran RDs told us that they ended up spending too much time with the relatively small group of learning community students at what they felt was the expense of the other residents. Several first-year RDs told us that they had to spend so much time figuring out their new job that they felt they shortchanged the learning community students. Based on those responses, as well as additional feedback from extensive debriefing of all the RDs, we went back to the drawing board.

In spite of our reluctance to move learning communities that were in spaces that worked for them, we decided to cluster learning communities in buildings with experienced RDs, putting a learning community in a building with a new RD only as a last resort. There are multiple challenges associated with this strategy. One is meeting the academic and programmatic needs of the learning communities with many fewer spaces from which to choose. Another is that decisions about where to place the learning communities have to be made in October, and the RDs don't have to let residence life know whether or not they are returning until February. (The hiring season generally begins in early spring and may continue up to the opening of school.) Once an RD has committed, he or she can express a building preference. So, each year we have to make our best guess four months in advance about who will return and what building they will prefer. It has not, of course, worked out perfectly. Each year, there has been at least one new RD who has multiple learning communities. We try to put new RDs with previous learning community experience in those halls. When that is not possible, we add extra support for the RD and rely more heavily on the resident advisors (RAs). It is a far from perfect system.

HOUSING SELECTION

Returning students who want university housing participate in a housing lottery. Some locations (smaller north campus residence halls, south campus) and room types (singles, suites) are much more attractive than others. In many cases, these are also the most appropriate spaces for learning communities. Add to this mix that learning community housing is assigned before the lottery, and you have the predictable problem that there are a number of students who request a learning community not because they are interested in the experience but because they want the location or room type. Students who select a learning community for this reason can have a significant negative impact on the community, and because housing is tight, it is in most cases impossible to move someone to another location. As a consequence, it is important that we try to make sure that students who are placed in a learning community have a genuine interest in that community.

Most of our learning communities that are open to returning students now require an application. Some also require an interview. Interestingly, the mere fact of having to fill out an application, although in most cases it is not onerous, discourages the majority of students who don't have at least some genuine interest in the community. For those communities where participation is particularly important and students are asked to move farther out of their comfort zone (e.g., interfaith and multicultural), the application is more extensive and the responses to the questions are evaluated more carefully.

It is unlikely that we will make much of a dent in the housing culture in the short run, and maybe we can't even make a significant difference in the long run. There are, however, some bright spots. The number of returning students who choose not to be active in a learning community after joining it is down significantly. And 36 freshmen in the Arts Adventure Learning Community committed to living and taking arts-related courses together as sophomores without having any idea where they would be housed. Happily for them, the most appropriate available space turned out to be in one of the most highly desirable locations on north campus.

ADVISING AND REGISTRATION

Advising and course registration for first-year students present complex and difficult issues. It is very important that students get off to a good start their first semester, both academically and personally. Learning communities are designed to promote a good start, but if students don't understand what is expected of them as a member of a learning community or how a required learning community course fits into their academic program, participating in a learning community may have the opposite effect.

First-year students elect to live in a learning community when they fill out their housing application, which is due May 1. Admissions materials provide descriptions of each learning community, and additional information is available on the learning community web site. Students are invited to consult with an academic advisor before choosing a learning community, but many do not. Students who visit campus have the opportunity to talk with students about learning communities and ask questions about course requirements, but not all students visit campus. How then can we be sure that students understand the implications of any learning community choice that they make? We can't. What we can do, though, is work closely with schools and colleges to make sure that we are providing appropriate and accurate information to their students, make learning community information available to advisors, and continue to encourage students to consult an advisor before choosing a learning community. We also work closely with the schools and colleges in making placements. When we have the learning community selections from the housing applications, we make tentative learning community placements. We then provide this information to the schools and colleges so that they can review the placements; only students who have been cleared by their home college will be forwarded to housing for placement. One of the criteria by which schools and colleges determine whether a student should be placed in a learning community is whether the required learning community course or courses fit with the student's academic program.

Even if the learning community course requirement fits with a student's academic program, it is not necessarily the case that the course fits into the student's schedule. Incoming students select first-semester courses over the summer through a mail registration process, and staff in each school and college build students' schedules from the courses they select. At the time students fill out their course selection sheet, however, they don't know whether they have been placed in a learning community. In building a schedule for a learning community student, therefore, a staff member may have to make some decisions about what the student would want to do. For example, if a student wants to take a Chinese class that is only offered at the same time as the required course for the learning community she selected, would she, given the choice, join the learning community or take Chinese? In many cases, the staff member can contact the student and ask that question, but it is not always possible to do with over 800 first-year students requesting a learning community and less than two weeks to build schedules for all 2,500 freshmen. As more learning communities come online with more required courses, this problem will only grow. Solving it requires a major rethinking of how we schedule classes and/or the timing of our housing and registration processes.

Sandra N. Hurd is professor of law and public policy in the Whitman School of Management and director of learning communities for academic affairs at Syracuse University.

PART II

Learning Community Profiles

We asked participants from a representative sample of Syracuse University's learning communities to share their experiences, good and bad, in creating, implementing, and evaluating their learning communities. We hope these profiles will help you in your own learning community work. A list of all of the learning communities appears on the following page. For descriptions of all of SU's learning communities, visit the learning community website at http://lc.syr.edu.

List of Learning Communities for 2004–2005
   Arts Adventure Learning Community
   Arts Adventure 2 Learning Community
   Creativity, Innovation, and Entrepreneurship Learning Community
   Discovery Learning community
   Education Living/Learning Community (ELLC)
   French Learning Community
   Freshman Forum Learning Community (10 sections)
   Higher Education Graduate Learning Community
   Human Services and Health Professions Interprofessional Learning
       Community
   Interfaith Learning Community
   International Living Center (ILC)
   International Relations Learning Community
   Leaders Emerging and Developing Learning Community (LEAD)
   Light Work Learning Community
   Management Integrated Core Learning Community (3 sections)
   Management Learning Community (2 sections)
   Maxwell Citizenship Education Learning Community
   Michelangelo Learning Community
   Multicultural Living/Learning Community (MLLC) (2 sections)
   Native American Studies Living/Learning Community (NASLLC)
   Newhouse Learning Community (5 sections)
   Psychology/Writing Freshman Forum Learning Community (5 sections)
   Service-Learning Community
   Student SUccess Initiative Learning Community
   Summer College Learning Community
   SUNY ESF Learning Community (2 sections)
   Wellness Learning Community
   Women in Science and Engineering Learning Community (WISE)
   Women in Science and Engineering 2 Learning Community (WISE)

9

The Management Learning Community: A Lesson in Innovation

Sandra N. Hurd and Steve St. Onge

The School of Management Learning Community, the first implemented at SU, is a residential community that links two three-credit courses and a one-credit learning community seminar.

How It All Began

It began as two theme floors (one for men and one for women) in Brewster Hall, a 470-bed coeducational (by alternating floor) residence hall facility. The School of Management theme floors were founded in 1996 with faculty and student support. In 1998, when Syracuse University decided to develop residential learning communities, the School of Management Learning Community (MLC) was born as one of two pilot residential learning communities and moved to Boland Hall, a slightly smaller facility with more appropriate academic space. The MLC has evolved significantly since that first year. With steadily increasing demand, the program has more than doubled in size. The instructional group, comprised of faculty in the School of Management, the writing program, and staff in the Office of Residence Life, has solidified into a team. The connections among the linked courses have become clearer with each iteration while the boundaries between living and learning have become more and more blurred. There is still work to be done, of course, but we can now confidently call the MLC a successful innovation.

LEARNING COMMUNITY DESCRIPTION

The School of Management Learning Community combines three linked first-semester academic classes with a significant residential component. All students in the MLC coregister for three classes: the freshman management gateway course (3 credits), the freshman writing course (3 credits), and a learning community seminar (1 credit). In addition to these classes, there is a series of writing workshops developed for learning community students but open to any freshman in the School of Management. All classes and workshops meet in the residence halls, and enrollment in each cohort is limited to 20 students in order to meet writing program enrollment guidelines. We started out with one cohort the first year, and expanded it to two and then three to meet demand. The number of sections of the learning community that can be offered is constrained, however, by the additional faculty resources needed to staff sections of 20 rather than the usual 25, and it is likely that we have reached maximum capacity at 60 students. The same management faculty member teaches all three sections of the management class; the same writing instructor teaches all three of the writing sections. Two residence life professionals co-teach the three sections of the learning community seminar. While the students continue to live together for the whole year, they are not enrolled in linked classes during the second semester.

The 60 students who enroll in the MLC live on one of three floors (two male, one female) in Boland Hall. Each floor has a resident advisor (RA), a paraprofessional staff member who is also an upper-class management student. The RAs assist the residents with their transition into the university and provide them with educational programs and opportunities. The RAs also work in collaboration with the learning community instructional team to complement in-class experiences with out-of-class experiences consistent with the educational mission of both the MLC and the Office of Residence Life.

One of the continuing challenges of the MLC is the size of the community, both in absolute numbers as well as numbers of men and women, in relationship to the available residence hall space. Historically, and in contrast to learning communities in general, significantly more men than women (75/25) have requested the MLC, in spite of the fact that the gender split in the School of Management is closer to 55/45. The only residence hall on campus that can accommodate the MLC's academic and community space needs is single gender by floor. As a result, we use parts of floors for learning community students. The rest of the residents on each floor are randomly assigned from the entire university pool of incoming first-year students. The mix of residents has a significant impact on the RA's work in building community as well as developing and delivering programming. In the first year, we used one men's floor and one women's floor. As the community grew, the number of spaces for non-community residents decreased, resulting in a sense of isolation for those students who were not part of the community. Shifting to three floors has created more balance and made it easier for the RA to manage the two groups of students.

How We Got It Together and Keep It Together

Critical to the success of the development process was involving people who were very positive about and committed to the experience of working collaboratively with others. The initial development group consisted of senior management, education, and writing faculty and a senior residence life professional. The high level of commitment by each individual involved, however, although it sustained us, did not guarantee a smooth process.

We had been persuaded by a review of the literature that it was important to have a theme for our learning community. The theme that emerged in our preliminary discussions was diversity—a topic that seemed, on its face, as if it could be easily connected to the management (managing diversity, both in terms of employees and customers), writing (multiple perspectives and diverse audiences), and residential life (living with people who are not like you) curricula. Although we acknowledged and understood at the outset that we had different spins on the concept of diversity, we did not completely understand either the depth of those differences or how tangled up in the multiple meanings we would get when we tried to meld these different understandings into a coherent curricular whole. The result was a series of strained conversations that led, not surprisingly, to equally strained connections that we didn't understand well and were virtually incomprehensible to the students. After the first year, we abandoned our self-imposed requirement of a theme and worked instead on capitalizing on the connections that emerged naturally from the content of the three curricula.

Going into our early discussions, we also failed to understand the impact on our working relationship of our Office of Residence Life partner's deeply felt but unarticulated perception that she was in a position of less power than the faculty partners. It took several meetings of talking past each other before we all understood the extent to which our communication struggles were the result of the faculty members not understanding her need to convince us of the important contributions residence life professionals could bring to the learning community. Once we all realized what was getting in the way, we could have the conversation about whether or not the faculty needed convincing. Following that conversation, the layer of powerlessness fell away, and we could work together comfortably. These issues did not, however, go away forever.

The development team's membership changed after the first year. The education faculty member was no longer part of the process, an additional management professor joined the team, and the two residence life professionals who would be teaching the following year replaced the original residence life representative. This time, though, we were smart enough to talk through and resolve issues around power imbalance and second-class citizenship before we got down to working on the substance of the learning community curriculum.

During the spring planning for the second year of the learning community with our newly constituted team, we found our greatest success when we created a matrix depicting each course and the residential component week-by-week for the academic semester. (See Chapter 5 on using grids as a curriculum development tool.) When we could visualize the MLC in grid form, the connections virtually jumped off the page at us. With all of the instructional team present, we broke down and then reassembled the curriculum week-by-week for each course, creating a weekly residence life curriculum in the process, so that both the in- and out-of-class experiences were coherent and complementary to each other. This work carried through into the summer as the connections among the courses were made more specific and opening weekend and ropes course activities were planned. Integral to this part of the planning process were our efforts to incorporate our belief that learning community students could come to see their peers as a valid source of knowledge and understand that they could create knowledge together if we structured appropriate experiences to enhance and celebrate the voice of students in the learning process.

During opening weekend, all instructors in the program make a special effort to be visible on the MLC floors and to talk informally with students as they move into the residence hall. (Several management and writing faculty have even joined the "Goon Squad," the group of over 300 students, administrators, staff, and faculty who help our 2,500 incoming first-year students move in over a two-day period.) The instructional team leaves a welcome letter and gift in each student's room and hosts a welcome dinner intended to start building community among the students as well as between the students and the faculty.

As the academic semester begins, the faculty meets weekly to discuss curricular connections, student development and floor issues, and any specific planning or alterations to the schedule that may be necessary for the coming week. These weekly meetings have been an invaluable part of our process. They have not only proved instrumental in improving the MLC curriculum but also in identifying and helping students with academic or social concerns that might affect their success at the university. We have found the combination of this early warning system and the opportunity to triple-team (involve the management, writing, and residence life instructors), challenge, and support a student who is starting to exhibit inappropriate behavior a most effective intervention.

Two or three weeks into the semester, the faculty and students go on an overnight ropes course experience at a nature center about 50 miles from Syracuse. The experience begins with a series of community building games and activities followed by low ropes challenges designed to enhance teamwork skills. Student may elect to do high ropes, which are individual challenges. After dinner, which is prepared by the students, additional community and team building activities take place. We have found that an overnight away from campus, with carefully designed activities, is a critical element in making the community a cohesive whole.

LEARNING OBJECTIVES

All learning communities at Syracuse University are required to have learning objectives. Articulating the learning objectives for the learning community proved surprisingly difficult. Although all faculty and staff participants had an intuitive sense of what we were trying to do, putting that sense into words that everyone agreed upon took a great deal of time and effort. It was not, in fact, until the end of the second year of the learning community that we had a set of learning objectives we believed accurately reflected our aspirations for our students:

The School of Management Learning Community seeks to help students develop academic and personal confidence and success through the following initiatives:

- Building connections with faculty and staff

- Enhancing peer support and building community

- Understanding the interconnectedness of living and learning environments

- Taking responsibility for their own learning

- Promoting effort, involvement, integrity, and citizenship

- Identifying and making appropriate use of resources

The process of talking through our learning objectives, however, was a critical part of the development process for this learning community. It allowed us to reflect on the curriculum and floor activities, see connections more clearly, and understand better what we were trying to achieve. It also graphically demonstrated that academic affairs and student affairs personnel speak different languages and operate in different conceptual frameworks: A significant early obstacle was that the concept of learning objectives operated very differently in the two spheres, and we got tangled up in what were goals, what were outcomes, and what were objectives. Finally, we decided to abandon the definitions used by academic affairs and student affairs and simply articulate what we wanted for the students. Although the learning objectives capture where we are now, it is important to revisit the learning objectives each year as our understanding grows and as different faculty and staff participate in the learning community.

RECRUITING STUDENTS FOR THE LEARNING COMMUNITY

Recruiting students for the pilot year of the MLC was a difficult process. With a product that was in its very earliest stages of creation and no history of success, it was almost impossible to interest prospective students who visited campus in signing up. We had to resort to calling admitted students in May and trying to convince them one by one. We got the learning community filled, but just barely.

After that first year, however, recruiting students was no problem; students in the learning community became our best recruiters. MLC students participate in the fall and spring receptions that the university hosts for prospective students and make themselves available for tours of the residence hall. They also publish their phone numbers and email addresses on the MLC website, inviting prospective students to contact them with questions about the learning community.

Although we now rely primarily on students to do our recruiting for us, information about the MLC is included in information mailed to admitted students as well as in the university's learning community brochure and website. While recruiting students directly remains our focus, it is in fact often parents who show initial interest in having their daughter or son join the learning community. This is a mixed blessing. On the one hand, it does help increase demand for the learning community as well as aid recruitment for the School of Management. On the other hand, students who join the MLC because of parental pressure have sometimes been less than fully contributing members of the community.

ASSESSMENT INITIATIVES

The assessment of the Management Learning Community has been a collaborative effort among learning community faculty and staff, Higher Education faculty and students, and the Center for Support of Teaching and Learning (CSTL). Assessment efforts have evolved over time. In the first year, we attempted simply to describe the program as experienced by students, faculty, and staff. Although we did get some helpful information, these efforts gave us relatively little to go on in terms of trying to improve the experience for the following year. We developed a much more ambitious assessment plan for the second year that included more in-depth qualitative and quantitative measurements of program impact. Students wrote reflective essays, filled out questionnaires, and were asked to participate in focus groups led by students in the Higher Education graduate program whose curriculum focused on learning communities.

At the end of the second year, we discovered, however, that we had overcorrected. The students reported feeling that they were constantly being asked about their experiences, and it felt like being in a fishbowl. For the third and subsequent years, we developed a strategy of embedding the assessment in both their curriculum and their residential experiences so that providing feedback became simply a part of their regular academic and social life. So, for example, a short paper for their learning community seminar asks about their learning and curricular connections in a way that allows us to gauge whether the linkages we have made are sufficiently visible to the students. And a floor program is structured to give us insight into how the students are blending their in-class and out-of-class experiences. Higher Education graduate students gain experience with assessment by helping us analyze the results of these assessment initiatives. In addition, the graduate students have used the learning community as a research site, and one doctoral candidate has researched the intellectual development of the learning community students for his dissertation. Throughout the process, CSTL staff have helped the learning community faculty and staff develop, implement, and coordinate the various pieces of the assessment plan. They also tracked institutional demographic, retention, and grade point average data for us.

ASSESSMENT RESULTS

Five years of assessment data demonstrate that students, faculty, and staff participating in the Management Learning Community have been positively affected by the experience. Over and over again, the students report that being a part of the MLC eased their transition to college, increased social connectedness, allowed them to develop relationships with faculty and staff, and provided substantial peer and faculty support for their learning. The following quotes, taken from student reflection papers, are representative of what each year's students say about their participation in the MLC.

> *Being a part of the Management Learning Community has helped me in so many ways. I've developed closer friendships with students in the learning community than with those who are not in the program. Having the same classes with my floor-mates has helped me academically as well: Discussions about how we learn, work, and interact with one another have given others and myself a way to express our feelings about college life.*

> *The Management Learning Community is very close-knit, and it made the transition to college much easier. I got to know everyone right away, and it's really a lot of fun. It's also helped me academically; you can always try to hunt someone down for help from one of your classes, but it's a lot easier when they're right outside your door.*

> *The Learning Community has had a great impact on my learning. It has provided me with the bond of friendship; in addition it has opened me up to new cultures and ways of learning. There is an extremely diverse group of individuals within this community; each one has given me insight about myself and allows me to learn along with them.*

> *The faculty members of the Management Learning Community are a more important factor in my classes than my other teachers. I view the faculty as a means of help and comfort in my first year here at Syracuse University. I feel that I can go to*

any one of the faculty members for help in any of my classes, not just management.

When I began classes, it was comforting to see familiar faces in my classes, and have people to walk to class with and talk to. On the first day of class, I looked around in my 8:30 lecture and saw many people just sitting in their seats and staring forward, not talking to anyone. I, on the other hand, talked to my new friends excitedly, as I now felt like part of a group.

I chose to be a part of the learning community because I thought it would provide me with an easier transition into both the academic and social aspects of college life. I was right, but I had no idea exactly how much of an impact my experiences in the MLC would have on me. As I now reflect on the first five weeks of my new academic career, I am very happy with what I see. I have more confidence in my schoolwork than I ever have before.

I learn better when I am comfortable with my classmates. Being a member of the learning community has allowed me to feel comfortable with my peers. Asking questions in class and participating in discussions helps me to learn because I do well with verbal teaching. If I did not know the other students in my classes, I would be much more reluctant to offer my insight and ask questions to better my own understanding of the class material.

Assessment data indicate that MLC students spend more out-of-class time than their non-learning community peers on academics and are more satisfied with their college experience. In addition, proportionately more of them become resident advisors, management peer facilitators, and leaders in the management school and the university. Grade point averages for students in the learning community sections of courses are higher than for students in non-learning community sections of these same courses. Retention rates are also higher.

The enthusiasm and satisfaction of the students are mirrored by the faculty and staff participants. They point specifically to involvement with and impact on students and building collaborative partnerships around student learning as being the most satisfying aspects of their learning community work.

CAVEATS

We would not be presenting a fair, balanced picture of the Management Learning Community experience, however, without sharing a few of the continuing challenges that we face.

A learning community experience is not for all students. We have had, on occasion, a student who prefers a more solitary existence, would rather not work collaboratively, feels that faculty and staff attention is oppressive, and is generally unhappy being part of a learning community. It is possible, if it is very early in the semester, to move a student into non-learning community classes although moving to another residence hall floor is not an option. When, however, the realization doesn't take hold until later in the semester, university add/drop policies preclude making other arrangements and the continuing presence of a very unhappy student can have a negative impact on the rest of the community. We try to head off these problems by being clear about what joining the learning community means. We provide information about what to expect in the MLC, we encourage prospective students to talk to MLC students before deciding whether to participate, and we send a letter over the summer reminding those who have been placed in the MLC about our expectations. When all of this is not sufficient, the faculty and staff find themselves spending a disproportionate amount of time and energy trying to make the best of a bad situation. We haven't yet figured out a solution to this problem.

Additionally, turnover in residence life staff is a fact of life. Staff in the Office of Residence Life at Syracuse are a particularly upwardly mobile group of professionals. Thus, each year we face the possibility of a new residence director (RD), either one who has shifted from one residence hall to another within the university or one who is just starting at Syracuse. This situation presents several challenges. One is the challenge that is always present when introducing a new team member into an existing mix. Another is that the timing of RD appointments, which is driven by national norms, falls quite late in the process of reviewing the assessment data and making adjustments in the learning community for the following year. We need continuity, we want fresh ideas, and we want the RD to feel part of the process. The timing makes reaching all those goals difficult.

Faculty turnover is not an issue that we have yet had to face, but it is not reasonable to expect the faculty teaching in the learning community to take this on as a lifetime commitment. We are always on the lookout for faculty who might be interested in joining the MLC some day. When that day comes, there will be significant transition issues to deal with, from introducing a new member into the team, to finding ways to allow that person to put her or his own mark on the learning community while still preserving the experience that the students have come to expect.

CONCLUSION

We are fortunate, as one of the pilot learning communities, to have had a chance to make our mistakes and learn from them in a very forgiving environment. We have learned much over the years about how to make a learning community an exceptional experience for students, and it is important to note that much of our learning comes from listening to the lives of our students. It is their experiences, hopes, and dreams that have taught us what we need to know. We are grateful to them as well as the many faculty and staff who have given us feedback, ideas, and help over the past five years.

Sandra N. Hurd is professor of law and public policy in the Whitman School of Management and director of learning communities for academic affairs, and Steve St. Onge is associate director of the Office of Residence Life, both of Syracuse University.

10

Leading for Change

Mariana Lebron

The LEAD Learning Community provides students the opportunity to learn leadership theory and hone leadership skills. The community strug-gled in its first two years to align the participants' multiple perspectives on leadership and understand its focus and goals. The extraordinary commitment of the learning community students, staff, and faculty to making LEAD a success has resulted in a vibrant community dedicated to leadership development.

INTRODUCTION

"You must be the change you wish to see in the world." Gandhi's words cap-ture the essence of the Leaders Emerging And Developing (LEAD) Learning Community. A residential-based learning community, LEAD utilizes the Social Change Model of Leadership Development (Higher Education Research Institute, 1996), which views leadership as a force for positive change in society. By combining this model with Kouzes and Posner's (2003) leadership theories, students learn specific skill sets that help them take risks, work with others, and motivate team members to be successful in a diverse and challenging society. The LEAD Learning Community meets a campus need for student leadership development.

EVOLUTION OF THE LEAD LEARNING COMMUNITY

Dr. Bill Coplin, a faculty member in public affairs, proposed the leadership challenge floor in December 1999. In a concept paper describing his vision, he said, "My challenge is to develop, test, and eventually implement products and activities that will increase the willingness of people to be committed to the principles of the Athenian Oath. The operating section of the oath is that we will 'transmit the city as greater, better, and more beautiful than it was transmitted to us.'"

Year One

The Leadership Learning Community began in 2000. The project team, which designed and implemented the curriculum, consisted of residence life staff and two faculty members, all of whom had various and differing perspectives on leadership development. Our biggest challenge the first year was to manage effectively this multifaceted approach and negotiate the different expectations of faculty and staff while maintaining effective collaboration among the team. It was hard work and at times extremely frustrating, but it was ultimately successful.

In the fall, students were required to take a three-credit course, Focus on Leadership, co-taught by Professor Marvin Druger, a faculty member in science teaching with a strong interest in leadership, and Professor Bill Coplin. Dr. Druger's component of the course explored various styles of leadership through presentations by academic, community, and military guest speakers. Students wrote a reflective commentary and analysis about each speaker's presentation. Dr. Coplin's component of the course consisted of six class discussions of readings in the required text, his book *How You Can Help: An Easy Guide to Doing Good Deeds in Your Everyday Life.* The residential component, which included a daylong ropes course, various floor programs and initiatives, and speaker presentations, was designed to enhance the students' class experiences and highlight discussion of how to serve the greater society by incorporating Dr. Coplin's Genuine Dogooder™ philosophy.

During the spring semester, residents chose from two academic options: 1) the one-credit GOLD Leadership Class, which focused on personal improvement and skill development, or 2) a two-credit public affairs practicum consisting of an independent project advised by Dr. Coplin.

Year Two

For the second year, the project team focused primarily on refining class components; further development of the residence life curriculum became secondary. During the planning process, conflicting notions of leadership theory had to be renegotiated, and the relative weights to be given public service and leadership development worked through. Although the community retained both of these concepts in its vision, it became clear that it was evolving more in the direction of leadership. As a result, the project team agreed to concentrate on one model of leadership and redefine the faculty and staff roles.

The three-credit fall course used the text *Exploring Leadership* (Komives, Lucas, & McMahon, 1998) and supplemental readings highlighting the Social Change Model of Leadership Development to examine how students can have a positive impact on change as leaders within a college or university community. For spring semester, the students developed and implemented a service project, which I co-advised with Dr. Druger, for which they received one to three academic credits.

Dr. Druger and I co-instructed the course. Dr. Druger arranged for and worked with the guest speakers, while I developed the course content and experiential-learning activities. Dr. Coplin worked with the students to help promote public service and proposed another learning community that focused on his primary interest, citizenship education (see Chapter 16). At the request of the students, the community was renamed Leaders Emerging and Developing (LEAD).

Year Three

The third year of implementation brought still more modifications. The learning community shifted from recruiting students who were already student leaders towards targeting a diverse group of students with varying leadership objectives and career goals. As a result, the learning community's core philosophies had to shift in order to establish an effective foundation from which activities and learning could be constructed. At the same time, our faculty and staff resources became constrained.

The learning community had to find its place as the campus-wide leadership development program underwent a strategic planning process and the Student Activities Office was restructured. As part of that reorganization, staff from the Office of Residence Life and the Office of Greek Life and Experiential Learning were given the responsibility of coordinating the learning community. This in turn led to an increased emphasis on connecting student participants to leadership opportunities on campus. Change was not, however, limited to reorganization in student affairs.

Due to increasing demands on his time, Dr. Druger had to withdraw from direct participation in LEAD, which meant we had to find an alternative academic component. The project team decided that the best option was to switch back to the one-credit GOLD Course, housed in the public affairs department, that we had used the first year. Dr. Coplin agreed and appointed two residence life staff members as adjunct faculty to teach the course, which underwent another collaborative revision to increase the public service component. The shift from a three-credit to a one-credit course allowed staff more time to try new ideas and supervise student development and implementation of optional projects. These optional projects allowed students more flexibility in matching leadership opportunities with their individual interests.

At the same time, student affairs human resources became an increasing concern. Although enrollment doubled on the floor and funding increased, staff resources decreased. Office restructuring and increasing demands in primary job responsibilities left student affairs staff with limited time to contribute. Rather than discontinue the learning community, we added to the team with the promise that each staff member would have only one or two carefully bounded responsibilities. Although this strategy presented some communication and coordination challenges, it has proven successful.

Looking Ahead to Years Four and Five

As we look forward to our fourth and fifth years of existence, we plan to combine and build upon the successes we have experienced in course curriculum, residential curriculum, and expanded support. In the fifth year, we will stabilize successful components, enhance assessment plans, and explore additional funding sources.

We will continue to model the important lesson we learned during the evolutionary process of our first three years—that a successful leadership learning community focused on creating positive change in society must have a core leadership team willing to walk the talk of effective leadership. The leadership team must be willing to change and adjust ideas and structures in collaboration with students and other campus constituencies in order to foster our students' development.

DEVELOPING LEARNING OUTCOMES

Developing learning outcomes appropriate to a leadership learning community requires the involvement of a diverse campus team, discussion about what success means, and an understanding of what is reasonable within the limitations of time, budget, academic requirements, and staff resources.

In the first year, goals (supported by more detailed objectives) for each part of the learning community experience were developed by the member of the project team responsible for that area. Dr. Druger's goal was that students learn different leadership styles and recognize their own inherent leadership traits. Dr. Coplin's goal was that students learn about and implement the Genuine Dogooder™ philosophy. My goal was that students increase their understanding of the links among academic, residence life, and cocurricular experiences. Our shared goal for the course was that students explore their potential as leaders and formulate strategies for becoming more effective in their leadership. We defined success as a learning community that facilitates:

- Leadership skill development within a diverse society (communication, conflict management, motivation, ethical decision-making, program planning, implementation, and evaluation, goal-setting, and vision development)

- Connections to the campus community

- Service to the community

- Connection with community leaders and employers as partners in enhancing leadership development for students

- Successful academic leadership

In the second year, informed by assessment data from the previous year and guided by the shift to the Social Change Model of leadership, a team of two learning community residents, the director of the Student Activities Office, and two Residence Life staff members revisited and revised the learning outcomes.

For the third year, a diverse campus community team, consisting of the Office of Greek Life and Experiential Learning, Career Services, the Center for Public and Community Service, and Residence Life, as well as student leaders from the campus community, engaged in a larger leadership discussion. Because these constituencies had varying approaches to preparing leaders for life after college, the team decided that LEAD students should be introduced to multiple models of leadership development. At monthly project team meetings, a team of administrators and students again revisited the community's objectives.

At the end of this process, learning outcomes crystallized around the vision of enhancing leadership development by involving floor participants both as individuals and as a group; by collaborating with other student leaders, faculty, and staff in creating learning opportunities; and by having a positive impact on society through intentional programming and individual interactions. Separate sets of learning outcomes were developed for the course and for the cocurricular experience.

RECRUITMENT AND RETENTION OF STUDENTS

We had to take multiple complicating factors into consideration in formulating our recruitment and retention plan. These factors included students' and administrators' perceptions of what leadership is, congruence between students' expectations of their involvement in the learning community and administrators' expectations about the learning community experience, whether or not the course would count for credit within a student's plan of study, understanding the motivations of our target population, and the necessity of providing individual interaction to help connect student participants to campus leadership opportunities.

Administrators' and students' views of leadership are not always the same. For example, as administrators we assumed that interested students would already be involved in leadership organizations on campus (e.g., student government, Residence Hall Association), so we recruited at student organizations' meetings. We subsequently discovered, however, that a large percentage of those applying for LEAD had never had any leadership training and were not involved in student organizations, so our recruiting strategy was not effective. As a consequence, we revised our strategy to recruit from a broader student population and focused on encouraging students to talk to other students. This approach, combined with the learning community materials sent out by the admissions office and recruiting efforts by the campus learning community coordinators, has significantly increased our applicant pool.

The second complicating factor was that students' varying understandings of leadership, largely influenced by their intended majors of study and career fields, had a significant impact on their expectations of what they would learn and what kinds of activities they would be expected to participate in. During the first year, these varying expectations resulted in significant tension and conflict on the floor. Of equal importance is clarity about the level of involvement expected of the students living in the community. Students interested in leadership tend to be involved in multiple projects on campus that compete for their time; sometimes they are so involved that they are unable or unwilling to give time to learning community activities. To address these issues, we included a brief phone conversation with each applicant in our application review process. During these conversations, we clarified the nature of the experience and expectations about learning community involvement, maximizing the likelihood that the learning community would be a good fit for each student selected to live there. We reminded students of our expectations in a welcome letter sent out to the students from the project team. We also included an agreement, highlighting mandatory expectations (e.g., enrollment in the course, participation in specified outside of class experiences and activities) that students signed and returned.

The third complicating factor is whether or not the required course counts toward graduation requirements in the student's home college. This is a serious issue for a learning community open to students from all the university's schools and colleges. Each school and college has a different set of curricular requirements, determined by the faculty and/or accrediting body mandate. Some schools, for example, don't count courses designated as experience credit toward graduation. Care must be taken during the recruitment process to provide students with appropriate information and access to advising by their home college so that they understand the curricular implications of being part of the learning community.

Another issue of concern is the motivation of the student choosing the community. Because learning community students are assigned housing first, some students may request a learning community solely for the residence hall in which it is located. A student who is in the community for this reason may have a significant negative impact on the dynamics of the community. Dealing with differences in motivation, however, can give rise to important learning opportunities. Involving students in solving motivation problems allows them to apply what they are learning. For example, one semester, faced with students who resisted taking the spring class, the coordinators decided the best approach was to allow students to make their own choices about fulfilling their leadership commitments. A few students decided not to take the course. A number of the other residents were frustrated by that decision and felt the students should be kicked off the floor. Instructors facilitated conversations about the conflict from which the students learned a real world leadership lesson: not everyone will fulfill commitments and the challenge to leaders is how to manage that situation—what consequences to impose and how to continue to focus on the greater goal.

Finally, individual interactions between administrators and students are critical in retaining students in leadership initiatives. Retention depends on the opportunity students have to use their leadership skills, to be recognized for their efforts, and to be accepted as individuals who have something special to offer. This process was facilitated by the project coordinators' intentional efforts to recommend students for opportunities, as well as to encourage their involvement efforts. Approximately 88% of those living on the floor became involved in some outside leadership opportunity that involved significant interaction with an administrator by the end of the year.

Although we understood some of the recruitment and retention dynamics when we developed the learning community, not all of them were obvious to us. And even the ones we knew about played out in unexpected ways. Developing an effective recruitment and retention plan required that we work constantly on the process of understanding and responding to multiple environmental factors.

Assessment

Our assessment plan for years one and two had multiple streams. The first stream focused on helping the students assess the extent to which they improved the effectiveness of their own leadership style. The second stream focused on assessing whether we had successfully met the learning outcomes for the community. A final stream involved gathering improvement suggestions from faculty and staff.

Assessment of skill enhancement was conducted in various ways and at multiple stages of the course. The first assessment was done, anonymously, during the first class period. Students were asked to evaluate themselves on specific leadership skills (e.g., ability to set goals, ability to motivate a group). During the course, students were given three formal leadership style/skill assessment instruments. The DISC (a personal assessment tool that generates profiles) helped students understand how their personalities influenced their effectiveness in leading diverse teams. Blake's Leadership Grid helped students understand that effective leaders have varying styles of leadership and why certain styles are appropriate to various situations. The Student Leadership Practices Inventory (Kouzes & Posner, 2003) helped students understand how their self-perceptions as leaders differed or were similar to the perception of others.

Learning outcomes were assessed in multiple ways. After the first class, students were asked to react anonymously to the learning objectives and provide information about themselves as learners. This assessment provided rich information about the needs of the students that the instructor used to adjust course content to support the learning objectives more effectively. For example, we learned that students most valued educational experiences that were stories, activities, and opportunities for them to get involved. We then modified the curriculum to incorporate more of these types of learning situations. Subsequent student input revealed both an increase in the level of students' satisfaction with the course as well as an appreciation that their voices were heard. At mid-semester, we gathered informal anonymous feedback to assess how well the course was meeting learning outcomes. Students were asked to comment on strengths of the course and areas in which instructors could improve the course. We discovered that while students enjoyed course content and presentations and appreciated the opportunity to think about what they were learning in their cocurricular experiences, they needed even more experiences outside of the course that connected them with other student leaders and with campus offices. At the end of the semester, a formal assessment was conducted to determine which topics and presentations were most useful to participants and which sessions yielded the highest levels of satisfaction. Questions designed to find out how each student had grown as a leader were also included. Finally, students were required to write a final course paper in which they reflected on their skill learning and their own changes. In these papers, students gave examples of how they had changed during the year and what they had learned. A number noted they had grown from being closed-minded, unmotivated, lacking in confidence, and scared to fail to being more open-minded, patient, determined, confident, and wanting to take initiative to make a difference in the world. Many emphasized that they now felt they could make the changes they wanted to see in the world by taking it step by step and by focusing on understanding themselves first and then how they have an impact. Finally, feedback from faculty and staff was very helpful in understanding what we were doing well and what needed improvement. Among the suggestions for improvement were putting more emphasis on practicing leadership skills, finding more ways to harness the students' energy and diversity, developing a more comprehensive collaboration between faculty and staff, incorporating more ways for students to understand their skill levels, and setting clearer expectations for recruiting and training the resident advisor. We used this information to enhance course curriculum, redesign the residential component, and make structural changes.

SUMMARY

The leadership learning community has overcome a number of obstacles. Conceived in student affairs, it struggled before it found a consistent academic home that could provide stability. At first there was skepticism, even among student affairs staff, about its potential. Since then, enthusiasm about the community has grown even though the human resources to support it have diminished. Despite these obstacles, the community has persevered and is successful. It has brought students, faculty, and staff together in a leadership learning experience that not only helps students succeed during and after college, but also helps the campus leadership development program grow. It has challenged all those involved to work together in making the world a better place. We see Ghandi's words of being the "change you wish to see in the world" come to life in the words and actions of our leaders of today and tomorrow.

Mariana Lebron is former assistant director of the Office of Residence Life at Syracuse University.

REFERENCES

Coplin, W. D. (2000). *How you can help: An easy guide to doing good deeds in your everyday life.* New York, NY: Routledge.

Higher Education Research Institute, University of California–Los Angeles. (1996). *Social change model of leadership development* (Guidebook Version III). Los Angeles, CA: Author.

Komives, S. R., Lucas, N., & McMahon, T. R. (1998). *Exploring leadership: For college students who want to make a difference.* San Francisco, CA: Jossey-Bass.

Kouzes, J. M., & Posner, B. Z. (2003). *The leadership challenge* (3rd ed.). San Francisco, CA: Jossey-Bass.

11

Multicultural Living/Learning Community: By the Students, for the Students

James Duah-Agyeman

Diversity is one of the core values of Syracuse University. The Multicultural Living/Learning Community supports this value by providing a safe place for students to explore the complexities of multiculturalism; learn to respect, appreciate, and celebrate diversity; and understand and act on their power to create positive change.

*I*n recent years, higher education has significantly addressed the need to promote ongoing development of multicultural knowledge, awareness, and anti-oppression skills to function within the ever-diversifying campuses across the nation (American College Personnel Association, 1994; Pope & Reynolds, 1997; Tierney, 1993). Tatum (1997) notes that despite perceptions of ethnic equality, we live in a racist society in which individuals are systematically advantaged or disadvantaged in relation to their racial and ethnic identities. According to Levine and Cureton (1998), students across the country from all cultural backgrounds have expressed a significant amount of frustration, discomfort, and even hostility towards cross-cultural discussions. The climates created around campuses to discuss freely the complexities of multiculturalism should be safe for students to unpack their observations, questions, and emotions about their experiences (Levine & Cureton, 1998; Tatum, 1997).

Enriched by a three-credit course that blends theory and practice, the Multicultural Living/Learning Community (henceforth, MLLC) offers students (of all races and ethnicities) a nonthreatening environment for such discussions to take place with the ultimate goal of assisting them to respect, appreciate, and celebrate multiculturalism and diversity in all its forms.

SETTING UP THE MLLC

To establish the MLLC, organizers needed a documented student need, student buy-in, and support from the faculty, staff, and administrators at Syracuse University. A group of undergraduate students provided the much needed student support and documentation of student need. What started out as a debate on the perceived segregation on the SU campus turned into a conversation about the richness of their respective communities. This group saw the parallels in their cultures and their paths to succeeding at SU. They became a cohesive group looking to create a richer educational environment for their university and each other. In the spring of 1999, these students proposed the idea of a learning community where people of different ethnic, cultural, and religious backgrounds could live together in a community that fostered individual growth and unity. With strong support from the Office of Multicultural Affairs (OMA) and the Office of Residence Life (ORL), the MLLC was established in fall 2000 as a collaborative initiative between the Divisions of Academic Affairs and Student Affairs. Under the guidance of OMA and ORL, the students took the important first step of developing the MLLC mission which is to nurture the spirit and growth:

> Of utility . . . not novelty
> Of enthusiasm . . . not reluctance
> Of pride . . . not arrogance
> Of inquisitiveness . . . not prejudice
> Of enlightenment . . . not ignorance
> Of camaraderie to blossom . . . not division
> Of life . . . not disillusionment
> Of each other and to you.

This mission connected closely with the university-wide goal of multicultural competence (the knowledge, attitudes, skills, and protocols that assist an individual or community in understanding others with respect to cultural differences). Cultural competency permits individuals to respond with respect and empathy to people of all cultures, classes, races, religions, and ethnic backgrounds in a manner that recognizes, affirms, and values the worth of individuals, families, and communities (Laib, 2002).

The next steps in the process of getting started were to work out appropriate residence hall space and create a timeline for developing the learning community. With space and a timeline, we turned our attention to putting into place a multi-layered support structure for the MLLC that fostered the widespread participation of students, faculty, and staff. A multi-layered support structure as first conceptualized included an advisory board (25 faculty, staff, and student members who meet at least three times a semester to provide overall guidance and direction to the MLLC), the Office of Multicultural Affairs, the Office of Residence Life, faculty and staff mentors, affinity group mentors (individuals who provide a structured support system for 10 to 12 MLLC students and hold weekly group discussions on selected topics), student mentors, a resident advisor, an undergraduate programming assistant, and the graduate assistant/coordinator for the MLLC.

Figure 11.1

Multi-Layered Support Structure

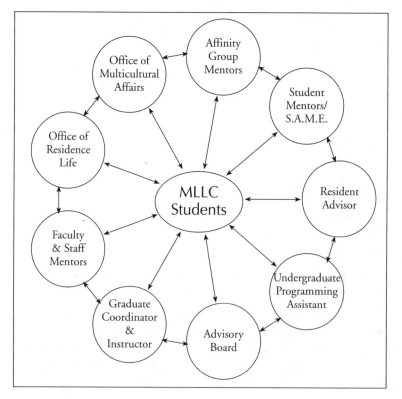

With the support structure conceptualized, we were ready to turn our attention to articulating goals and objectives for the MLLC.

LEARNING OBJECTIVES

All learning communities at SU are required to have learning outcomes or objectives. A collaborative process resulted in the development of these objectives and goals for the MLLC:

- Students will have an increased sense of themselves and of how they relate to other cultural groups. They will share personal histories, clearly identify where in the cycle of personal oppression they define themselves, articulate commonalities and differences with others who identify culturally with the same umbrella expression, understand racial identity concepts, recognize the legacy of our diverse cultural perspectives, and celebrate the contributions of the varied groups within our community.

- Students will understand the effects of privilege and marginalization. They will understand the cycle of personal oppression, understand the ways in which they and others are privileged and/or marginalized, and understand the various levels of human interaction at which oppressions can play out. They will be able to articulate the ideas of the interrelatedness of oppressions and be able to articulate the idea of institutional oppression.

- Students will understand and act upon their power to effect positive change and influence the environment. They will understand and utilize the concept of reflection and action and will understand different ways to organize and create change such as networking. They will define ways to establish and support allies across identities, express a commitment to eliminate social injustice, and learn ways in which the environment supports/hinders development. Additionally, they will learn the basic skills involved in intercultural communication, conflict management and resolution, mediation, negotiation, anti-oppressive behavior, and participate in floor and community activities that address social justice issues.

As one might imagine, developing these goal statements was a tough process. Their very existence is a tribute to everyone's commitment to the collaborative process and the MLLC. Each year the MLLC staff revisit the learning objectives in light of participants' feedback, but thus far they have not had to revise them.

RECRUITMENT

The first year of the MLLC, a group of students already on campus who had proposed a multicultural learning community wanted to live in the MLLC. Incoming first-year students were recruited through the university's regular housing application process. Since the first year, MLLC residents have been recruited by word of mouth, by flyers posted in the residence halls, and by information provided in the admissions brochure.

Students wanting to live in the MLLC for the first time were asked to respond to the following questions: What is your interest in living in this particular community? What do you think you could contribute to this community? What do you hope to experience and learn from being a part of this particular community? What types of programs would you like to see in this community? What are your interests and hobbies? Please explain why diversity is important in your life. (See Appendix 11.1 for sample responses to these questions.) Staff from Residence Life and from the Office of Multicultural Affairs reviewed the applications and selected students to live in the MLLC. This approach, which resulted in rejecting some applicants to the MLLC, created confusion for a few incoming first-year students who felt that their excitement about being admitted to the university had been tarnished by being denied their request to participate in the MLLC. As a result, we quickly abandoned this approach. Though we require responses to these questions, they are not the basis for acceptance to the floor, which is filled on a first-come, first-served basis. The staff of the Office of Multicultural Affairs and Office of Residence Life read the responses to help in programming for the floor/community, establishing affinity groups, and as a starting point for conversation and counseling around issues of diversity and multiculturalism.

We are also cognizant of the fact that some students consider terms such as "multiculturalism" and "diversity" to be references to experiences of students of color only and believe that the MLLC is only for students of color. We need to be even more intentional in our effort to dispel this perception and attract students from all backgrounds, especially our White/European American students. Our participating white students have been instrumental in the recruitment process, and we need to work much more closely with them to make the program attractive to more Caucasian students.

OVERNIGHT RETREAT

To provide MLLC residents with the opportunity to bond with each other, the residents participate in an off-campus overnight retreat during the second weekend of school. The components emphasized at the retreat are programming, mentoring, community building, advocacy (advocating on their own behalf and on behalf of one another), education (educating their peers and the larger community about diversity), and leadership (developing and practicing their leadership skills). The retreat is designed to set the stage for establishing a sense of trust and for feeling comfortable expressing feelings, thoughts, and experiences with one another. Most importantly, it is intended to facilitate a sense of bonding and connectedness with each other and with the faculty, staff, and administrator participants involved in the MLLC.

At the end of the retreat, participants are asked to reflect on the retreat in terms of what they have gained from the experience and what they will take from it. Responses include the following comments:

> *The experience that I will like to take from this retreat is that I am not alone. That I have so much to offer to this world and that the MLLC is my family away from home. This experience has made me aware of people that I never really noticed had as many problems as I. I have experienced a whole new rebirth within myself that I would like to share with the rest of the world, and I have gained such a closeness with everyone here. I thank all of you for this privilege.*

> *I hope to get to know each individual in this community more than just this weekend's worth of sharing. I've learned about what other people value to be things that shaped them, but also to look at myself and my own values/beliefs. I am privileged to be a part of such an amazing group of young women and men!*

> *I am more aware of the problems minorities face on a daily basis and of how segregation continues to occur. . . . I have learned that sometimes groups self-segregate to form a support group of people who have shared similar experiences and not to exclude other groups.*

> *If nothing else, I will leave knowing that the idea of racial harmony isn't just an idea. I will know that it is not an us-against-them world. I am ridiculously happy to see that everyone is*

*comfortable enough to let their hearts spill and I know the best
is yet to come.*

*Through this retreat, we built trust and respect. We shared our
experiences; we learn from each other's experiences. We understand each other's experiences. We understand each other's needs
and feelings, that we are able to support each other. This is our
home, our shelter. I can really get the backup and support I have
never had.*

ASSESSMENT

We have initiated systematic collection of information about activities, characteristics, and outcomes. This assessment generally has been more qualitative
than quantitative, with students' anecdotal reports, reflective journal(s), and
learning logs as primary data sources. We use feedback gleaned from these
sources to make improvement in the community.

One area we discovered needed improvement was the course. The learning community academic component was initially an independent study that
consisted of readings and discussions led by the graduate coordinator and
instructor and monitored by an adjunct faculty member from the Department of Psychology in the College of Arts and Sciences. It also served as the
forum for planning group activities and field trips. Early assessment revealed
that because it was an independent study, the course would not count toward
graduation for students in several schools and colleges. This operated to
exclude students who otherwise would be able to participate. In addition, students wanted a better balance between experiential learning and more traditional academic coursework. The course environment was described by one
student as "a little bit to read, a little to eat, a little to watch, a little to listen
to, and a lot of talking." Armed with this information, we approached the
director of the Latino/Latin American Studies program (in the College of Arts
and Sciences) who put together a three-credit course titled "Living in a
Diverse Society" (LAS 300). This course provides an introduction to different
cultural forms, life styles, political ideologies, religious traditions, philosophies, artistic expressions, sexual orientations, and worldviews that together
make up a general panoramic vista of the diverse structure of life in contemporary American society. (See Appendix 11.2 for the new syllabus.)

Another area that we found that needed improvement was the relationship between OMA staff (MLLC coordinator) and ORL staff (the resident
advisor). With the MLLC coordinator living on the floor and the resident

advisor participating in the MLLC as a resident, it was not clear who had primary responsibility for the various community activities. As a result of this feedback, we moved MLLC coordinators (graduate assistants) off the floors, and their responsibility now is to assist the faculty member in teaching the course. The biggest challenge that remains is integrating the class readings and discussions into programming for the floor. Both the resident advisor and the graduate assistants are in constant communication regarding floor programming, which remains the responsibility of the resident advisor.

Addressing these concerns has helped us build a stronger learning community. We note several indicators of success. One is that the high level of enrollment in the MLLC has led to the opening of another MLLC community. Another is the number of students who have chosen to live in the community a second year. A third indicator of success is that students from the pilot year of the MLLC established a student organization called "S.A.M.E." (Students Advocating Multicultural Equality), which is made up of former and current residents of the MLLC. The mission of this group is to establish a working relationship with current and future MLLC's and to be inclusive of students on campus who have not had the opportunity to be a part of the MLLC.

Next Steps

As we move forward, we find it important to seek more funding for programming outside the residence hall. We plan to write grants to get funding for off-campus trips for special educational and cultural experiences. The grant writing process will include MLLC students collaborating with existing student groups on projects as well as soliciting funds from other sources within the university. In addition, we need to continue to be very intentional about our recruitment efforts to make the MLLC more attractive to all students. As importantly, we need to seek more collaboration with other learning communities on campus.

Conclusion

Initiated by students, the Multicultural Living/Learning Community (MLLC) is a collaborative endeavor between academic affairs and two units of student affairs, the Office of Multicultural Affairs, and the Office of Residence Life. The MLLC serves to advance student learning through a unique faculty-enhanced residential experience integrating cultural identity development, complex multicultural and intercultural communication, and anti-oppression work. This diversity initiative aims to educate students to become culturally competent and to respect, appreciate, and celebrate multiculturalism and diversity in all its forms. The former director of multicultural affairs and the founding director of MLLC, Irma Almirall-Padamsee, put it well. She said:

> *I understand that this floor won't be for everyone. If you live on this floor, you will be challenged to do many things simultaneously; challenged to take the time and make the effort to deeply explore what it means to identify in the ways that you do, to open your mind and your heart to learning about communities other than the ones you may be most familiar with. Participants will be challenged to understand and commit to the notion that in order to make real social change regarding diversity issues, you must ally yourself with others also committed to change for the better (even if they do not look like you), and define significant change, and then set out to make that significant change (in your own life and/or in the life of the community you connect with). I hope there are at least 40 brave men and women out there willing to take the risk involved in participating in this new effort—they will reap the benefits of being the leaders of a basic norm shift on our campus.*

The journey—to understand "privilege" and "marginalization," to understand and act upon one's power to effect positive change and influence the environment—has indeed been a challenging one for those students brave enough to join the MLLC. But the benefit of achieving an increased sense of themselves and how they relate to other cultural groups has been worth the struggle:

> *This floor represents the true meaning of synergy! Every culture we represent has intertwined to create something valuable, and that's the ability to adapt, respect, and be open-minded about our world. Everyone should have the MLLC experience. The only regret I have is that all the floors on campus have not had this experience because it will help us understand and realize that there's only one race, and that's the human race!*
> —A. C., Arts and Sciences, Class of 2002

And in the MLLC, the struggle—the struggle to get our undergraduate young men and women of all races and ethnicities to appreciate, respect, and celebrate diversity in all its forms—continues.

James Duah-Agyeman is director of student support and diversity in the Office of Multicultural Affairs at Syracuse University.

REFERENCES

American College Personnel Association (ACPA). (1994). *The student learning imperative: Implications for student affairs.* Washington, DC: Author. Retrieved February 25, 2003, from http://www.acpa.nche.edu/sli/sli.htm

Laib, C. J. (2002, March). Increasing our culture compeetence. *The Diversity Campus Report,* 1.

Levine, A. L., & Cureton, J. S. (1998). *When hope and fear collide: A portrait of today's college student.* San Francisco, CA: Jossey Bass.

Pope, R. L., & Reynolds, A. L. (1997). Student affairs core competencies: Integrating multicultural awareness, knowledge, and skills. *Journal of College Student Development, 38,* 266–277.

Tatum, B. D. (1997). *"Why are all the black kids sitting together in the cafeteria?" and other conversations about race.* New York, NY: Basic Books.

Tierney, W. G. (1993). *Building communities of difference: Higher education in the twenty-first century.* Westport, CT: Bergen and Garvey.

Appendix 11.1

MLLC Application Questions

What Is Your Interest in Living in This Particular Community?

"I, myself, coming from a mixed ethnic background of two South East Asian countries, have always valued and seek interest in diverse community. I would like to learn about other cultures I am not aware of, and at the same time get to know more about myself."

"As an African-American, I would like to learn more about the Latin and Jewish cultures. I have always known that the three cultures had a lot in common, but I have yet to see these cultures acknowledge their differences and similarities by living together in celebration of their histories, traditions, and values."

"I have spent my entire life in Harlem surrounded by people of color. This experience has left a gap in my life. I strongly desire a more rounded group of people to be with. In this global society, we all need to have exposure to all kinds of people. Through this way of living, we can all learn to understand our differences as well as our similarities."

"My interest is as a freshman, that I will be able to relate to many different people in this community. We will all be there to help and guide each other. I feel that this is an important and very useful tool for college. I will meet people in my classes that will also be in the community I live in. If I need help, I will have people who live with me to go to, and I will be there for them if they need help. I think this idea is really a good one."

"I think that this particular community better enables minority students to grasp a sense of who they are. Like the Philosopher Tao Te Ching said: 'He who knows others is wise, but he who knows himself—is enlightened.'"

What Do You Think You Could Contribute to This Community?

"In this community, I think I can contribute my perspective of a Chinese-American girl being raised in Harlem. I think that being a Chinese girl and being able to speak three languages—English, Chinese, and Spanish—is something valuable to contribute."

"What I will contribute to this community is my interest in learning about other peoples' cultures. I will also contribute my understanding of my culture and share it with others, so that they could learn from it, as I learn from theirs."

"Since I am a first-generation American and the only American citizen in my family, I feel that I have a fairly balanced outlook as to what it means to not only be part of the American culture but also the African culture. I can contribute my experiences of being bicultural and what this means to my current and future goals."

"I can contribute my honesty and my friendship. If ever someone needs someone to talk to, I will be there for them. I can also contribute my friendliness, caring, and supportive ways to this community."

"I feel I could contribute my own experience of having lived in India for 11 years and also share my experiences with culture shock, etc. I would like to put in the time and effort to educate others about diversity as well."

"I can contribute a lot to this community. I believe I'm a very open-minded person as well as energetic. I'm always willing to try new things and I can try to encourage it, if it's not already there, with others. I have good interpersonal communication skills and will use it to make others feel comfortable around me and thus, be more willing to open up."

What Do You Hope to Experience and Learn From Being a Part of This Particular Community?

"I hope to become exposed to other cultures, especially to find out where a lot of the stereotypes of each culture originated. I hope to clear up some of my own misconceptions."

"I hope that the MLLC will give me an individualized account of what it is like to be a person of Latin, African and/or Jewish descent. The personal stories and experiences to be (hopefully) shared will make a very strong impact on my perceptions of the Latin, Jewish, and African cultures. I hope to grow more comfortable with sharing the smallest details of my Owambo (Namibian) culture to any number of people. Also, I would like to learn about the traditional values and beliefs that motivate and/or influence these cultures. And, for those who are also of mixed cultures, I would like to learn how these students, much like myself, are coping with the constant struggle of having to balance their ways of life amidst all the traditions and beliefs."

"I hope to gain understanding for other cultures by living on the multicultural floor. I think at times people do not get along because they can not see where the other person is coming from. By living on this floor, I hope to gain the ability to live and interact with people with a different perspective on life."

"To learn about all the different cultures, to have stereotypes about these different cultures corrected. Also to learn how to get along with other cultures, because in the future you never know who you might be working with in your career."

What Types of Programs Would You Like to See in This Community?

"A mentoring program, small group discussions, monthly cultural dinners, an international festival, guest speakers, and performances."

"I would like to see the establishment of not only extracurricular groups, but study groups as well. Students should be able to have academic study groups. I also think open forums are necessary. Everyone should have a chance to express themselves."

"I would like to see programs where the residents play an interactive role in the process of learning about each other's cultures. This can range from storytelling to cultural performances by residents/students, professors, speakers, storytellers, etc. To conclude the MLLC experience at the end of the semester, there should also be an "International Night and Potluck Dinner." This event could be an avenue for students to express their comfort and confidence in all the cultures they've just learned about through performance. They could read a favorite poem, sing a powerful song, or dance a traditional dance—any of which illustrates an important aspect of their culture. The dinner would consist of international dishes created by the residents, students, or SU faculty to highlight the important role that food plays in the many traditions of these cultures."

"I would like to see programs that require students to work in groups that they would not pick themselves. Programs that take trips off campus to museums, theater, and even different kinds of restaurants. For example going to the Folk Art Gallery to see the exhibit on the Harlem Renaissance. Having dinners in the penthouse where we have different theme dinners for each nationality. Study sessions are always helpful. Movie nights that feature films with various ethnic groups that are positive and not stereotypical. I would also like to have sessions where students can talk about themselves and express their feelings about controversial topics that deal with their ethnicities."

"I hope to see that there are programs that deal with ethnic themes like oppression and discrimination, or even racial programs."

"The type of programs I hope to see in this community are programs where we can better learn about important issues like oppression, discrimination, and how we can use the resources we have to help make things better for ourselves and others."

What Are Your Interests and Hobbies?

"My interests and hobbies include reading, writing, dancing and—most importantly—learning how to communicate with others, and develop social skills."

"Listening to music, learning about anything that has do with the struggle or oppression of a certain people, and relaxing."

"I like to play volleyball and am in the process of learning other sports. I like dancing and learning new ones—salsa, merengue, swing, and even break dancing. Since I have been at Syracuse I've taken up learning photography as well."

"I'm involved in, and have always been involved in student government. I write for an African-American publication, volunteer at center village, and would like to host an international student. Other hobbies include eating! Dancing! Classic movies! Music! Alternative modern rock, lape verde, drum and bass, Spanish, Reggae/jazz."

"Some of my interests and hobbies are listening to music, reading, dancing, and spending time with family and friends. I also like doing well in school, so that I can accomplish my goals."

Please Explain Why Diversity Is Important in Your Life.

"I have come to a point in life where I believe diversity is a way of life and also being a university student at this point in life, most of us seem to forget the real meaning of the word, "university" = unity + diversity."

"Diversity is important in my life because I feel that everyone should learn and get along with people of different cultures. This allows people to learn new things and realize that they have a lot to offer to one another."

"My field of study is nursing, and within this field you come in contact with people from various cultures. In order for me to succeed in my nursing career, I need to be able to recognize, understand, and respect other cultures."

"I think the more I learn about diversity, the better I will be prepared for life. I love learning about and meeting new people."

"Diversity is important in my life because I was raised with it all around me. I have always had friends of many different backgrounds whom I have learned from. My neighborhood, Washington Heights, must be one of the most diverse Latino communities in New York. My parents have friends from around the world who are family friends and who I have grown up with. Diversity keeps my friendships interesting, and it helps me learn about other people and their perspective of things. I could not imagine living in a world or in a community that is only of one color, or race, or people."

"After moving from a different country, I have realized that learning about others different from us is crucial. Learning about others helps to eliminate stereotypes. Different cultures offer different experiences and to learn and become knowledgeable."

"Diversity is very important in my life because I am able to capture the whole beauty of human life. Instead of experiencing and living in one environment, I can experience everything and thus, not be left out with the gift diversity has for me. Diversity is what creates a multicultural world, and that for me is what I want out of my life. I want to gain synergy."

Appendix 11.2

LAS 300
LEARNING COMMUNITIES: LIVING IN A DIVERSE SOCIETY

Fall 2002   Prof. Silvio Torres-Saillant
3 credits   405 Hall of Languages
Meets Monday, 6–9 p.m.   Phone: x 9475
                                                 E-mail: saillant@syr.edu

SYLLABUS

Course Description

This course provides an introduction to different cultural forms, lifestyles, political ideologies, religious traditions, philosophies, artistic expressions, sexual orientations, and world views that together make up a general panoramic vista of the diverse structure of life in contemporary American society. The course explores the tension between the fact of diversity and the resilience of paradigms of homogeneity in the construction of national identity in the United States as well as in the country's rapport with foreign nations in an increasingly global world. The course will survey several ways of looking at the American experience depending on contrasting philosophies of history. We will look at definitions of the family in light of an awareness of sexual and personal realities that challenge nuclear and heteronormative assumptions.

We will examine various understandings of the here and hereafter in light of dissimilar conceptions of the divine. In addition, the course will compare the varied scales of value implicit in capitalist, socialist, theocratic, and other socioeconomic systems while also considering the experience of everyday life as it applies to able-bodied, disabled, and extraordinarily endowed people. We will study representations of the beautiful with a focus on cross-cultural and epochal appreciations of attractiveness in the human body as well as the extremes to which people would go to conform to prevailing standards. We will peruse culturally specific worldviews and philosophies such as Western metaphysics, Confucianism, and orisha thought, with their varied emphases on human destiny, the purpose of existence, the value of a human life, progress, civilization, and the place of the individual, while assessing the ideas of love and goodness in different religious cosmologies. Overall, the course will explore the inevitable coexistence of dissimilar, distinct, and contrasting value systems in the cultures, constituencies, linguistic groups, class origins, and other differentiated subsections of the population of the United States, a nation made up overwhelmingly of immigrants that plays an active role in the lives of people around the globe, thus exacerbating the preponderance of diversity in American society.

Method
The course will consist of 14 class meetings, each devoted to a particular theme or topic and taught in collaboration with a specialist in the pertinent field. The guest lectures will be drawn from a wide range of interdisciplinary areas of expertise, bodies of knowledge, intellectual approaches, and ideological perspectives. The areas represented will include history, anthropology, religion, sociology, art, and literature, as well as African-American, Native-American, Film, Latino, and Gay and Lesbian studies.

Requirements
Students will be responsible for assigned readings, film screenings, research assignments, oral reports, writing projects, regular attendance, and class participation. The successful students will be those who through their completed assignments demonstrate a command of the aspects of diversity covered in the course.

Schedule of Classes

Week 1: Introduction. Overview of the concept of diversity and its relation to homogeneity. Announcement of the topics covered in the course. Handouts for discussion in next class meeting. Short reading for discussion. Screening of film clip. Students write a one-page presentation of their understanding of diversity or any experience with someone who is different.

Week 2: Introduction to comparative genocides. Examination of Elie Wiesel's *Night*, a poem by Leonard Cohen on Adolf Eichmann, excerpts on the decimation of the Native-American population, and newspaper clippings of lynchings of blacks in the South. Class discussion. Writing assignment.

Week 3: Sexual orientation and the family. Presentation by Professor Roger Hallas, who specializes in film and gay studies. Screening of a short film on AIDS. Essay by Douglass Crimp. Class discussion. Writing assignment.

Week 4: Construction of national identity, the history of U.S. ethnic violence, racial othering, and cultural conflict. Presentation by Professor Monika Wadman guiding the class through a reading of key documents of

Native-American culture, including selections from Sherman Alexie's *The Toughest Indian in the World.* Class discussion. Writing assignment.

Week 5: Complexity of achieving fairness when situations have been created by legacies of violence. Guest lecture by Andy Mager from the Neighbors of the Onondaga Nation. Discussion of former efforts to strip Indians of their native identity ("Kill the Indian; Save the Man") and current unresolved land claim cases. The history of U.S. ethnic violence, racial othering, and cultural conflict. Class discussion. Writing assignment.

Week 6: Differing and competing ways of understanding human culture. Presentation by Damian Baca (Ph.D. candidate, composition and rhetoric) on the pitfalls of monolithic narratives of the genius of the species. Writings by philosopher Enrique Dussel and cultural historian Martin Bernal. Class discussion. Writing assignment.

Week 7: Rapport between oral culture and scribal culture. Guest speaker Arthur Flowers, a fiction writer devoted to preserving folk traditions of African-Americans in the United States, reads from his novel *Another Good Loving Blues.* Class discussion. Writing assignment.

Week 8: Immigrant experience of Caribbean women in New York. Guest presenter Professor Linda Carty (Arts and Sciences) surveys the geopolitics of U.S.-Caribbean socioeconomic and political relations. Class discussion. Writing assignment.

Week 9: Architecture, the use of space, and the making of one's surroundings. Guest speaker Professor Scott Ruff (architecture) talks about his interest as an African-American in conceptualizing an architectural use of space that accords with the cultural identity of the people inhabiting the structure. Class discussion. Writing assignment.

Week 10: Difficulties encountered by people with disabilities when structures, spaces, and functions are imagined without their needs in mind. Guest lecturer Cindy Linden is a disability studies expert. Class discussion. Writing assignment.

Week 11: Ways in which individuals can intervene in the public sphere in pursuit of social transformation given their dissimilar ideological leanings, intellectual formations, and social sensibilities. Guest presenter Professor Marcia Robinson (religion) examines speeches and excerpts from the fiction of 19th century African-American abolitionist Frances Watkins Harper and the introduction of *Souls of Black Folk* by W.E.B. DuBois. Class discussion. Writing assignment.

Week 12: Screening of Doubles, *a documentary film on the experience of Japanese Americans who were the children of "war brides."* Exploration of comparative belief systems by Indian novelist Brinda Charry through an essay by A. K. Ramanujan, a creation story from the *Rg Veda*, and ancient poems. Class discussion. Writing assignment.

Week 13: Review of concepts and links among classes. Discussion of performance by stand-up comedian Margaret Cho. Discussion on institutional racism by Cynthia Fulford, associate director of the Office of Multicultural Affairs. Writing assignment.

Week 14: Problems of racial classification. Guest presenter Matthew Edward, a law student, provides an overview of the Zapatista Movement in Chiapas, Mexico. Paul Buckley, a doctoral student in education, discusses the difficulty of classifying people racially and the inadequacy of defining human beings on the basis of only one of the various characteristics that could serve as markers. Class discussion.

Week 15: Overview of course, concepts, and connections. Class discussion.

Required Texts:
Assigned readings will be selected in consultation with the Office of Multicultural Affairs (OMA), the guest lecturers, and Professor Sandra Hurd.

12

Amazing Growth at SUNY ESF

Janine M. DeBaise and Julie R. White

The State University of New York College of Environmental Science and Forestry campus, with 1,800 undergraduate and graduate students, adjoins that of SU, and its first-year students live in SU residence halls. Creating a learning community for first-year students that connects their required botany and writing classes has improved both the students' academic experience and their connection to their school.

GETTING STARTED

What is the college experience? It was the answer to this seemingly simple question that guided our creation of the State University of New York College of Environmental Science and Forestry's (ESF) Learning Community. We quickly realized that the characteristics of learning communities translate into good education. A learning community structures the college experience in just the same way students live it: as a whole. Traditionally, we have compartmentalized and kept separate academics and student development. The ESF learning community has blurred these boundaries, and the result has been better education defined by community, personal growth, and enhanced academic performance.

Our motive for initiating a learning community was better education. But, truth be told, extraneous factors encouraged us to move quickly to this initiative. ESF students live in Syracuse University residence halls, and, traditionally, our students were clustered into three residence halls near our campus. This had been working out fine for our students in that they were housed in pockets and could find each other quite easily. Syracuse decided that as of fall 2001, however, first-year students would be randomly assigned to all residence halls. This meant that we would no longer be able to cluster our students. While the ESF student affairs staff was hearing and worrying about this new housing arrangement, academic affairs was learning about theme housing and learning communities. Our problem was suddenly met with a solution that would move us beyond old ways of doing business.

The evolution of the ESF learning community is best characterized by buy-in. The academic and student affairs partnership was solidified in the beginning as the deans of each division worked together to solve our housing problem. Next, we identified two courses that most of our first-year students are required to take (botany and writing) and contacted the faculty to assess their level of interest. This was quite possibly the most simple part of our learning community initiative. We knew that the faculty members teaching botany and writing shared a student-centered philosophy that would be well served by such an effort. The faculty members not only agreed to learn more about learning communities, they enthusiastically began to identify connections between their courses at our very first information meeting.

After solidifying the academic components of the learning community, we formalized our relationship with the SU Office of Residence Life by securing a residence hall floor on which our learning community students would live. It was at this point that the concept really started to take shape and the learning community team was established. We had the support of the director of residence life who immediately put us in contact with the residence hall director (the actual go-to person). Again, this was an easy pitch. Learning communities, by their very nature, address issues of student development and link academic learning with life learning—a central mission of the SU Office of Residence Life. We met regularly during the spring of 1999 to create what we referred to as THE Syllabus, which was comprised of three complementary and integrated curricula: botany, writing, and student life.

It was at this juncture that we needed wider support and feedback regarding the initiative. How would we fund the programs we would offer? How would we inform prospective students of this opportunity? How would students react to this concept? In order to answer these and other questions, we developed a road show that we took to the executive administration, faculty governance, admissions personnel, and to student government. These efforts yielded broad-based enthusiasm and ownership. Among the biggest fans of our learning community is our college president. Needless to say, his endorsement of and excitement about this project doesn't hurt.

RECRUITMENT

Our admissions staff helped us to devise a recruitment plan. In addition to the normal print advertising in admissions and housing materials, we decided to do some more active advertising and recruiting. Fortunately, we had completed planning in time to promote the learning community at our spring receptions for admitted students. In our first year these presentations depended on our aspirations and plans.

Of course, the second time around, recruitment was much easier. The current learning community students were eager to share their experiences with incoming students. Several of the students had put together a Power-Point presentation of music and photographs for our end-of-the-semester gathering in December; the dean recognized that this glimpse into student life was exactly what prospective students needed to see. During our second round of recruiting, we actually had to turn students away.

The lesson learned here is that experience is the best recruitment tool we have and the voice of participants is the most influential. During the second year of presentations, we essentially got out of the students' way. They had experienced the benefits of learning community membership, and they enjoyed talking about it. The pride they had in their community and their school was exemplified in their encouragement of prospective students to sign up.

In addition to this live promotion, our dean of instruction sent a letter to all first-year students inviting them to participate in the learning community. This letter highlighted the academic benefits of community involvement, and it was presented as a special opportunity for ESF first-year students that would be filled on a first-come, first-served basis. This letter included an application to be completed by interested students, and it outlined the requirements for membership (e.g., courses to be taken). Upon receipt of the students' applications, we sent them a learning contract that documented students' rights and responsibilities as members of the learning community. To be placed in the community, students had to sign this contract and thereby commit to being active and contributing community members.

DESCRIPTION OF THE LEARNING COMMUNITY

Interlocking Circles
The symbol we used for our learning community was three interlocking circles: one circle for writing, one circle for botany, and one circle for residence

life. All 58 students were registered for two courses—botany and writing—which were integrated with each other and with residence life activities on their floor to create a seamless learning environment. The group was broken into three sections of fewer than 20 students each for their writing class—which met three times each week in their residence hall—and these same three groups made up three botany lab sections, taught by a teaching assistant who was part of the learning community team. All the students attended botany lecture as part of a class of two hundred plus students. The students were required to attend weekly floor meetings and mandatory student life activities that included such topics as stress relief, diversity, and ethics.

Linking Courses With Each Other and With Student Life

Linking a hard science course—botany—to a writing course sounds a bit crazy at first, but once we started discussing the idea, it made a lot of sense. Scientists cannot succeed in their field if they don't know how to write. The biggest challenge for a writing teacher is often to get students involved with topics so that writing is not an artificial exercise with no context. The integration with the botany course and with the residence life activities handed the writing teacher topics that had already been discussed and explored by the students. Writing class, because it was small, became the place for questions and feedback and for planning projects like retreats, coffeehouses, a student assessment project, and a collaborative art mural. It was the writing class that served as the conduit through which the other two circles were connected. Writing assignments ranged from botany-related topics such as genetics and plant diversity to residence life-related topics like alcohol use and human diversity.

We took advantage of the overlap wherever we could. For example, in September the students took a botany field trip to a nearby county park. Their assignment was to compare vegetation found on an east-facing slope to the types of vegetation found on a north-facing slope to determine whether or not the amount of sunlight the slope received affected the plant growth. While they were taking notes for the botany lab, they also took notes for a writing assignment for writing class. Botany labs are written in a highly specific and technical form for other scientists. For writing class, however, the students had to write a paper for a lay audience. They had the choice of writing a narrative of the day, explaining the lab to a high school audience, or doing something creative. In writing class the next week, students read aloud their essays and also spent some time talking about the science writing component, the formal lab that they were writing up for their botany course. By taking advantage of this opportunity for overlap, the students discovered what both the botany teacher and the writing teacher wanted them to learn—that a good writer will write in different ways for different audiences.

During residence life programs, students talked about topics such as ethics, diversity, and drug/alcohol abuse. In writing class, these topics became vehicles for thinking, reading, and writing. Monday morning class often began with the teacher asking, "So how did the floor program go last night? Let's write about it today." The residence life programs were also a huge time-saver for the writing teacher: It's wonderful to work with students who have been given a topic and who have already had stimulating discussion and learned lots of information about the topic.

Careful choice of reading materials for the writing course helped further emphasize the overlap among the three circles. For example, the book *Dwellings* by Native American poet Linda Hogan (1995) discusses traditional knowledge of plants, ethical responsibilities of humans to the earth, a community that includes plants and animals, the role of science in our culture, the idea of objectivity in science, types of human communication, ecological destruction, and the role of language. It stimulated wonderful discussions that touched both botany and student life issues.

LINKING LIVING WITH LEARNING

Integrating the three circles was often as simple as considering the physical space. Writing class was held in the residence hall, sometimes in the classroom on the first floor and sometimes up in the students' floor lounge. The writing teacher spent one afternoon each week in the lounge, reading the group journals and chatting with students. Before big tests, the botany teacher held review sessions in the residence hall. The study lounge on the floor was equipped with three computers and a printer. The students requested (and received) a white board so that they could hold study groups in their own lounge. Faculty members were given meal tickets so that they could go to the hall and eat meals with the students on occasion. The team—the writing teacher, the botany instructor, the two ESF administrators, and the residence director—met with the students during finals week for a pizza study break. To emphasize the learning part of community life on the floor, the administration supported tutors for chemistry, calculus, and botany, who held hours right in the lounge.

When we interviewed students as part of our ongoing assessment, most of them saw the integration of botany, writing, and student life as a natural fit. "I think writing is really important to botany because in botany you learn

concepts that have to be applied to the world, and you have to get the information out through writing," said one learning community student. Similarly, students often connected residence life issues with their writing class. More
often than not, the content of papers and reflections required by the writing
instructor dealt with community issues and personal concerns.

The topics the students chose for their final projects in their writing class
show a huge overlap with residence life: alcohol abuse, marijuana use, suicide,
advice for incoming learning community students, advice on how to go
camping, animal rights and veganism, hunting, tattoos and piercings, and an
analysis of the positive/negative effects of the Internet. Two students, for
example, wrote and performed a skit on the cultural differences between
urban and rural life. After the skit, one student shared her experience growing
up in a rural area, and another student talked about what it was like to grow
up in the Bronx. Then the presenters led a discussion about the tensions on
campus between those from rural areas and those from New York City. Every
topic the students chose was a topic that had been hotly debated in class, at
floor meetings, and in their rooms.

LEARNING OBJECTIVES

The learning community team brainstormed goals at one of the early meetings, but we soon realized that defining our learning objectives would be an
ongoing process. It wasn't until we were actually working with the community of students that many of our objectives became clear. Goals were solidified
during our biweekly team meetings, our overnight retreat, class discussions,
our review of student reflection papers, informal social gatherings, and other
experiences we shared as a community. The learning objectives that the learning community team agreed upon fall into three categories—learning, community, and personal development:

Learning

- Students will show enthusiasm for learning and writing which will be
  measured not only by the quality of work they produce, but also by the
  process they used to create their work.

- Students are aware of and can demonstrate the connection between in-
  class and out-of-class experiences.

- Students will be enthusiastic and take responsibility for learning.

Community

- Students will express enthusiasm about being an ESF student.

- Student demand to participate in ESF learning communities will increase.

- Students will feel a sense of ownership for their community.

- ESF will become a more caring community—one that fosters the appreciation of diversity as well as provides a forum of discussion on diversity.

Personal Development

- Students will gain confidence in their ability to learn and feel empowered to take on risks and new challenges.

- Students, faculty, and student affairs staff will develop authentic relationships.

- Students will develop their leadership potential.

- Students will develop a sense of power and authority in their environment; they will move from buy-in of the learning community to a sense of ownership.

- Students will discuss and understand the long-term consequences of drug/alcohol use. We will create an atmosphere in which drug and alcohol use is not a taboo topic.

- Students will learn to be respectful of differences. Students will engage in frank and in-depth discussions about racism, sexism, and homophobia. They will listen to each other even when they strongly disagree with each other.

GETTING IT DOWN ON PAPER

Part of the process of developing learning objectives was simply to put down on paper many of the unspoken goals we all had. The conversations during our weekly meetings revealed the common goals pretty quickly. "We need to get students to take responsibility for learning," one faculty member would say, and we would all nod in agreement. At one meeting, a residence life staff member asked, "Which students are emerging as leaders?" When the writing teacher stopped to think about which students took charge of a collaborative project, she realized that developing leadership potential was a goal in the classroom as well as in the residence hall.

One thing we learned quickly is that faculty, administration, and residence life staff often do have the same goals and concerns—we just use different language. The residence life people would talk about setting community standards, the writing teacher would talk about classroom atmosphere, the botany teacher would talk about rules for the lab; we were all talking about the ways we teach these students to create an environment in which they can live and work together. Writing everything down forced us to negotiate the language and the goals.

SUPPORTING EACH OTHER

The high level of interaction among the team formed an atmosphere in which we supported each other's learning objectives and discovered many shared objectives. When, for example, students in the classroom came up with great ideas ("Let's have a second retreat" or "Let's do a collaborative mural"), the writing teacher would send the students off to talk to the associate dean of student life and experiential learning. Her response was exactly what writing teachers love to hear: "Put it in writing. Give me a proposal."

The writing teacher was trying to teach the students that writing was a way to organize their ideas, think through projects, and persuade an audience—and the other members of the team supported that goal. The students quickly discovered that the way to get what they wanted—whether it was getting the administration to pay for a second retreat or the dean to pay for art supplies for a mural they wanted to paint—was to put their ideas in writing, to write a proposal that was specific and convincing. In writing class, we talked about how this is the kind of writing they will do in their careers; scientists, for example, have to learn how to write grant proposals to get money for projects.

The shared objectives of all three circles became obvious to the students as the semester progressed. The residence life staff talked about citizenship and setting standards for living in a community; the botany teaching assistant talked about standards for working together in a lab situation; the writing teacher talked about setting rules for class discussion and collaboration. It may have taken weeks of meetings for the teaching team to learn each other's language and make these connections, but the students were quick to see the overlap.

Group Journals

Another tool for promoting the shared objectives for the three circles of this learning community was the group journal. During the first week of class, the writing teacher separated the students into groups of about five students per group, trying to keep the groups as diverse as possible. Each group was given a binder full of loose-leaf paper that would serve as the group's journal. The journals were kept right in the lounge on the floor, and each student was required to write at least one page in the journal every week. In these pages, they responded to class discussions, to residence life activities, to the books they were reading, and to each other's entries. They talked about being homesick, they shared stories about their hometowns, they vented their frustrations about difficult courses, they analyzed current events, they gave each other advice, they did soul-searching about their careers and the meaning of life, and they informally assessed the learning community environment. These journal entries informed our work. The writing teacher was able to share her perceptions of student development issues with the residence life staff. She could tell—from the tone of journal entries—when students were feeling overwhelmed with academic work or worried about a botany test, and accordingly, she could keep the botany teacher up to date on student morale.

Overnight Retreat

An important element of the learning community was the overnight retreat during the third week of the semester. Attendance was mandatory: We had the whole team and 100% of the students. With sleeping bags and notebooks, we piled into two big buses and drove off to spend 24 hours together. The students began bonding before we even left the parking lot: The loud songs continued the whole way. Students, divided into teams, were responsible for meals and clean up. Since the students were already divided into three groups for writing class—sections of about 20 students each—we were able to use groups that seemed natural. The 8:30 writing class was in charge of breakfast, the 10:40 writing class took lunch, and the 11:45 class made dinner.

During writing class the week before, we planned Friday night's activity: a nature walk in the dark, some creative writing, and then a coffeehouse in front of the roaring fire. For the nature walk, the students chose to stay in their journal groups. After wandering around under the stars for half an hour or so, they stumbled back in, ready to sit on the floor of the lodge and do some writing. It's a scene that a writing teacher has to love—all 58 students, still breathing heavily from their hike, settled down with notebooks, writing furiously, while a fire crackles in the background.

The coffeehouse, organized and run by the students, gave the students a chance to see each other's talents. Students read poetry, sang songs, played guitars and violins and the digeridoo, and performed skits. It's amazing how open the students will be during this kind of event: The poems (often about unrequited high school love) were heartfelt and the audience applause sincere.

The retreat continued with late night conversations, card games, and music. In the morning, the botany teacher and teaching assistants sent us all into the woods on a plant scavenger hunt. Sitting on the grass in the sun talking about the plants we've picked is a great way to learn botany. By afternoon, as we all participated in a ropes course, we felt like we'd known each other for years. The writing and botany teacher were just as thrilled with the ropes course as the residence life staff members were. After all, teamwork and communication are important to both writing and science.

BENEFITS OF COMMUNITY

The writing and botany teachers discovered that one of the wonderful things about teaching students who live together is that they could require them to work together outside class. In the case of the writing teacher, by the time students came to class with their essays, they had often read each other's work and given each other feedback. The learning community situation is ideal for collaborative work. Even the floor meetings at times became an extension of writing class. For example, in class we read *The Age of Missing Information* by Bill McKibben (1992), a book that compares a day spent in the Adirondacks with a whole day's worth of cable television and which led to a spirited discussion about the effect of television on our culture. One group of students proposed turning off the television in their lounge for a whole week, much to the horror of other students. The debate found its way to a floor meeting where, after much talk and a few dramatic monologues, they all agreed to the experiment. The negotiations included talk about what students might do instead of watching television (card games, guitar playing, and even a squirt gun war, although perhaps we are not supposed to put that one in print). They rearranged the furniture in the lounge and all pledged to support those students who admitted to being television addicts.

The benefits of this collaborative community also extended to the campus as a whole. The ownership students felt, not only for their learning community, but for the college was impressive. Many of the graduates of our first learning community are now the backbone of our student leadership in government and clubs and organizations. Most of the orientation staff is made up of this population, and they are the group we often look to as a barometer of student sentiment.

In addition, the learning community initiative provided the administrative team with an ideal environment for collaboration. It wasn't long until we understood each other's language and began to integrate others' perspectives into our individual work. We found professional support and challenge, and the result has been a wonderful experience that we otherwise would not have had. The learning community has given us a reason to learn about each other, our work, our motives, and our aspirations.

ASSESSMENT

Our method of assessment was a bit haphazard, at least during our first year. Part of what made assessment complex was our commitment to qualitative assessment, in addition to the more easily measured quantitative assessment. Of course, the selling points of the learning community would come from the grade point average and retention data. The powers that be on campus tend to be bean counters, and quantitative data tell the type of stories they seem to be able to hear.

So what did we learn? Our learning community makes a difference! During our first year, 98% of the participants in the learning community persisted to their second year (compared to an overall rate of 78%). Similarly, learning community participants outperform their peers academically by an average of one-third of a point. Needless to say, our bean counters are impressed with these numbers!

What the quantitative measures don't tell us is how satisfied students are with their experience or specifically what is good or what needs tweaking. For this information we turned to qualitative methods. We engaged graduate students from the higher education program at Syracuse University to facilitate student focus groups. As anticipated, this information was invaluable as we planned for year two. For example, students suggested that we have tutors on the floor for especially difficult courses. We implemented this suggestion in year two.

The student interviews reaffirmed for us that many of our objectives were on target. One student, for example, said: "Learning communities are so great for student-teacher relationships because students get to know our teachers on a more personal and relaxed basis." Knowing that this sense of community was important to the students made us confident that this objective was an important one. Almost all the students characterized the environment on the floor as supportive and nurturing. "What I like best about the learning community is the family structure and support I get from my peers and professors," said one learning community student.

The high level of interaction between faculty, staff, and students led to informal forms of assessment that were discussed at our regularly scheduled meetings. For example, the writing teacher was able to report 100% class attendance almost every day of the semester, even during her 8:30 section. Toward the end of the semester when the students were giving presentations, students would go to other sections to see their friends presenting: Class attendance was sometimes 200%. This high level of enthusiasm toward learning has been one of our objectives. The group journals and the reflective pieces assigned by the writing teacher were an important source of continual feedback from the students. The writing teacher was able to track student satisfaction during the semester by simply reading what they wrote.

During the first year of our learning community, the students themselves were very conscious that they were part of a grand experiment. When the writing teacher suggested assessment of the learning community as a project for writing class, the students were eager to participate. During the first semester, the students interviewed all the students on the floor as well as all the members of the learning community team. Each student wrote a reflective paper about his or her experiences. They held several focus groups, conducted two surveys, and then pulled all the information together with a big presentation that included numerous charts, graphs, and a slide show that showed student life on the floor. While students were critical (and fair) in their assessment, they were also very constructive and interested in helping to facilitate an even more successful experience for those who followed.

Many of the students, for example, felt that having a residence life activity in addition to a floor meeting every single week was too much of a commitment. After discussing this issue amongst the team, we concurred with the students and cut the number of required activities in half. Students also asked for stronger links to the botany course. One of their suggestions—that the huge botany lecture be split into several sections—we sent to another committee on campus because the implementation would have ramifications for the entire freshmen class. In the short term, the team came up with other ways to strengthen the links. For example, the botany teacher and the writing teacher will both include in their course the book *The Botany of Desire* by Michael Pollan (2001). Because the book has a whole section devoted to marijuana use, the book will lead to a residence life discussion of drug use on campus.

Whenever possible, we tried to involve students in making change happen, putting the responsibility on them, giving them ownership. When the students asked for a second retreat (presenting us with a petition signed by all the floor members), we agreed to go ahead with it as long as they planned the retreat and carried it out themselves. Several outgoing students took charge: They formed committees, talked over major details at floor meetings, and approached the dean for funding. The second retreat, an overnight trip in December, included a coffeehouse, a game of Capture the Flag, a slide show, and an afternoon of improv.

The students were adamant about including a creative or nontraditional form of assessment as well: To this end, they convinced the dean to give them the money to pay for a 4' by 8' canvas and acrylic paints. They painted this fairly abstract work of art during the second retreat and during several late-night sessions in the lounge. The mural included quotes, images, photographs, and abstract designs—contributions from all 58 students.

Of course, the assessment continues. On a small campus, we are able to track student growth and involvement by simply watching closely. As the first group of learning community students became sophomores, we were thrilled to watch them joining clubs, becoming orientation leaders, and taking leadership positions. We continue to watch their growth with pride.

CONCLUSION

The success of our first learning community exceeded our own expectations. By the second year we had already expanded the program, and we hope eventually to have all of our first-year students involved in a learning community. Simply put, we are providing a more integrated and comprehensive experience for our students, faculty, and staff. We've perforated the artificial boundaries between classroom learning and residence hall learning.

At our very first meeting with the students in August, we gave them each a plant to nurture, joking that their grades would depend on whether or not the plant lived. We knew that taking care of the plants would require negotiation among community members because some of the rooms faced north and didn't get enough sunlight. The plants moved about the floor, sometimes in the students' rooms and sometimes in the lounge where a big window provided necessary light. There were a few difficult situations—one plant lost a lot of dirt when it got knocked over by rowdy students—but for the most part, the plants flourished and grew, reaching heights that amazed us all. And these plants remain as the appropriate symbol of our learning community: For faculty, staff, and students, this has been a time of amazing growth.

Janine M. DeBaise is a writing instructor in the College of Environmental Science and Forestry, and Julie R. White is associate dean of student affairs, both of the State of New York College of Environmental Science and Forestry.

REFERENCES

Hogan, L. (1995). *Dwellings.* New York, NY: W. W. Norton.

McKibben, B. (1992). *The age of missing information.* New York, NY: Random House.

Pollan, M. (2001). *The botany of desire.* New York, NY: Random House.

13

Constructing Concentric Communities

Stacey Riemer and Leah Flynn

The Service-Learning Community is closely associated with SU's Center for Public and Community Service, which facilitates service-learning placements for over 30 courses per year and makes community service referrals to over 2,000 students. Students in the learning community participated in over 660 hours of service at ten different community agencies.

*I*n the fall of 2000, the Center for Public and Community Service at Syracuse University faced an exciting challenge. Students and faculty were becoming more aware of service learning as a viable pedagogical option and therefore were demanding more sophisticated service-learning opportunities. During the same time period, academic affairs and student affairs were expanding their learning community program, responding to a challenge by the chancellor to create residential learning communities for 25% of the students on campus. Based on these two trends, professional staff members from the Center for Public and Community Service (CPCS) and the Office of Residence Life met in the fall of 2000 to brainstorm ideas for a Service-Learning Community (SLC) to be piloted during the 2001-2002 academic year. This working team became the advisory group for the initiative. The collaboration was partially supported by grant resources received by the Center for Public and Community Service from the University Vision Fund, a university-sponsored initiative that provides support for creative curricular innovation.

THE SERVICE-LEARNING COMMUNITY OVERVIEW

Service learning is an educational experience where participants learn through active participation in thoughtfully organized service experiences that meet community needs. The practice of critical reflection provides the transformative link between the service experience and the learning relative to a student's course of study and personal development. The Service-Learning Community provides sophomores, juniors, and seniors with the opportunity to explore their service experiences through coursework while living together in apartment-style housing. Participants reflect on their personal service experiences with peers from other disciplines, build relationships with faculty and community leaders, and explore their roles in various communities.

Figure 13.1.

Structure of the Service-Learning Community

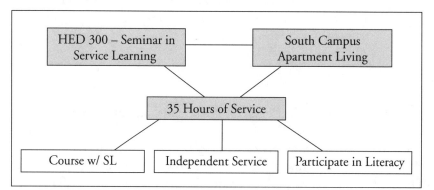

Twenty-two students applied for the learning community during its pilot year. Students in the Service-Learning Community enrolled in a one-credit course (HED 300) that acted as an interdisciplinary seminar and participated in a service experience of their choice for 35 hours. Five of the 35 hours were devoted to a service project in the South Campus community where they lived. Each class session examined students' ongoing service experiences as they related to weekly class topics. Reflection, a key component of service learning, was structured in a variety of ways, including class activities, discussions, and journal writing. From this class and the concurrent service experiences, students explored personal philosophies of service and developed skills through experiential learning.

RECRUITING STUDENTS

Recruitment efforts began the semester before the Service-Learning Community was piloted and included distributing flyers to faculty and staff who were asked to share the information with students. For example, a writing instructor who used service learning in his class announced the opportunity to his students. The Center for Public and Community Service also publicized the opportunity to all students who took part in service initiatives during the spring semester. Information about the SLC was also included in the university's learning community brochure, which was distributed to incoming students and current students interested in learning communities.

Recruiting efforts for the pilot year were not entirely successful. The Service-Learning Community is the only learning community on SU's South Campus, which has apartment-style living available only to sophomores, juniors, and seniors. Demand for housing on South Campus is high. During the course of the pilot semester, a number of students articulated that the main reason they joined the Service-Learning Community was to be able to live on South Campus.

Based on this feedback, the advisory group made two changes in the recruiting process for the second year. First, recruiting was more tightly targeted to students who were involved in service activities or who wanted to continue their freshman learning community experience. Brochures were sent to student groups that were involved in service on campus; brochures and personalized letters were sent to faculty and students who were currently involved in a learning community. Second, we added an essay question to the application process. The essay question was added not only to better gauge a student's level of commitment to the community, but also to help the advisory group understand student expectations and learning goals for the upcoming year.

LEARNING OUTCOMES

The Service-Learning Community advisory group identified a set of learning outcomes specific to this learning community. We decided that through their experiences, students would be able to:

- Develop a spirit of partnership with the community

- Understand the nonprofit sector while exploring their roles and responsibilities as citizens

- Develop an awareness of larger societal issues (e.g., literacy, hunger, homelessness) and the local resources relative to them

- Develop an awareness and understanding of diversity (e.g., learning styles, race, class, gender, socioeconomic status, ability) as well as prejudices, stereotypes, and different realities

We also identified outcomes associated with skill acquisition in addition to service-specific learning outcomes. These skills included oral and written communication, ethical decision-making, problem solving, and critical thinking. For example, students may make use of applied ethics in confidential situations and/or when relating with staff and clients, or they may develop critical thinking and problem solving skills as well as practice and develop interactive reading if they are placed in classrooms in the community.

These learning goals were developed during a collaborative planning meeting and further refined during subsequent group meetings. At the outcome level, our group came to consensus quickly. As the group started to develop specific activities related to the outcomes, it became clear that for some of the outcomes we, in fact, meant different things. For example, when using the term "community," residence life meant the immediate South Campus community while CPCS meant the greater Syracuse community. This distinction not only had a direct impact on where students in the learning community completed their service hours, but also on the nature of their service work.

ASSESSMENT PLAN

After negotiating outcomes, the advisory group developed an assessment plan based on these outcomes. Because reflection is a key component of a service-learning experience, the group agreed that the various forms of reflection used during the seminar (e.g., journals, focus groups, reflection papers, discussions) could also be used as assessment data. Focus groups, conducted by graduate students in the higher education graduate program, provided an open forum for SLC students to exchange and express feelings about their learning community experiences while providing anonymity. Document analysis on students' reflective journals and focus group transcripts was conducted to identify areas of learning prevalent for students.

In addition, we decided to use existing CPCS assessment tools. An experiential learning matrix (Cabral, 1995) was administered at the beginning and end of the semester to evaluate students' perceptions of skills (e.g., communication, problem solving, applied ethics) developed through their SLC experiences (see Appendix 13.1). Also, CPCS post evaluations were administered to assess students' expectations, personal, and educational enhancement through their service experiences, and ways they believe CPCS can improve its services.

As with outcome construction, assessment plan development went smoothly for general skills, outcomes, and service theme measures. However, when the group met during the fall of the pilot community to finalize the seminar evaluation, each group was working on independent evaluations for their respective activities. Staff members from residence life, as part of a South Campus assessment process, intended to administer an evaluation of South Campus activities and CPCS intended to administer a seminar evaluation. When we each viewed the respective evaluations, we agreed that the seminar evaluation could include questions from each area. We then constructed a common evaluation, designed in a Likert scale format, to obtain student feedback about the interdisciplinary seminar linked to the community, the seminar objectives, and South Campus aspects of the community (see Appendix 13.2). By combining the assessment instruments, each office received the desired information, and students devoted time and attention to one instrument instead of having to fill out several.

Assessment Results

Learning for students extended beyond the goals of the classroom seminar and is best characterized as a transformation of multiple, independent goals to concentric ones (see Figure 13.2). As assessment data indicate, students reflected on their learning relative to seminar outcomes, provided examples of

Figure 13.2

Transformation from Individual to Interdependent Goals

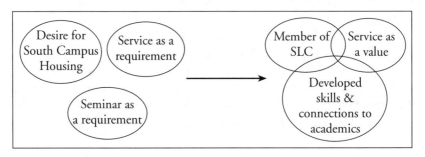

how they developed experiential skills, and thought critically about how their service applied to their academic studies. Further, they examined their initial, independent rationale for joining the community and developed the desire to socialize with fellow learning community members.

Through in-class reflections and journal writing, students thought critically about community needs and issues encountered at their site, their membership in various communities, and how their experiences related to their course of study. An analysis of these reflections, as well as other assessment data, demonstrates the students' learning around the intended seminar outcomes. For example, with respect to the "develop an awareness and understanding of diversity" outcome, one young woman articulated her thoughts about and awareness of diversity issues raised through her service experience:

> *We were the only two Caucasian people in the room, and I had never felt so uncomfortable to be a blond-haired, blue-eyed girl. At this point, it was the last thing that I wanted to be. . . . I learned a lot about myself and my willingness to open up in new situations, which is something that I never thought I would be comfortable doing.*

A second student appreciated the opportunity to process such issues during class:

> *One of the highlights from class was the exercise we did on [diversity]. It was great to have an open talk about these subjects, which can still be very taboo. . . . I think one could have a seminar just on those topics alone. I was surprised that even though the majority of students in the room were white Americans, we could have an open and insightful discussion about race and culture without people shouting or people just being politically correct.*

In fact, based on student responses to the seminar evaluation, 83.3% of students felt that they developed an awareness of diversity issues as a result of the seminar.

Assessment information was received not only for content outcomes, but also for skill outcomes. At the conclusion of the semester, based on responses to the experiential learning matrix, we found no significant change in how students rated the importance of the various skills developed in their service settings. What did change, however, is how students described those skills. They were able to provide actual examples of how they used skills at their sites instead of speaking more generally and without example as they did at the beginning of the semester.

The seminar evaluation and CPCS post evaluations provided additional information relative to components of the learning community. Not only did 77.7% of the students feel that the service requirement contributed to their learning, but interest in service increased for 83.3% of the students. Participants recognized that a community need existed: 94% of the students felt that the service benefited the agency and they would, in turn, participate in service again.

Given the majority of participants' interests in independent apartment-style living, we did not find it surprising that their responses, on average, to the residential goals for the community were not as positive. For example, only 22.2% of the group felt connected to each other as a result of their living together and only 11.11% participated in social events together. While most of the students joined the community for housing purposes, they wished that they had gotten to know others in the community better and hoped to do so during second semester. A student reflected, "One aspect of the SLC that I am looking forward to next semester is working together as a group within our community. The first semester we really didn't get to know each other that well as a group." Others recognized the unique challenges that our learning community with apartment-style living posed:

> *[At the beginning of the semester], I reflected how I didn't expect everyone in the LC to become friends. The cold hard fact is that we lived together and shared a class, but still hardly know each other. The fact that we live on South Campus in apartments and have varied class schedules didn't help our bonding.*

By the end of the semester, student goals for independent living evolved to a desire for interdependence with their learning community peers.

REFLECTING ON EXPERIENCES/IMPROVING ALONG THE WAY

Based on informal and formal assessment efforts during the pilot program, the advisory group planned mid-semester changes as well as larger changes for the following year. It became clear during the pilot semester that students were primarily interested in independent South Campus living, which conflicted with the focus of and service rationale for the learning community. Service and reflection were not priorities for them, and therefore their initial commitment to academic work tied to the seminar was low. The combination of mismatched expectations and rationale for SLC membership challenged seminar instructors to transform student attitudes and understanding of service. Instead of exploring participants' service commitment and related civic concepts in more depth during class time, we shifted part of the curriculum to introduce many participants to service. This allowed us to challenge the few participants who were already committed to service while exposing others to first-time service experiences. At times, this was frustrating for those who joined the community to explore their value for service at the next level intellectually. However, integrating their experiences into the seminar discussions allowed the experienced service learners to process their experiences in more depth and motivated others to explore the ideas.

To build community among the group, we did not alter the quantity of service hours required, but allowed and encouraged students to take part in group service projects. In fact, one of the most successful service projects, from the community agency and the students' perspectives, was when a group of eight SLC members volunteered for a nature center's Halloween event. This project was brought to the seminar by one of the participants, and she took responsibility for organizing the efforts of the group. Informal observations of this project as well as other alterations to class discussions and formal assessment data helped our advisory group formalize changes for the upcoming year.

CPCS and residence life staff realized the need to integrate respective programmatic components into a seamless whole and added service-centered, teambuilding activities on South Campus to the seminar syllabus for the following year. For example, participants were asked to participate in a welcome dinner and a South Campus carnival event at the beginning of the semester to model the community commitment expectation. Not only were students encouraged to use group service projects as a way to complete their service hours and get to know other students in the learning community, but two group service projects were added to the seminar syllabus to integrate these respective learning community goals. Because an essay was added to the application process, the advisory group was better able to gauge past service experiences and commitment to learning community goals. This led us to allow more time in class for participants to process how their past and current service experiences applied to topic areas so that all participants were engaged and intellectually challenged.

INDIVIDUAL COMMITMENT AND COMMUNITY GOALS COALESCE

While the number of students who participated in the Service-Learning Community during its second year decreased to12, the commitment level of participants to overall learning community goals was much higher. Preliminary analysis of second-year program evaluations indicates that 100% of the students participated in social events together and felt connected to their fellow SLC members. All participants felt that they took initiative and responsibility for their learning relative to community goals, developed transferable skills, and made connections between course assignments and their service. The group service projects organized at an area soup kitchen and with the local Habitat for Humanity received overwhelmingly positive responses from participants, suggesting that it allowed them to bond as a group, learn from peer reflections on the experience, and serve a genuine community need. One student stated, "Participating with Habitat for Humanity brought our learning community together as we worked to better the Syracuse community." Several students were sad to see the semester come to an end. "We are now at the end of the semester and to be honest with you, I am really sad. This class has been fun, informative, and a completely positive experience in every way. I liked how we discussed controversial topics because it allowed me to see other people's points of view and the differences always related back to the idea of service and what we can learn from it."

CONCLUSION

All of the individuals and programs involved in the creation and development of the Service-Learning Community have learned much during its evolution. Not only did students learn to move from individual to interdependent goals, but faculty and staff did also. The guiding characteristics of a service-learning experience—reflection, reciprocity, and a community defined need (Kendall, 1990)—were enacted in many ways. There was a give-and-take among all participants, and everyone's goals were met; a community need was served, both on the South Campus as well as in the greater Syracuse community; and reflective and assessment strategies enhanced learning for everyone. These characteristics coalesced with the general goals of learning communities, creating remarkable synergy.

Stacey Riemer is former associate director of the Center for Public and Community Service, and Leah Flynn is coordinator of student programs, both of SUNY College of Environmental Science and Forestry.

REFERENCES

Cabral, A. C. (1995). Evaluation of transferable academic skills. *Integrating community service and academics: A manual for faculty.* Rochester, NY: Nazareth College.

Kendall, J. (Ed.). (1990). *Combining service and learning: A resource book for community and public service* (Vol. 1). Raleigh, NC: National Society for Internships and Experiential Education.

Appendix 13.1

EVALUATION OF TRANSFERABLE ACADEMIC SKILLS

Instructions:

Read each skill definition carefully

Rate each skill in terms of its importance to your success in the program

For each skill, identify and describe one incident or example from your experience that shows how you applied that skill

Use the two blank rating areas to identify other skills which you were able to transfer from your academic coursework to your experience

Sign and date the form and return it to_____by_____

Importance Scales:

1= not at all important for success in this experience, never or rarely used

2= used only occasionally; not critical even when used; other skills more important

3= an important skill; used often; it would be tough to succeed in this experience without this skill

4= essential for success in this experience; used more often than other skills and effectiveness in it is critical

SKILL	IMPORTANCE	EXAMPLE

Critical Thinking

Analyze information, behavior or
quantitative data; synthesize information or
important elements; evaluate information or
data in order to make meaningful conclusions

Problem Solving

Identify critical elements of a
problem (something to be learned,
a gap in performance, etc.); search
out information to resolve the problem;
develop practical recommendations that address
the need or close the gap completely and expediently

Spoken Communications

Formally or informally; express
ideas; teach; make inquiries; give advice;
persuade others; or otherwise engage in
presentations or dialogues related to the duties

of your experience (be specific
concerning type of communication and
audience for it)

Written Communications

Express ideas, facts, or opinions
In a form that is understandable,
professional, and grammatically
sound (be specific concerning type
of communication, its audience
and the purpose for it)

Interactive Reading

Learn tasks, facts or other features of your
experience by reading and retaining material
from manuals, books, journals or other
documents (be specific concerning type of
document, purpose for reading it, and how
you applied what you learned)

Applied Ethics

Accomplish tasks and make decisions
based on your personal set of values and definition
of ethical behavior (your examples should
describe a situation in which you used ethical
principles or values to make a decision or a
situation in which your values were compromised
by a decision you or your organization made)

Other

EXPERIENTIAL LEARNING

Evaluation of Transferable Academic Skills

Below are some examples that illustrate each of the academic skills on the evaluation. Study the examples to see how they fit the definitions on the form itself. Then, write an example or two from your own experience that relates to each skill.

Critical thinking

"When the children act a particular way, I try and figure out what it was that was making them act that way. Then I think of an activity that helps us to refocus them."

"I had to write an informational letter which provided prospective students with an overview of the school. I had to analyze audience and purpose, plus compile the necessary information to produce the piece."

Problem solving

"I helped to pick a potential advertisement to be aimed at a very specific audience. I had to determine how to interest them and to help them learn about the topic."

"If a child expressed a feeling that we weren't able to address, we would work together to think of a game or activity that would draw out the feeling."

Spoken communications

"In talking with my supervisor to get information or feedback, I always had to clarify my thoughts systematically."

"I participated in team meetings as well as a case audit within the team setting, I had to be assertive and articulate to make sure my points were listened to."

Written communications

"All researchers keep lab books so that others can repeat their experiments or use the information."

"We had to fill out forms for each child at the end of each session. It gave us an idea of how well they were doing and if any progress is happening."

Interactive reading

"I had to read and refer to several manuals and journals that are essential to doing my job—policies and procedures, technical information, etc."

"In order to get a quote done, I had to familiarize myself with printing terms. Having had no experience with printing, I used a glossary of such terms to help me learn."

Applied ethics

"A client of mine began flirting with me and calling me 'cutie.' This violated professional ethics, and I had to confront him and explain why it had to stop."

"All the children's records are confidential. We had to be careful when sharing information to help each other out not to violate the privacy of the children."

Appendix 13.2

HED 300—Seminar in Service Learning

Fall 2001 Course Evaluation

Please circle your response to the following statements using the rating scale provided.

1 = Strongly Disagree, 3 = Agree, 5 = Strongly Agree

1. Your interest in service has increased as a consequence of the class.   1 2 3 4 5

2. The instructors were enthusiastic about teaching the class.   1 2 3 4 5

3. You gained important feedback and learned from the instructors and your peers to assist you in being a more critical thinker.   1 2 3 4 5

4. The organization of the class responded to various learning style needs.   1 2 3 4 5

5. You felt encouraged to contribute your ideas to the class.   1 2 3 4 5

6. You took initiative/responsibility for your learning by fully investing in sessions and assignments.   1 2 3 4 5

7. As a result of the seminar, you developed:

    a. A variety of transferable academic skills including critical thinking, communication, applied ethics   1 2 3 4 5

    b. A spirit of partnership with the community, a belief that through shared effort, both the organization and the community will benefit   1 2 3 4 5

    c. An awareness/understanding of diversity issues   1 2 3 4 5

    d. Living/life skills and the larger societal issues that surround them   1 2 3 4 5

8. You felt the assignments contributed to your learning:

    a. 30 hours of service at your site   1 2 3 4 5

    b. 5 hours of service at South Campus   1 2 3 4 5

    c. Book (*A Hope in the Unseen*) Synopsis   1 2 3 4 5

    d. Journals   1 2 3 4 5

    e. Reflection Papers   1 2 3 4 5

9. You feel that by living in the learning community students felt connected in some way.   1 2 3 4 5

10. You feel that students living in the learning community communicate, care and show respect for one another.   1 2 3 4 5

11. You feel that the students in the learning community are able to rely on one another.   1 2 3 4 5

12. You feel that students from the learning community participate in social events with each other.   1 2 3 4 5

13. You feel that students from the learning community participate in academic studies together.   1 2 3 4 5

14

From Theme Floor to Learning Community: The Wellness Experience

Terra Peckskamp

The Wellness Learning Community emphasizes an overall mission of health and well being. The residence life staff work with other offices such as the SAPHE Office, the Office of Health Services, and the Office of Recreation Services to provide educational, personal growth, and social opportunities for students to learn more about leading a healthy lifestyle.

BEGINNINGS

The Wellness Learning Community has a unique history at Syracuse University and, like most learning communities, is constantly evolving. The story starts in the fall of 1992, when the Office of Residence Life (ORL) put into operation Syracuse University's first healthy living environment called CHEERS (Chemical Health Education Encouraging Responsible Students). Funding for the floor came from a federal grant (FIPSE) with the goal of creating and implementing a substance-free living environment for students in recovery. A partnership to support CHEERS was formed between the Office of Residence Life (ORL) and the Substance Abuse Prevention and Health Enhancement (SAPHE) Office, and staff from these two offices supported students through programming, mentorship, and advising. The floor continued to grow and change, evolving into a community with a more holistic approach to wellness, addressing the social, intellectual, spiritual, physical, and mental dimensions of one's being. The floor formerly known as CHEERS changed to the Wellness Floor in December 1996, emphasizing an overall mission of health and well being.

The learning community program was initiated a few years later, and conversations began during the summer of 2000 about transforming the Wellness Floor into a learning community. People were excited about and interested in the prospect of creating a more academic atmosphere on the Wellness Floor. Although the Wellness Floor, in its then current form, did a good job in focusing on the cocurricular and residential aspects of students' lives, adding an academic component would provide a way to blend academic and cocurricular experiences and increase the impact on student learning and development.

Adding an academic component was attractive to residence life staff because it also offered the opportunity to work with an academic unit. A professor from the Department of Health and Exercise Science had indicated interest in working on a learning community and agreed to collaborate in designing the academic component and integrating it with the wellness residential programming.

LEARNING OUTCOMES

Meetings were held throughout the fall of 2000 to design a wellness course and connected programming for the Wellness Learning Community. The learning community took shape on paper, and funding for the project (including a stipend for a graduate student to serve as the course coordinator) was secured through a Syracuse University Vision Fund grant. The learning objectives for the community were developed after discussion about what students should learn in the Wellness Learning Community, what the faculty and staff involved thought wellness was, and how the programmatic and academic goals could best connect and relate to each other. The objectives for the Wellness Learning Community are that:

1. Students will determine one wellness goal they want to achieve while living in the Wellness Learning Community.

2. Students will develop a plan to actualize their wellness goals.

3. Students will learn how to support each other in their wellness goals.

4. Students will become aware of wellness concepts, and of how these relate to each other.

5. Students will become aware of Syracuse University resources.

6. Regular opportunities for students, faculty, and staff to interact around wellness themes will be provided.

7. Students will have input in the development of wellness programs and will take progressively greater responsibility for the development of these programs.

The Wellness Floor became the Wellness Learning Community (WLC) in the fall of 2001, with HEA 100: Student-Centered Holistic Wellness as its academic component. Programmatic events in the residence hall were linked to course topics.

THE WELLNESS LEARNING COMMUNITY ACADEMIC COMPONENT

HEA 100 is a one-credit introductory level course open to all undergraduate Syracuse University and SUNY College of Environmental Sciences and Forestry students, and it is taught in the residence hall where the Wellness Learning Community is located. Students living in the WLC are strongly encouraged to take HEA 100, and many of them do, although it is optional due to other academic program requirements that students may have. HEA 100 is offered through the Department of Exercise Science in the School of Education. The graduate student who serves as the course coordinator selects discussion topics, develops the course syllabus/assignments, and recruits discussion leaders in collaboration with the Wellness Learning Community faculty member, staff from ORL, and staff from the SAPHE Office.

A different topic is discussed each week. The topics include sessions on physical activity and health, nutrition/eating disorders, financial wellness, mental and emotional health, drugs, alcohol, substance abuse, and medical health issues, to mention just a few. Each topic focuses on developing, enhancing, and maintaining a high level of wellness as well as supporting each other's wellness goals. Course assignments include a final four- to-five-page reflection paper and group activity project. Other course activities include a theme dinner (e.g., Exploring our World: A Feast to Celebrate Diversity and Nutrition) and a ropes course exercise that requires physical activity and teamwork. Many of the group activity projects are events that the students design and implement for the entire community, so that those students who are unable to attend the class are still able to benefit from what others are learning.

THE WELLNESS LEARNING COMMUNITY RESIDENTIAL COMPONENT

The Wellness Learning Community is a coed environment open to all undergraduate students. Two resident advisors (RAs), who are both supervised by the residence director (RD), live with the students in the WLC. Hall staff members work with other offices such as the SAPHE Office, the Office of Health Services, and the Office of Recreation Services to provide educational, personal growth, and social opportunities for students to learn more about leading a healthy lifestyle. The RAs work closely with the WLC course coordinator to supplement class discussion topics during floor meetings and programs. Other RA responsibilities include fostering community and implementing team-building activities on the floor. At the start of the semester, residents participate in a team building retreat, for example, a ropes course or a white water rafting trip. Other signature activities include a class dinner, wall climbing, yoga, healthy relationship discussions, Sex Jeopardy, and massage therapist sessions on the floor.

WELLNESS LEARNING COMMUNITY RECRUITMENT

Prior to fall 2001, recruiting students for the WLC had not been a difficult process. Wellness was one of only two theme-housing options for many years, and student interest was generated by word of mouth and a short description in housing information materials. Four new learning community options were added in the fall of 2000, and the number of learning communities had increased to 13 by the fall of 2001 when Wellness was officially designated a learning community. As the number of learning communities increased, the number of students applying for the WLC decreased. To learn more about this, we decided to conduct a focus group. One of the questions we wanted to answer was how students decided to participate in the WLC.

The information we gathered from that focus group had significant implications for how we do recruitment for the WLC. "I don't remember signing up for this, but I am really happy I'm here," was the response of one student when asked how she heard about the WLC. Other students in the room echoed her sentiment, and it appeared as though some of the students had not intentionally made the decision to sign up for the WLC. A parent may have signed them up for the WLC, or they didn't remember signing up for it, or they were placed there randomly to fill an empty space. Additionally, many of the students indicated that they had never heard about the WLC before arriving on campus. "You guys really need to tell more people about Wellness—I had no idea until I got here." These responses clearly indicated to us that we needed to have a more intentional and better constructed recruitment plan, so that not only would we get the number of students we needed, but also that the students would know what they were signing up for.

A new recruitment plan for the WLC was implemented in the spring of 2002. This plan included students from the WLC attending housing informational sessions for current SU students to tell them about the WLC, giving tours during the spring receptions for newly admitted students, and publicizing the WLC in areas of campus such as the Health Center, the SAPHE Office, and the academic office for the Department of Health and Exercise Science. We also scaled back on the number of spaces we designated for the WLC. Previously there were 70 spaces for the WLC; for the 2002–2003 academic year, 40 spaces were held for the WLC. We hit our target number for 2002–2003, and we are now in the process of evaluating and fine-tuning our recruitment process.

WELLNESS LEARNING COMMUNITY ASSESSMENT

Success in the WLC focuses on the attainment of the WLC goals, student satisfaction, the development of a positive community, and student learning about wellness concepts. Short answer surveys, a focus group, and a course evaluation are the primary vehicles for gathering assessment information about the WLC.

The pre- and post-surveys (see appendices 14.1 and 14.2) focus on how well students understand content from the HEA 100 course, as well as from the programs and activities presented as part of the WLC. Overall, the findings indicate that upon completion of the HEA 100 course, students have a good understanding of wellness concepts and can relate these concepts to a personal wellness philosophy. They were also able to identify campus resources for information on nutrition, health, spirituality, substance abuse, and debt management. One hundred percent of the 20 respondents (a 50% response rate) indicated that the WLC had met or exceeded their expectations after one semester.

The focus group yielded information that was helpful to us in planning for the following year. As mentioned earlier, one of the themes that came out of the focus group was that students weren't necessarily aware of the WLC and/or didn't understand what it meant to be part of the WLC. We believe this issue was successfully addressed through better publicity and recruitment, but we will need to reassess it each year and develop additional strategies if necessary. In addition to information about publicity and recruitment, students indicated that the WLC helped them feel connected and eased the transition for first-year students. "Making new friends is hard, and the WLC really helped. It is so much easier making friends, people are open to knowing everyone else, and it feels better knowing everyone else." Another student commented on the perceptions of other, non-WLC students. "People in other classes are mad they aren't on the floor when they find out what kinds of things we do. Other people in Shaw want to be on this floor; it's more social and open." Students also indicated that they really enjoyed the white water rafting trip that was held early in the semester. The trip met its goal of creating an opportunity for students to get to know each other and have some physical fun at the same time.

Overall, the assessment information indicates that the students are learning about wellness concepts, are connecting with each other socially, and are viewing their community positively. Of course, there are many ways to improve. Our assessment efforts are somewhat inconsistent; we need to develop a comprehensive assessment plan and then implement it. We are committed to getting more input from the students when developing programs, although we recognize that this can be a difficult process to manage, especially if the students aren't completely aware of community expectations. Finally, connecting more with the recreation services department on campus is something the students would like to see, and we, too, think it is a good idea. Overall, we are satisfied with the evolution of the WLC and are excited to take on the challenge of improving it each year.

Terra Peckskamp is director of learning communities for student affairs and associate director of residence life at Syracuse University.

Appendix 14.1

THE WELLNESS LC INTRODUCTORY QUESTIONS AND PRE-ASSESSMENT

This questionnaire is not a test; answer the questions to the best of your ability and knowledge. This is designed to help faculty and staff working with the Wellness Learning Community develop a good program and make sure we are meeting our goals.

Thanks for your help in creating a strong learning community!

1. What are your expectations for the Wellness LC?

2. What are the seven spheres of wellness? How do they relate to one another?

3. Give an example and describe the impact your lifestyle/living choices have on others in your community.

4. Please list health and wellness resources on campus for the following topics, including where these resources are located and how to access them. Also indicate how likely you are to use or access these services if you needed to.

   Emotional/mental health (i.e., depression, stress management, etc.):

   Nutrition information:

   Spiritual guidance:

   Help with a substance abuse problem (yours or a friend's):

   Debt management:

5. What is your personal wellness philosophy?

6. List three physical activities you have done or tried in the last three months. What prompted you to try/do these activities?

Appendix 14.2

THE WELLNESS POST-ASSESSMENT

This questionnaire is not a test; please reflect on your experiences this semester, and answer the questions to the best of your ability and knowledge. This is designed to help faculty and staff working with the Wellness Learning Community develop a good program and make sure we are meeting our goals.

Thanks for your help in creating a strong learning community!

1. a)   What were your expectations for the Wellness LC, prior to the start of the academic year?

   b)   Looking over the semester, would you say your experiences with the Wellness LC (circle one):

   exceeded your expectations

   met your expectations

   have been less than what you expected

2. What are the seven spheres of wellness? How do they relate to one another? How do they relate to you?

3. Give an example and describe the impact your lifestyle/living choices have on others in your community.

4. Please list health and wellness resources on campus for the following topics, including where these resources are located and how to access them. Also indicate how likely you are to use or access these services if you needed to.

   Emotional/mental health (i.e., depression, stress management, etc.):

   Nutrition information:

   Spiritual guidance:

   Help with a substance abuse problem (yours or a friend's):

   Debt management:

5. What is your personal wellness philosophy? Has it changed over the last semester? If so, how?

6. List three physical activities you have done or tried in the last three months. What prompted you to try/do these activities?

15

Arts Adventure: A Work in Progress

Martha Sutter interviewed by Ruth Federman Stein

The Arts Adventure Learning Community brings together undergraduate students from all the university's schools and colleges to explore their interest in the arts and discover the rich cultural environment on campus and in the Syracuse community. Adding two academic courses has substantially increased the level of participation in and commitment to the learning community.

CONCEPT OF LEARNING COMMUNITY AND HOW IT STARTED

When my dean in the College of Visual and Performing Arts (VPA) said that we needed to have a learning community and asked me to come up with a plan, I started thinking about what would be an appropriate model for us. Our college is comprised of four areas: art and design, drama, music, and speech communication. What could we do that would work for this range of students? Then I thought about the Arts Adventure program that the university already had in place, which introduces students to cultural opportunities on campus and in the surrounding community by providing free or substantially reduced tickets to sponsored events and free transportation to off-campus performances. That program seemed to be floundering a bit, and I thought this might be a quick and easy way both to get our students to attend events and bring some more prominence to the Arts Adventure program itself.

Deciding which students would be invited to join seemed like it should be pretty straightforward, but in fact there was a lot of conversation about it. Our early discussions were about whether or not we should open the learning community to everybody at the university. The directors of the various programs in VPA liked the concept of having the learning community open to all SU students; they were concerned about residential learning communities limited to, for example, drama or music students because those students already spend so much time together their first year. Although I agreed with that argument at the time, I am, in fact, having second thoughts about it. They all end up living together after the first year anyway, so I'm beginning to think it might not be a bad idea. We also talked about not letting any VPA students join the Arts Adventure learning community and then creating a second, more highbrow learning community for our own students, but that was going to be too complicated to get going right away. Finally we decided to make the learning community available to all students, including VPA students. We didn't want to exclude them, and we thought the learning community would be generic enough so that we could show them what was available on campus and in town, and it would give them opportunities to attend events.

THE FIRST ITERATION

The first year that we did the learning community, we planned it for one semester and relied on a series of activities rather than requiring the students to enroll in a course. Home base for the learning community was Lawrinson Hall; the 58 students lived on the 19th (female) and 20th (male) floors of the hall. Four students who lived on the floor were not enrolled in the learning community. The lounges on each floor provided good programming space for community building. We learned, however, that the 20th floor lounge is shaped differently and is slightly smaller and less open than the other floors, and sometimes this different configuration posed difficulties for community building. Having activities in the 19th floor lounge worked best. We also had some programs on the 2nd floor lounge, but we tended to get fewer participants there, just because it was further away from the living areas.

There were specific events that were considered Arts Adventure events. For example, Syracuse Stage produced *A Streetcar Named Desire*, and we intended to tie it in with programming on the residence hall floors, both before and after the performance. We had faculty from the drama department come in to talk with the students about listening to things before they went to the show. They discussed the answers to questions like: "What do you do when you go to something?" "Why do you critique it?" "What do you get out of it?" "What do you bring to it?" The follow-up programming, however, never occurred because of 9/11 when everything else was shoved aside to deal with that catastrophic day.

We intended to use the questions posed by the drama faculty as a framework for other events, but that didn't work out. After *Streetcar* we were going to see *The Wiz* as part of our conversation about diversity. Then we planned to take students to the Schine Student Center to hear the Syracuse Symphony play Mahler. But we ran into a significant problem scheduling these events. Faculty teaching the Freshman Forums (one-credit first semester courses taken by Arts and Sciences students) were taking their students to several of those events, which we didn't find out about until it was too late to do anything about it. Unfortunately, this presents a recurring problem because faculty don't necessarily decide what they are going to do in their Freshman Forums until quite late. We finally resolved this issue by having the students choose the outside performances they wished to attend.

Another problem that we encountered was having a learning community without any specific course requirement. Some students did not have the same willingness to participate without an academic sword hanging over them. There was a core of about 20 students who were committed to doing things, and they'd come to all the hall meetings and the discussions. For the others, having a test or a paper due the next day frequently took precedence over a learning community event. It was understandable but frustrating. I remember one music student who ran into a music professor who was coming to speak to the learning community. The professor said, "So, are you coming to our meeting?" The student acted as if he had no idea that he was living on the learning community floor. We tried to get the no-shows to participate by giving them more latitude in picking their own events, which could even be a rock concert at the Schine, but that didn't work. We also hoped they'd go to some events because they'd hear "Wow, that was neat, let's all go there," but that didn't happen either.

We really struggled with the learning community the first semester. We were all fumbling around trying to figure out who these students were and what we were doing. The public perception was that it was going wonderfully, but in reality we had a lot of problems. During the second semester, we continued to advertise events, but we didn't track whether or not the students participated.

The first year we planned one special session at the Cayuga Nature Center Ropes Course near Ithaca. It was scheduled on a Sunday from 10:00 a.m. to 6:00 p.m., and about 38 students signed up. Because it was early on a Sunday morning, only 18 students showed up. The core of students who went were the same 18 who were involved in everything in the learning community. At the ropes course, they did community-building low ropes activities in the morning and high ropes personal challenges in the afternoon. However, there was no integration between the ropes course and the arts even though that had been requested ahead of time. Feedback from the activity was that the ropes course was a cool activity, but it didn't really relate to the arts. This year the learning community did not repeat the ropes course activity. Instead they are taking a required one-day bus trip to New York City to visit the Guggenheim Museum.

LEARNING OUTCOMES

We developed more of a goal statement—exposing students to various kinds of cultural events—than learning outcomes for the first iteration of the learning community. As we developed a clearer understanding of what we and the students wanted out of the learning community, we worked on articulating actual learning objectives. Currently, we have three:

- *Students will have access to a diverse array of visual and performing arts activities on campus and in the Syracuse area.* To meet this objective, the students are expected to attend seven events during the course of the year. Four of the events are scheduled for the fall semester: a dramatic production, a staged musical, a symphony, and dinner theatre. The three spring events are student events: a musical theater production, a dance production, and a fashion show. We also distribute a comprehensive calendar of arts activities for the spring. The students are also expected to attend presentations by guest speakers.

- *Students will gain in their appreciation and understanding of aesthetics, traditions, and histories of various forms of artistic expression.* This outcome was to be achieved through pre-event lectures and symposia and attendance at a variety of venues.

- *Students will be able to articulate and incorporate the availability of social alternatives.* For this outcome, we expected the students to keep both a log of attendance at arts activities and a reflective journal.

SECOND ITERATION OF THE ARTS
ADVENTURE LEARNING COMMUNITY

Academic Component

For the second year, we made some significant changes in the learning community. Approximately the same number of students lived together, although we moved to a different residence hall. Most importantly, we added two required three-credit courses to address the participation issue.

The first course is a music-based fine arts class, FIA 195: Performance Live. It meets once a week in the evening, and about every third week, during class time, students attend a concert, which is part of the Tuesday Night Concert Series in Crouse College. The instructor also has some in-class performances. In addition, the students attend optional events outside of class (e.g., Brahms concert, Syracuse Opera). We have had to be flexible in allowing certain students to be part of the community without taking this course. For example, students in the School of Architecture and students in the School of Art and Design in the College of Visual and Performing Arts have first semester schedules full of required classes and can't fit it in. We created a one-credit independent study for the Art and Design students who had room for one more credit, and we waived the requirement entirely for the architecture students who had no room at all.

The second class is a writing studio, WRT 105, that is linked to the fine arts class. The writing studio uses American music as the focus for exploring academic literacy, practicing writing, analysis, and argument. The writing class is a very popular one. In fact, one student who was living on the floor but was not a part of the community asked to join the community in order to take the writing class and adjusted his schedule in order to take the fine arts class as well.

RECRUITING STUDENTS

We haven't taken special steps to recruit students for the learning community. We use the material that is sent out to admitted students about housing and residence life, and we talk about it on campus at various events such as spring receptions and auditions, and, of course, our Admissions Office at VPA always talks about it.

Initially, 70 students signed up for the second iteration of the learning community. During the summer the numbers dwindled a little. We filled up two writing sections (limited to 20 students per section); a third section only had a few people in it. Because there weren't enough students to make a class, we were told we either had to switch those students out or add outside people. The Writing Program agreed to let us exceed the 20-student limit, so we decided to switch the students into the two other sections. So, out of the 60-plus students, we had close to 50 in the two writing sections. We also have four or five sophomores in the learning community, but I'm not sure if they joined primarily because of their interest or because they wanted to live in Boland Hall. We also have one transfer student who is one of our most active students. Again this year we have a mix of students from VPA and other SU schools and colleges and a few students on the floor who aren't actually members of the learning community but who have participated in some of the concerts and activities on the floor.

One event that was extremely successful in the residence hall was "The 3 P's: Pizza, Painting, and Performance." It was advertised several weeks in advance to the students as an event with floor painting and food. Each floor had time before the event to plan their painting. Both floors worked separately but in the same room. They each had a 3x4 canvas on the floor to paint. The event was planned to last a little over an hour, but students were still there after two hours. While the paintings were drying, students performed on a temporary stage. For example, one student played a guitar and sang, another read his own poems, and two young women danced and lip-synched. All the faculty from the learning community attended the event. This activity truly captured the spirit of the Arts Adventure!

ASSESSMENT

The first year we didn't have a formal assessment plan, but we did collect significant anecdotal evidence from students, through conversations and through reading their journals, that, coupled with our own observations, gave us significant insight into what was happening in the learning community.

We quickly became aware of the participation problems that resulted from not having an academic component. Adding the courses for the second year has substantially increased the level of participation and commitment to the learning community. It has also contributed to students' academic success. The block of students in the linked writing studios, when compared to all other students in the music class (nearly 100), consistently wrote better papers. The instructors had hoped for a synergy in learning outcomes—the music instructor hoped that her students would write better papers, and the writing instructor hoped that that his students would show a grasp of the sonic dimension of music (in other words, show a willingness to discuss music as sound, and begin to develop a vocabulary of concepts and terms to do so). In their most recent conversations, both instructors felt students grew in those key areas.

We also discovered, as we looked at what students actually went to, that productions put on by student groups—for example, First-Year Players and Dance Works—were the most popular. Knowing that, we now use those events as a way to get students in the habit of attending other cultural events.

We are encouraged that the changes we made between the first and second year are contributing to a stronger, more successful learning community by the fact that a group of our most active students has proposed the creation of another arts adventure floor for upper-class students. Housing has provided a floor for them, and they are currently in the process of identifying an academic component. Although they would prefer to take one course together, they understand the scheduling difficulties inherent in that strategy, and they are working with the faculty coordinator to develop a list of three or four courses—in fine arts, religion, English, and music—from which to choose.

WHAT'S NEXT?

In their feedback about the course components, the students suggested that we provide more balance in the topics covered in the fine arts course, which focused primarily on music. As a result of that feedback, students next fall will enroll in the writing class and then choose between Performance Live, which has a music appreciation focus and another fine arts course, Arts and Ideas, which has an art history focus. We will again make exceptions for students who don't have room in their schedules for these courses or who are enrolled in a school-based non-residential learning community that includes WRT 105 as one of its linked courses.

The fact that some students choose a learning community primarily because of its location rather than its subject matter is a problem shared by all learning communities open to upper-class students. To discourage selection based on location, we want to add a screening process for upper-class students who want to join the learning community. We will likely ask them to write about their background with the arts, why they want to be in the AALC, what they hope to gain from the AALC, and what they can contribute to it.

One of our continuing challenges will be to find ways to get busy students to take better advantage of what's happening on campus as well as in the community. We must present the arts in a way that students know what's available, enjoy it, and pursue it on their own. With the numerous events occurring in Syracuse, we want to construct the learning community in such a way that students learn all they can from this culturally rich environment.

Ruth Federman Stein is a teaching consultant at the Center for Support of Teaching and Learning, and Martha Sutter is assistant dean of students in the College of Visual and Performing Arts, both of Syracuse University.

16

A Lesson in Citizenship: The Maxwell Citizenship Education Learning Community

*Sandra N. Hurd with William B. Coplin,
Rosalie Carpenter, and SaraKate Kirk*

The Maxwell Citizenship Education Learning Community is unique among learning communities at Syracuse University. An outgrowth of the Maxwell School's Citizenship Education Conference for high school seniors, it was designed and implemented by students with minimal supervision by faculty and residence life staff. The goals of the community are to promote citizenship and service.

HOW IT BEGAN

The Maxwell Citizenship Education Learning Community almost didn't get off the ground. Professor Coplin had participated in the Leadership Learning Community but wanted to launch a community with more of a public service focus than the leadership community provided. When he first proposed a learning community around the theme of citizenship education to his work study student, SaraKate Kirk, she wasn't sure it was such a good idea and worried that nobody would want to live on the floor. There was very little structure proposed, and she wasn't sure how to explain it to prospective residents. But Professor Coplin thought it was worth a try and assigned SaraKate and several other policy studies students were assigned RA positions for the following year. SaraKate would be an RA and design the learning community as an outgrowth of the Maxwell School's Citizenship Education Conference.

Every year in April, the Maxwell School hosts its Citizenship Education and Scholarship Competition under the direction of Professor Coplin, director of the Public Affairs Program. High school seniors who have already applied to Syracuse University are invited to participate and compete for one of 25 four-year scholarships to SU.

Conference participants, approximately 100 each year, are required to submit a four- to six-page paper presenting a public policy proposal on the year's conference theme in advance of the conference. (A recent theme, for example, was "Public Policy Proposals to Increase Opportunities for Children in Poverty in the United States.") They then attend the one-day conference (a peer group exercise in which they defend their proposal), which consists of individual presentations and group discussions. Scholarship awards are based on the quality of the student's paper and her or his score on the peer group exercise. Students who participate generally need financial assistance, have good time-management skills, and have strong academic records. They may or may not have a strong interest in public policy. They are, however, highly motivated, often by parents who want them both to have a good learning experience and a chance to win a scholarship. It is from this group that the Citizenship Education Learning Community students are recruited.

The first year of the community, the residence director (RD) talked to students and their parents at the conference about the learning community. Less than one-third of the conference attendees asked to be placed on the floor. The next year, 15 of the previous year's residents participated in the conference and joined the RD in the recruiting effort, talking to the students and their parents about their experience in the learning community. Over 50% of the conference participants asked to join the learning community although several fewer than that actually attended SU and lived in the community.

How the Community Works

The Citizenship Education Learning Community is unique among SU's learning communities in that it is run almost entirely by the residents under the direction of the resident advisor with minimal supervision by Professor Coplin and the residence life professional staff. In fact, the faculty member and the residence life staff member who coordinate learning communities for the university had to sign a non-interference accord, in which they agreed to limit their involvement as long as the floor governance and activities were consistent with university policies and rules, before the planning could begin. With that precondition in place, SaraKate and several of her fellow policy studies majors who had participated in the previous year's conference became the planning group and designed the learning community.

All learning communities at SU are required to have an academic component. When the planning group began developing a proposal for the community, they thought about making Professor Coplin's public affairs class the academic component. But the students who attend the conference are from all
different majors and not all would be able to take the class. They decided that
maintaining the diversity of participants was more important than having the
academic component be a course, so they looked at other ways to structure
the academic component. They decided that the academic component should
be facilitated floor discussions. Every other Sunday night at 9 p.m. after the
regular floor meetings (the community is housed on two floors, one female
and one male), SaraKate would lead a discussion about citizenship. The students began the semester by trying to create a definition of citizenship and
then explored the various meanings of citizenship. Later in the semester, the
discussion shifted to connecting the various community service experiences
the students were engaged in to their earlier discussion of citizenship. Professor Coplin attended these meetings several times each semester and participated in the discussion. He also brainstormed ideas for community service
projects and helped students make contact with appropriate placements for
their particular interests.

The structure of the learning community calls for a student board to
oversee the service work of the floors. The members of the learning community chose, through a democratic process, four of their number to be on the
governing board. During the first semester, the actual service work of the
floors was done by committees. The students in the community self-selected
into committees, with each group working on a separate project. In retro-
spect, SaraKate believes it was a mistake to let the students form their own
groups. As is often the case with that strategy, like-minded, committed students clustered together and were extremely productive while other groups
struggled.

At the end of the first semester, the board met with Professor Coplin to
evaluate the first semester and decide on programming for the spring. Several
changes to the structure of the community were made. The most significant
was that they abandoned the committee structure. Instead, students did considerable community service through individual service projects, and the governing board selected several projects for the entire community. Although they
developed ambitious plans, only one major service project actually happened.

The RAs continued to lead the community spring semester. In spite of
the ambitious plans made by the board, the RAs were careful not to try to do
too much. They were concerned that if the students over programmed the

floors, they would feel overwhelmed by their learning community obligations and become frustrated or lose interest. The RAs also believed that an important part of the learning experience is taking initiative and accepting responsibility and that prescribing too much can get in the way of such learning.

Although taking initiative is a value of the community, the planning group recognized that there are limitations on the ability of freshmen to govern themselves. So, while the freshmen take on some additional governance responsibility in the second semester, their role remains limited.

COMMUNITY ACTIVITIES

In addition to individual and small group community service activities at such venues as Habitat for Humanity and the Veterans Administration Hospital, the learning community participated as a group in two activities and two significant community service projects. The first group activity was the ropes course they went on early in the fall semester. The purposes of the ropes course were to build community and foster teamwork. The second group activity was a trip to New York City to observe how citizenship was being played out in the aftermath of September 11, 2001.

The two community service projects were an arts and crafts day at the Boys and Girls Club in the fall and a daylong cookout at Wilson Park in the spring. For the arts and crafts day, the students created nine holiday projects (gifts and/or ornaments) for the boys and girls to make. Putting the day together involved working as a team to figure out appropriate projects, raising money to pay for materials, ordering supplies, organizing space, managing participation, and cleaning up. Wilson Park is a small community center run by the City of Syracuse and located in a public housing project adjacent to the SU campus. Throughout the day, the learning community students grilled hot dogs, played games, and taught small groups of boys and girls about business with a computer game called Hot Dog Stand. They ended the day with prizes and awards.

LEARNING OBJECTIVES

The initial learning objectives were a collaborative effort among the RAs, Professor Coplin, the residence director, and the student planning group and evolved over time as they understood more about the learning community and clarified their own goals. By the end of the first year, the agreed upon objectives were that they wanted students to:

- Develop an understanding of citizenship and what it means to be a citizen
- Weigh the personal benefits and costs of working to help make a difference
- Appreciate the personal and organizational constraints on planning and implementing a project
- Recognize the importance of individual leadership in collective action
- Understand how the attempt to organize the community is similar to the role of government in society
- Complete 20 hours of volunteer activities each semester

The RAs, in addition, set informal goals of familiarizing the students with the campus and how the university works as well as having them get off campus and into the Syracuse community.

ASSESSMENT

The lack of structure for the learning community, although good for student learning and development around issues of citizenship and the evolving nature of the learning outcomes, made it difficult to design a comprehensive assessment plan. There are, however, some data from which to draw inferences about how well the community met its objectives.

The RAs kept track of the hours students spent on community service. About 30% actually performed 20 hours of community service each semester. This percentage, higher than expected but lower than hoped for by the RAs, confirmed Professor Coplin's previous observations that leaders are few and good citizens almost as rare. In his view, "That is the whole idea of the floor. What they did as a floor and as individuals is evidence of how a democracy operates."

There is evidence to suggest that the learning community was, in fact, a success. The learning community was attractive to the non-learning community students living on the floor, a number of whom asked to join during the first semester. An unusually high proportion of learning community students applied to be RAs the following year. Many of the students participated actively in residence hall government or other student organizations, and a handful of students have become very active in the public affairs major.

SaraKate collected vast amounts of informal information during the year. She concluded from her conversations with the students about the two floor community service projects that the students had learned a great deal about how to organize and manage a large community service project. She also concluded that her goal of connecting the students with the university was met, especially in terms of the close and trusting relationships they built with Professor Coplin. In her words, "[T]hese kids love him. They just love him." At the end of the year, a number of students communicated to both the RAs and the residence director their satisfaction with their experience in the learning community.

The learning community was certainly a success from SaraKate's perspective as an RA. Despite being heavily recruited by the Office of Residence Life, she vows never to be an RA again because she can't imagine that she could have a better experience than she had with the learning community. She admits to "having withdrawal anxiety. I can't seem to let Margot and Megan [next year's RAs] take it over."

The residence director also declares it a success as measured by her observations of the personal development of the students involved. The students connected quickly with each other. She credits these early, strong bonds with creating a different dynamic. She notes that the students held each other accountable in ways that simply didn't happen on other floors in the residence hall. They were quick to confront problems on the floors and treated each other respectfully as members of a true community. She also noted that the women assumed leadership roles in greater numbers than on other floors and attributes this to the support they received from each other and the rest of the community. Part of this may be attributable to the fact that the community was housed on two single gender floors.

Professor Coplin agrees that the community is a success. Although he estimates that only about 50% of the students are ready for the kind of learning experience the community offers, he believes it is important to continue to create opportunities for students to develop themselves into strong leaders and good citizens.

Sandra N. Hurd is professor of law and public policy in the Whitman School of Management and director of learning communities for academic affairs, William D. Coplin is professor and director of the Public Affairs Program, Rosalie Carpenter was the 2001–2002 resident director, and SaraKate Kirk was the 2001–2002 resident advisor, all of Syracuse University.

17

The Education Living Learning Community

Amie Redmond

The Education Living Learning Community, open only to first-year stu-dents enrolled in the School of Education, creates a supportive environ-ment in which students learn to live and work cooperatively, developing the academic and social skills necessary to achieve their goals. As part of their learning community experience, the students provide significant community service working with students at a public school in Syracuse.

How the Education Living Learning Community Started

I was sitting in one of my first Academic Coordinating Committee (ACC) meetings as the School of Education's assistant dean for undergraduate stud-ies, listening to a presentation about the upcoming 2001 Syracuse University Learning Communities. As I listened to the descriptions of the communities and the discussion of the benefits to students, faculty, and staff, I began think-ing to myself, "What about an education learning community?" I skimmed the handout that listed the schools and colleges and indicated their interest in developing learning communities for freshmen. It said that the School of Education was not interested in a residential learning community. After the meeting, I asked why. I was told that the faculty was concerned about further isolating and insulating what was already a fairly homogenous group of stu-dents from opportunities to experience diversity.

At the time, the university was moving to randomized housing assign-ments. (In previous years, students could indicate their residence hall prefer-ence on their housing application.) Incoming freshman who did not choose to live in a learning community would be randomly placed in one of the university's residence halls. Despite the reservations of the faculty, I had reason to believe that a learning community for education students might be a good idea. In my previous role as the undergraduate admissions coordinator for the School of Education for four years, prospective students often asked me if we had a residence hall for education students. Armed with that expression of interest as well as the knowledge that education programs in colleges and universities with whom we compete offered a learning community option to students, I began the process of convincing my dean that we should have a learning community.

I began by listing the advantages and disadvantages to having an education learning community. The advantages I saw were that students who lived together and had an interest in the field of education would form connections and friendships more quickly; it would be easy for the students to find partners and groups with whom to study; we would be able to put together a field experience in the freshman year; and students would have more interaction with faculty, staff, and administrators in the School of Education. The only potential disadvantage I saw was the concern raised by the faculty. Most education majors form small cohorts toward the end of the sophomore or junior year and take their classes together. Was the freshman year too early for the students to begin spending so much time together? Would they not meet students outside the School of Education? Would it be too much togetherness?

As I thought about the answers to these questions, it became clear to me that there were more reasons to have an education learning community than not to have one. I presented my list to the dean of the school. Hesitant at first, the dean recognized the positive aspects of the learning community and gave me the go ahead to create an Education Living Learning Community.

The next step involved an initial meeting with university learning community organizers, along with my dean, to go over the logistics of developing a School of Education learning community. We discussed possible models of learning communities being developed and implemented at Syracuse, and I walked away from that meeting with a conceptual framework of the Education Living Learning Community (ELLC).

MISSION, LEARNING OBJECTIVES, AND DESCRIPTION OF THE EDUCATION LIVING LEARNING COMMUNITY

The mission of the ELLC is to bring first-year education students together with School of Education faculty and staff members to ease the transition into the Syracuse University community and to contribute to the students' success within the School of Education and beyond. The ELLC is designed to alleviate some of the personal and academic tensions that many first-year college students experience when making the transition from high school to college so that the students become quite comfortable with the intellectual and residential aspects of university life in a short period of time. We achieve the mission by providing a close-knit and supportive environment that involves participating in activities designed specifically for education majors.

Once this mission for the community was established, I turned to developing specific learning outcomes. Fortunately, the advantages I saw in having the learning community transformed easily into the community's learning objectives:

- Meet and learn from others who hold similar academic interests, but whose backgrounds and values differ from their own

- Build a supportive community in which individuals learn to live and work in cooperation with each other

- Discover the unlimited opportunities available both within Syracuse University and in the surrounding area to get involved with and contribute to the community outside the academic curriculum

- Obtain the academic and social skills necessary to help students achieve their goals

The learning community is structured around three elements. First, the students take two courses together in the residence hall: WRT 105 (Writing Studio I) and EDU 100 (First-Year Forum). Second, residence hall programming promotes the students' success through floor experiences that support the goals of the ELLC. Third, students in the ELLC have the opportunity to engage in a number of activities outside the university environment such as performing community service within the local area, attending cultural events, and participating in activities centered around getting to know the Syracuse community.

ACADEMIC COMPONENT

The academic component of the ELLC consists of two required first-semester courses. WRT 105, the first-year writing studio, develops students' abilities to use writing for learning, thinking, and critical reading of complex texts and provides instruction in basic elements of the writing process. EDU 100, First-

Year Forum, facilitates students' transition to college life. Specifically, its goals are to:

- Facilitate interaction among students and faculty members

- Provide an opportunity for students to interact with School of Education students outside their own program of study and create a sense of community

- Create an environment in which students can ask questions and discuss issues that concern them

- Assist students in gaining some understanding of what university life is all about and the opportunities that exist on campus for academic and non-academic needs and pursuits

- Develop among students a sense of identity as a School of Education student within a supportive community of learners and educators

- Help students balance the freedoms and responsibilities that are part of college life

- Assist students in exploring the variety of campus issues that affect all students, but especially students in their first year of college

- Explore the purposes and importance of higher education and learn more about Syracuse University, its faculty, and staff

- Introduce students to the many educational opportunities and resources available at Syracuse University

- Improve students' academic skills such as writing, speaking before a group, using the library, studying, and taking tests

The instructors of WRT 105 and EDU 100 met together to discuss the topics to be covered in each class, uncover areas of collaboration, decide on the timing of shared materials, and determine how best to include the service-learning component of the learning community. The linked aspect of the courses helped the students tie the classes together and connect them with their residential experience. Holding the WRT 105 and EDU 100 classes in the residence hall right before dinner was particularly beneficial. Students would leave class and go to dinner together, continuing class discussions over their meal.

Living together and taking classes together created a supportive academic environment. One ELLC student commented to me that "study groups are a huge advantage to living with your classmates, and it's also very hard to sleep through a class that your roommate has to wake up for anyway!" I was extremely impressed to find out that non-ELLC students living in other residence halls would make their way over to the learning community floor to study with ELLC students or to work on homework. When I talk to people about this aspect of the learning community, which I did not foresee happening, I use the analogy of bees on honey. The non-ELLC students are the bees and the ELLC floor is the honey.

SERVICE-LEARNING COMPONENT

Service to the community is an important value in the School of Education. This value was clearly reflected in designing the service-learning component of the ELLC, in which the students took part in the Delaware Academy Extended School Day/School Violence Prevention Program. Delaware Academy is a K-6 elementary school with a population of more than 700 students who come from diverse racial, ethnic, and cultural backgrounds. It is a bilingual school serving a large Hispanic population; English is a second language for 32% of its students. Minorities make up 75% of the school population. Ninety-four percent of Delaware students participate in the free or reduced-cost lunch program, indicative of the high poverty rate among the families of its students. Delaware has also traditionally had the highest suspension rate of elementary schools in the district. The school's goal is to increase substantially the number of students who score at or above performance standards set by the New York State Education Department (NYSED).

In the fall 2001 semester, 18 ELLC students participated four days a week (20 visits per student) for a total of 340 hours in the Extended School Day (ESD) program, an after-school program for K-6 students. The program is comprehensive and comprised of three equal, one-hour strands: academic skills, social skills, and enrichment. Each day a group of ELLC students were transported by taxi to Delaware Academy to work with students who face severe challenges in achieving NYSED higher learning standards. Together they practiced academic and social skills, including conflict resolution, under the guidance of ESD staff. ELLC students also participated in enrichment activities such as chess, karate, and painting.

Current research highlights the importance of after-school programs and the important contribution made by communities like the ELLC who support them. In the past year Delaware's ELA (English Language Arts) test scores have increased significantly, their suspension rates have declined, and attendance in the Extended School Day has increased.

The ELLC students found their service experience at Delaware Academy valuable. One ELLC student said, "I have really gotten attached to the third graders and enjoy working with them twice a week to help them with their homework, and just to be their friend." Another student commented, " I really enjoy working with the students, and I feel as though they like having us there, too. It is a worthwhile program that enables us to gain experience in our major." According to one ELLC student, going to Delaware Academy is one of the best parts of the Education Living Learning Community. The ELLC students even comment on the taxi ride to and from campus to Delaware Academy. One student said, "We have also had some crazy and interesting taxi rides together on the way to and from Delaware Academy. It is just another neat experience we have shared together."

I am extremely proud that the Education Living Learning Community was selected to receive a Chancellor's Award for Public Service, an award given to students who exemplify the highest ideal of quality service in our community, for its work at Delaware Academy. The ELLC students were delighted to win the award and to be recognized by the chancellor at a celebration dinner.

RESIDENCE HALL PROGRAMMING

In addition to service-learning at Delaware Academy, the ELLC students were involved in a number of activities as a group. Residence hall staff met regularly with the instructors of the academic courses to develop programs that complemented those courses. Some of these happened away from campus, and some of them happened on the floor.

In September, the ELLC floor went to a ropes course at the Cayuga Nature Center outside of Ithaca, New York. The students participated in small-group team building and trust building activities such as working together to get every member of the team over a ten-foot wall and the leap of faith. One ELLC student said, "I gained a lot of knowledge about how to work together with people to get things accomplished not only faster but more efficiently." Another student reflected on the ropes course as "one of the most memorable activities" she did with her floormates. In October, the residence life staff hosted a School of Education Jeopardy Night to help the students learn about the School of Education. A discussion about the positive and negative features of the learning community followed. During that month, the students also created a poster of their living-learning experiences with pictures, quotes, and text. They used the poster as part of a presentation to parents during parents weekend. Near the end of the month, they visited a pumpkin patch to celebrate fall and Halloween.

In November, the ELLC hosted Suzanne Damarin, professor of education at The Ohio State University. She spoke on "The Mathematically Able as a Marked Category," discussing with the students issues of school reform, educational technology, and gender and multicultural equity. Throughout the semester, the learning community lounge became a popular place for ELLC students. They would get together for floor meetings, hold informal study groups, watch television, or just hang out.

It wasn't clear to me how important both the paraprofessional (resident advisor) and professional (residence director) residential staff would be to the success of the education learning community until we marked the halfway point of the first year of the ELLC. The Office of Residence Life asked me to review resident advisor applications to recommend an RA who would be most appropriate for the learning community. From the handful of applications I received, I chose an education major whom I knew to serve as the RA for the ELLC. It was a good choice. She was able to share information about the school that non-education students simply wouldn't know. She was also able to talk about the field of education—why she chose it, what direction she plans to move in, certification requirements, course-specific information, and whom to contact in the school should students need to seek out additional information. Besides being a resource for the students living on the floor, she was also a resource for me. When I had a question about a student or was planning a floor activity, I felt comfortable contacting her. We would often see each other around campus and strike up a conversation about the ELLC.

Not only is it extremely important to have an RA committed to the learning community concept, it is also essential to have a residence director who believes in the concept. The RD of the residence hall was a person who committed his time and energy to the success of the ELLC. He was a wonderful mentor for our RA, attended bi-monthly ELLC team meetings, was open to suggestions and ideas for social events, and had an open door policy for my involvement in the community as the coordinator of the ELLC. I didn't completely understand the importance of having an RD's commitment to a learning community until the second year of the learning community began with a new RD who was not able to spend as much time working with the ELLC as the former RD. (See Chapter 8 for the residence life staffing challenges presented by learning communities.) Without high levels of collaboration and commitment, it is easy for communication to break down.

RECRUITING STUDENTS

Fall 2001 was the first year of the Education Living Learning Community. It was difficult recruiting the first class of ELLC students, as I didn't have anything to go on other than the other learning communities that existed on campus. Although there were going to be some similarities, there were going to be more differences. We started with the goal of filling 30 spots, which was probably too ambitious for the first year. We ended up having 18 students interested in the ELLC.

The second year of recruiting was much more successful as the current ELLC residents did the bulk of the recruiting for me. They participated in the fall and spring receptions, talking to prospective students and their parents about the benefits of the ELLC. Who was I to think, as an administrator, that I could encourage prospective students to live on a floor full of education majors! It was the ELLC students themselves who were my best recruiters. They enjoyed talking to prospective students about the benefits of the ELLC and looked forward to every opportunity to give prospective students a tour of the floor. Parents of prospective students also responded enthusiastically to the concept of the learning community. One parent said, "I will feel much better about sending my daughter to Syracuse University if she can become a member of the ELLC." Parents often spoke about the safety aspect of the community, the importance of knowing that their children were part of a structured community where students have the opportunity to get to know one another quickly. Our student recruiters were so effective and the response from parents and prospective students was so enthusiastic that I feared we would have to turn students away. And turn students away for the second year of the ELLC was just what we had to do. Without committing to a larger size ELLC, which we were not prepared to do at the time, we had to limit ourselves to the 32 spaces we had available. As a result, we could not accommodate a few of the students who wanted to live in the learning community.

ASSESSMENT

As the first year of the ELLC came to a close, three assessment strategies were used to try to find out whether the learning community had been successful.

Personal Observations
The first and most simple assessment was my own personal observations of and conversations with the students about their experiences during the semester. In addition, I took the students out to dinner for an end of the year wrap

up session. At dinner I opened the dialogue up for discussion with an open-ended question, "As you know, this year was the first year of the ELLC, and I am happy to report we are making plans for the second year and I would like your feedback on what you liked and what you would change about the learning community if you were the coordinator." Here is what I learned:

- All the students were glad they chose the learning community.

- The best aspects of the ELLC were that it was easy to make friends early on, there was easy access to study partners, there were people watching out for each other, there was the opportunity to get to know faculty and administrators when they might not otherwise have been able to, and there were opportunities to do fun activities off campus.

- The students believed that they did better academically and developed a stronger interest in the field of education.

- They liked Delaware Academy, but some students felt there were too many hours of service required.

- They liked the special attention they got from faculty and administrators.

- They felt more connected to the School of Education ("a home away from home").

Academic Performance

The second type of assessment that was important for me was to find out how the students did academically. At the end of the first year, their cumulative GPA's together averaged 3.41. Fifty-six percent of the students, 10 out of 18, had a cumulative GPA of 3.5 or above; 28%, 5 out of 18, had a cumulative GPA of 3.0 to 3.49; and 3% of the students had a cumulative GPA of 2.5 to 2.99. I then did a random sample of 18 non-learning community School of Education students. Their cumulative average GPA was a 3.21. What did this tell me? It told me that we had been successful in fostering an academic environment in the community—the students took their academics seriously and benefited from the opportunities the community provided to study and learn together. I was also very impressed, as an assistant dean, that none of the ELLC had below a 2.5 cumulative GPA. The students' academic success made all the hard work of designing, developing, and implementing the learning community well worth the effort I put in as coordinator of the ELLC.

Focus Group Input

The third type of assessment was a focus group facilitated by two students in Syracuse University's Higher Education Program. Seven of the 18 students were present at the focus group session. The focus groups explored the following issues:

1. **Why did students sign up for the ELLC?** All of the students liked the idea of living and studying with other students interested in the field of education, they liked the idea they could form relationships with other students easily, and they liked the idea of living in Flint Hall.

2. **What were the floor relationships like?** The female students liked the easy access to other females as a way to form friendships. As a result of spending so much time together, some tensions emerged.

3. **Tell us about the classes and instructors.** Students felt a close, personal connection with the EDU 100 instructors, but felt the WRT 105 instructor wanted to know too much about the "personal stuff," which the students felt belonged in the EDU 100 class. The students felt the EDU 100 and WRT 105 classes belonged and fit well in the ELLC. Students liked the roles the resident advisor and I played in their ELLC experience.

4. **Tell us about your experience at Delaware Academy.** Although the logistics of their experience got off to a shaky start, the students appreciated the experience and felt it was worthwhile. They felt the time commitment was a little too much for their busy schedules. They liked the impact they had on the staff and students at Delaware Academy. It also increased their personal passion for teaching.

5. **Tell us about ELLC pride.** The students have a lot of pride in being members of the ELLC. They liked being the first members of the ELLC and that what they had to say could shape the future of the ELLC. They liked having the opportunity to meet the faculty and administrators as a result of being part of the ELLC and that these individuals knew them by name.

PLANNING FOR THE FUTURE

It was clear to me from my own personal involvement as well as from the assessment data that the ELLC was worth offering for a second year. As a result of the information we collected from the first group of ELLC participants, I made the following adjustments:

- **Service-learning component.** I realized having the students do 20 visits to Delaware Academy was too much given the time commitment. I cut the requirement in half.

- **WRT 105.** I decided to share with the WRT 105 instructor the concerns students had regarding the disclosure of personal information in a writing class.

- **Number of ELLC members.** I felt 18 was too small, which might have led to some of the tensions felt by students. My goal was to fill the floor, which we did for year two.

CONCLUSION

Coordinating the Education Living Learning Community is an extremely satisfying experience. It is gratifying to watch as students grow and develop, both academically and personally, as they become acclimated to the university and the School of Education. I have enjoyed developing collaborative relationships not only with the students but also among the faculty and staff learning community participants. I am convinced, from my personal experience and a review of the assessment data, that the ELLC is a valuable experience for our first-year students and well worth continuing.

Amie Redmond is assistant dean in the School of Education at Syracuse University.

18

Creating an Online Learning Community

Mary Ann Middlemiss and Maureen Thompson

The online graduate nursing curriculum does not meet the Syracuse University guidelines for a learning community because it is not interdisciplinary. We include it here, however, because it provides insight into how a successful online learning community might be constructed.

*T*his chapter describes the development of a learning community in a graduate nursing program delivered in an online environment. Our graduate program culminates in a Master of Science degree in Nursing and is part of the Independent Study Degree Program (ISDP) at Syracuse University. Students in the program come to campus for brief annual residency periods followed by yearlong periods of distance learning. This population of working, professional adults is motivated and self-directed, and they value the exchange of ideas, knowledge, clinical expertise, and learning experiences. But, just as in the face-to-face classroom, these students need a social context for learning, and attention needs to be paid to developing a sense of community in order for their learning to be successful. With mature and motivated students, such as our experienced professional nurses, online courses and distance learning degree programs can achieve excellent results.

Despite its popularity, online teaching and learning remains a recent development in American higher education. This chapter discusses the historical development of an online learning community at Syracuse University's School of Nursing, factors contributing to success, issues to consider before embarking in this direction, and potential difficulties with suggestions for minimizing their impact. The final section offers some best practices for creating an online learning community, including specific learning activities to facilitate student interaction, collaboration, and cooperation.

How the Online Learning Community Evolved

In the nursing program, the concept of a learning community in computer-mediated distance education evolved over time. Through its Independent Study Degree Program, Syracuse University has enjoyed a long history of providing educational programs to those geographically isolated. In 1992, the School of Nursing first offered its graduate nursing program through the ISDP structure. As the name implies, the courses offered in this early program were primarily independent study format—with course materials being exchanged primarily through the U.S. mail and supported by occasional phone contact with the professor. During the annual residency period, the students met with faculty, participated in community building activities, and attended classes. From 1992 to1998, the program continued in this format. The students formed a cohesive group while away—emailing and using instant messaging. Without intending to do so, these students formed their own learning community. However, faculty members were often left out of this connective loop. They were viewed as experts who delivered information but were rarely contacted or consulted. During this time, some of the nursing faculty became disillusioned with the ISDP format.

From a teaching and learning perspective, it became apparent that the design of the residency period was ineffective, and change was necessary. However, the faculty wanted to keep intact those components of the residency that proved highly effective—the community building activities. In 2000, the independent nature of course delivery was abandoned, and a total computer-mediated or online approach to teaching and learning was initiated. The phrases computer-mediated distance education and online instruction are often used interchangeably. For our first year of online instruction, the faculty were chosen carefully—a commitment to computer-mediated distance education and to learning new interactive methods of course delivery was essential.

Students in the program remained relatively constant throughout the three years of study. This provided a distinct advantage to the development of a cohesive group. They met each other in the initial residency period and then maintained relationships through the interactive course activities. However, courses offered in the distance-learning program were not restricted to students enrolled in the ISDP; any main campus or non-matriculated student could also enroll. Having students come and go from course to course did not detract from the formation and sustaining of the learning communities. On the contrary, new students brought additional richness to the learning activities and dialogue.

FACTORS CONTRIBUTING TO SUCCESS

Many factors contribute to the development of a successful online graduate program. Success was generally defined by faculty as student satisfaction, the achievement of course and program objectives, and the quality of the faculty-student and student-student interactions and dialogue. The fact that faculty had previous experience with distance education made it easier to make the transition to online teaching. We knew who our students were likely to be, and the courses, which had been adapted for distance education, needed only modification for online delivery. Furthermore, the university had in place the infrastructure for distance education and a good beginning on the infrastructure necessary for online instruction.

The logistics of creating learning communities within an online teaching environment can be complicated by the associated technology. While the design of the courses was the responsibility of the faculty, the university was instrumental in providing the essential technological support.

The following support was provided by the university:

Centralized University Support

- *Course management software.* The course management software used provided the capability for the development of an interactive learning environment and supported group work for assignment completion.

- *Technology support at the macro level.* Frustration caused by the technology of online instruction can impede learning. Therefore, it is important that students feel comfortable with the technology. The university provided technological training to the faculty and ran a help-line to assist students and faculty experiencing difficulty.

School of Nursing Support

- *Computer and media services.* The School of Nursing employs a computer specialist who is available to assist faculty and staff with the technological aspects of course delivery.

- *Faculty development.* Monies were available for faculty members to attend workshops related both to online teaching and to the use of interactive teaching/learning strategies within an online teaching environment.

- *Secretarial training.* In-service instruction was provided for staff to become familiar with the course management software and to learn web-authoring software.

- *Teaching assistant support.* A teaching assistant was assigned to the program to assist the instructor with email management and to help students with course assignments.

OBJECTIVES

All of our online courses include learning objectives describing the knowledge, skills, and attitudes students should acquire by the end of each course. However, the online environment also requires that both faculty and students view the learning process as dynamic and share the responsibility for learning. Consequently, both faculty and students must facilitate learning and shape the learning environment to accommodate individual needs and learning styles. Thus, we included the following objectives:

1. Develop and sustain supportive, caring, connected, and empowering relationships

2. Connect the personal and professional experiences of a diverse population of students

3. Appreciate diverse ideas, values, perceptions, and experiences

4. Explore knowledge, skills, values, and professional practice from a community perspective

LEARNING COMMUNITY DESCRIPTION

A learning community is not likely to happen unless it is planned, nourished, and encouraged by faculty. Many activities used to create online learning communities are similar to those used in face-to-face classroom settings. However, modifications are necessary to adapt the learning activities to an online teaching environment and to incorporate learning strategies that promote the development of learning communities.

Judith Boettcher and Rita Conrad (1999) describe the importance of interaction, collaboration, and cooperation when building a community without face-to-face interaction. Interaction is usually the first step in the process of establishing a learning community and can be defined as a communication exchange between two or more people. It is usually short and does not result in a lasting relationship between the learners. Collaboration involves more commitment from the learner and occurs when students work together in small groups to complete learning exercises or assignments during a specified time period. The learning activity is short, and the students may not become interdependent or mutually supportive. Cooperation goes beyond collaboration. Cooperative groups work together over a longer period of time to complete a series of learning exercises or assignments. In cooperative groups, the faculty member monitors progress and provides guidance and support as needed. As students become more dependent on each other, they become more responsible for their learning and move closer to becoming a community.

Minimizing the Impact of Potential Difficulties

Establishing learning communities in an online environment is not without its difficulties. Faculty and students must learn to interact without the usual physical and verbal cues of face-to-face environments. This difficulty may be lessening as many learners currently use email and instant messaging in their day-to-day interaction with others. Unfamiliarity with the involved technology may inhibit active participation. Providing a sound orientation to the educational software may allay any initial frustration. The availability of support staff to assist with students' technological questions is also important. Courses that are self-paced do not lend themselves as well to community building as courses with defined time periods for assignment completion and discussion. As in traditional classroom settings, some students may seldom participate if cooperation and collaboration are not perceived as valuable and essential. To offset this problem, faculty may choose to include participation, effort, and quality in the overall course grade. And finally, misunderstandings can occur more easily and may take longer to resolve until students feel comfortable disagreeing in a text-based environment. But with discussion structure and rules, faculty guidance and support, and a focus on caring communication and relationships, most students overcome this challenge within a few weeks.

CREATING LEARNING COMMUNITIES IN AN ONLINE ENVIRONMENT: BEST PRACTICES

It is the course faculty's responsibility to create opportunities for community building. Strategies to promote interaction can occur in both asynchronous and synchronous environments. Asynchronous environments allow participants to log on to class or to discussion at any time. Thus, class participation occurs at the student's convenience and allows students time to read, process, and respond. Synchronous environments or chat rooms provide an opportunity for all participants to log on to a course site at once and interact with each other in real time. Asynchronous activities were more predominant in our course design and provided opportunities for reflection and thoughtful participation. Synchronous activities were used for more functional purposes—clarification, office hours, and information sharing. Examples of activities used to promote learning communities in online instruction are summarized in Table 18.1.

The following section describes selected learning activities and provides specific examples to highlight best practices, effective teaching strategies, and successful outcomes for graduate students with some knowledge and professional experience.

Course Introductions: Student Biographies

The course started with each participant posting a biography and her or his picture. Once all the biographies were posted, students were to read them and post a response on the discussion board to one classmate's biography. Similar introduction activities are often used in face-to-face classroom settings. But their time is limited, and some students feel uncomfortable sharing about themselves. Online students had the opportunity to offer more detailed disclosures leading to a more personal and professional sense of one another. This early connection is important because new students join the group each semester. Students who had been very quiet in traditional classroom settings were more willing to engage and to share in an online environment. The student biographies and responses illustrated the sense of community and connection the students were beginning to experience. After reading the biographies, one student offered this response: "Wow! What a diverse group of people we are. The mix is amazing. Everyone has so much to offer. How lucky we are to learn from our peers. We all bring with us individual experiences that are priceless. By sharing with each other, we can build our knowledge." Another student wrote: "As I look at the bios, I feel more connected to all of you and more comfortable discussing issues relating to this class."

Table 18.1

Activities to Promote Learning Communities

Asynchronous Activities	

Course introductions
  Students
  Instructor
  Greetings
	Students and instructors posted their biographical information and pictures on the course web site. Students were required to contact at least one classmate through the discussion board.
	
	A welcome letter was posted on the course web site. This greeting welcomed the students, offered suggestions to facilitate learning, described course format, and outlined expectations for both students and faculty. Students were invited to comment on course format, expectations, and content.

Icebreaker activity	The instructor posted pictures on the course web site. Each student reflected on one of the pictures and wrote a metaphor about learning and posted it to the discussion board.
Debate teams	These teams facilitated group cohesiveness and introduced students to the literature. Each team posted their position on the course website. An interactive dialogue followed on the discussion board.
Web site of the week	Each student presented a critical evaluation of a web site related to a course discussion topic. Other students reviewed the site as well and responded to their classmates' evaluation via the discussion board.
Virtual poster session	Students presented their electronic posters on the course web site. Poster session attendees read the information posted and posed questions to the author, who then responded to the questions via the discussion board.
Discussion	Focus questions and a threaded discussion board were used to facilitate critical thinking, reflection, and discussion.
Learning teams	Learning teams were formed to complete selected course assignments.
Journal Club	Student journal reviewers posted their critical reviews on the course web site. Other "club members" participated in an interactive discussion with the review on the discussion board.
Synchronous Activities	
Learning teams	Chat rooms were also used for learning team members to engage in real-time discussion.
Clinical conferencing	Students and clinical faculty engaged in real-time discussion related to clinical issues. Relevant clinical experiences and application of current clinical standards were also included.
Guest speakers	Mini-lectures, references, and other support material were first posted on the course web site. The guest speaker then engaged in real-time discussion with the students via the chat room.

Several students were touched by some of the text from an international classmate. She wrote:

> *I decided to travel 25,000 miles from my country to Syracuse, U.S.A., to learn more about differences in hospital experiences from different cultures. Being a foreigner without an English speaking background, I had faced many difficulties in the first few months of my stay here . . . Life is a little difficult in the United States for an international student like me. So I try to find pleasures in hobbies like cooking, swimming, and shopping every moment I miss home or have a difficult time . . . I put up a lot of information about myself and I hope that everybody gets to know me well. I hope we can be friends in this class. In addition, although I always try my best to speak and write English, sometimes I cannot be perfect at it. I hope everyone will understand and is willing to correct me at all times so that I can learn. Thank you for having me in this class.*

In an online environment, this very quiet student was able to connect with her classmates. Several classmates responded that they admired her courage and her willingness to express some of her vulnerabilities to strangers. The introductions were valuable for students and faculty to get to know one another as well as to appreciate the diversity of knowledge, skills, and other professional/personal experiences they represented.

Icebreaker Activity

An icebreaker labeled "Writing a Metaphor" gave students an opportunity to think about the meaningfulness of the course and to share meaning with classmates. One picture of a small boy throwing a ball provoked the most responses. One student stated, "I could say that the picture meant that learning should be fun. There are rules on how to play the game, but it should not be without the pleasure of doing it." Another student wrote, "When you see the learner is ready to play ball, catch the opportunity." Yet another student used this picture to describe the teacher's role: "I see the little boy as the teacher. The teacher is holding a lesson plan that is well rounded. It is a soft ball that can be thrown without harming the learner. The learner gains confidence in catching different kinds of throws—different ways of understanding the topic. The boy's smile represents the teacher's glee when the learner understands she can throw back other ideas that the teacher can grab on to. Learning is a collaborative process."

Learning Teams

Learning teams were particularly useful in promoting interaction and collaboration in an online environment. Learning teams were either self-selected, assigned for specific learning activities, or assigned by clinical area of specialization. Teams were used to facilitate small-group discussion, complete small-group assignments, and engage students in group activities. Sometimes students were assigned team roles such as team coordinator/leader/facilitator, process observer, content commentator, or presenter. These assigned roles ensured attention to group process and facilitated interaction within the team. Group members were responsible for discussing course content, problem solving, providing feedback, and ensuring mutual success for meeting learning outcomes (Stein & Hurd, 2000).

Discussion Board

Regular, ongoing participation in the course seminar discussion was expected. The purpose of participation through online discussion was to gain a deeper understanding of the seminar topics and to develop a community of learners. The following guidelines for online discussion were provided:

- Students prepare for seminar through reading, contemplation, and reflection

- Students share knowledge, ideas, and questions

- Students actively contribute to the development of a caring dialogue, one that is respectful, spirited, relevant, and knowledgeable

- Students offer and accept feedback to advance learning

- Students participate in self and peer evaluation

To add structure, the discussion board was set up in forums of discussion, and there can be several threads or conversations within each forum. Because students have more time to think and reflect in an asynchronous discussion environment, their responses to the topic areas were often more complex and in-depth than those typically observed in a traditional classroom. Students also were able to add to the discussion by posting relevant articles or web sites to the discussion. In this way, the students also actively contributed to the learning environment rather than primarily depending on faculty. Table 18.2 is excerpted from the discussion board and demonstrates its interactive quality.

Table 18.2

Current Forum: Week 5 Hypertension/Hypercholesteremia
Date: Sat Feb 9 2002 2:36 pm
Author: MT. (instructor) >
Subject: Cholesterol Screening
Considering your advance practice settings, how do they rate in regards to the NCEP or AAP recommendations for the detection and/or evaluation of cholesterol?

Date: Sun Feb 9 2002 9:34 am
Author: LB (student)
My preceptor keeps a pocket guide from NCEP ATPIII (National Cholesterol Education Program Adult Treatment Panel Recommendations) with him and uses it each time he sees patients. I copied the following guidelines into my pocket memo book for reference. Each patient is scored depending on if they have coronary heart disease or at risk (diabetes or comorbidities). The end goals for lipid levels are then determined by the score: If they have CHD the goals for LDL <100, Total cholesterol <200, HDL at or above 60, and Triglycerides <150 are discussed with the patient. Major risk factors such as smoking, HTN, low LDL (<40), family history of premature CHD (<55 if male, <65 if female) and present age men >45 and female >55 are looked at. My preceptor also has these guidelines on posters in the exam room (from pharmaceutical company) so it is easy to refer to and discuss with the patients. He seems to be aggressive in the detection and treatment of hypercholesterolemia. He recently started obtaining homocysteine levels as well.

Date: Wed Feb 13 2002 2:24 pm
Author: EJ (student)
My facility has a health maintenance sheet in the chart of every patient, included on this page is a lipid profile section. Although all adults over 20 years should have total cholesterol measured every five years, I often find the lipid profiles blank and no record of lipid screening in the lab section. I think Laura's preceptor is a great role model in having the protocols handy to show patients. I do think the HCPs address cholesterol levels in high-risk cardiac patients, but not always. Yesterday, I saw a patient with HTN (on statin therapy) and looked specifically for lipid levels on her and couldn't find any. When I asked about it, the NP working with me said that a cardiologist also saw the patient and that the cardiologist would follow the lipid levels. When patients with multiple problems see multiple specialists, sometimes important things can fall through the cracks. I requested that we get the reports from the cardiologist and documented that when she is seen in follow-up in two weeks that lipid screening be performed if needed (after determining when it was last done). Even though she sees a specialist, when acting as primary care providers, APNs should make sure that guidelines are being implemented and appropriately followed up on. I have seen that patients with high LDLs are being

placed primarily on statins, which is the first choice. I have also observed patients with primarily high triglycerides are appropriately placed on fibric acid derivatives.

Date: Wed Feb 13 2002 2:45 pm
Author: SW (student)
Well said, Joy. I also see health maintenance profile sheets in front of the chart. My preceptor tries to keep them up to date in her practice. I've tried making it a habit, no matter what has brought the person into the clinic, to refer to the health sheet just to make sure they haven't slipped through the cracks.

Journal Club

The journal club activity provided students the opportunity to share current clinical literature with their classmates. The student assigned to the reviewer role summarized a current clinical journal article and reported her commentary and/or interpretation of the article on the course web site. The student reviewer then served as moderator for the discussion period that followed. The other students and course instructor served as the audience and posted questions and comments to the student reviewer. Table 18.3 shows student questions and comments that were posted to SW, a student who provided a review of an article on acute coronary syndrome.

Table 18.3

Current Forum: Week 6 Journal Club: Cardiovascular Disease
Date: Tue Feb 19 2002 1:39 pm
Author: LB. (journal club participant) >
Susan - I enjoyed reading your Journal Club article and found the information useful. I appreciate the decision regarding the acute coronary syndrome now more than ever since my mother in law had an acute MI just before Christmas. The guidelines talked about in the article were basically what she experienced. I think the information you presented was a reflection of the nuts and bolts information that was in the article...the "down and dirty" as JD would say. While managing acute MI seems out of my league, I appreciate that the rapid identification of acute coronary syndrome is essential.

Date: Tue Feb 9 2002 3:47 pm
Author: SW (journal club reviewer, moderator)
You're right, it is the nuts and bolts of what to look for in ACS. I appreciated the article very much for that reason although I thought it got too vague when it came to treatments. Basically, other articles have said that the causes of cp [chest pain] most common in primary care are not ACS (unless it's an elderly pt) but more like musculoskeletal (36%). GI is 19%. BUT cardiac is as high as 50% in the older

population. What that said to me is be careful to rule it out and that's basically
what the article seemed to be stressing

Date: Tue Feb 19 2002 7:37 pm
Author: MM (journal club participant)
Susan—I really enjoyed your article this week. This is a subject near to my heart.
Quickly recognizing ACS in the primary care setting is a must. This will prevent
further delay for thrombolytic therapy and/or invasive interventions (angioplasty
with balloon procedure or stent if necessary).

In the primary care setting we are more likely to see an individual present with
atypical chest pain. The female patient may present more with atypical chest pain.
As you pointed out, negative EKG findings DOES NOT rule out ACS. Women
are more likely to not have Q waves present on the EKG. We should continue on
and obtain the cardiac enzymes (CK, CK-MB, and Troponion T/I).

In primary care, risk modification is key: statin (if appropriate), ASA, beta-blocker,
ace inhibitor, diet, exercise, yearly stress test to monitor disease progression, etc.

ASSESSMENT

As the learning moved from faculty-centered to student-centered instruction,
traditional faculty and student roles were redefined. Faculty moved away from
being the sole source of information to becoming facilitators, mentors, and
guides. Students moved from being passive learners to active, engaged learners
who shared resources, led discussions, and provided feedback, support, and
encouragement to each other.

Online relationships were supportive, caring, connected, and empowering. Initially, one student wondered how interpersonal relationships could or
would evolve. As the semester progressed, everyone began to relax. The language and feel of conversations changed. Students often communicated
online just as they would in a face-to-face classroom. They added emoticons
or symbols, such as ☺ (smiling), ☹ (frowning), %-) (braindead), :-o
(WOW), '-) (winking), etc., to clarify meanings and/or to express emotions
in their dialogue. By the end of the course, rapport among students and faculty was evident. A student commented, "A person's voice, reflections, facial
expressions, eye contact are all missing; yet somehow this was all conveyed
over the Internet."

Regardless of the setting, the creation of community greatly enhances the
learning experience and the likelihood of successful learning outcomes. In the
online classroom, the learning community takes on different dimensions. In

this environment, it is the relationships and interactions among students and between students and faculty through which knowledge is primarily generated. Thus, a strong learning community is critical to the success of online education.

In conclusion, a learning community for graduate nursing students can work with different populations and environments. However, the learning community must be developed and nurtured through careful planning by the faculty. It also requires the commitment of the class community to make it work. But increased student satisfaction and improved student learning outcomes are well worth the extra time and effort.

Mary Ann Middlemiss, PhD, RN and Maureen Thompson, PhD, APRN are faculty in the College of Health Professions and Human Services, both of Syracuse University.

REFERENCES

Boettcher, J., & Conrad, R. (1999). *Faculty guide for moving teaching and learning to the web.* Mission Viejo, CA: League for Innovation in the Community College.

Stein, R. F., & Hurd, S. (2000). *Using student teams in the classroom: A faculty guide.* Bolton, MA: Anker.

Additional Readings

Draves, W. (2000). *Teaching online.* River Falls, WI: LERN Books.

Palloff, R., & Pratt, K. (1999). *Building learning communities in cyberspace: Effective strategies for the online classroom.* San Francisco, CA: Jossey-Bass.

White, K., & Weight, B. (2000). *The online teaching guide: A handbook of attitudes, strategies, and techniques for the virtual classroom.* Boston, MA: Allyn and Bacon.

19

Interprofessional Learning Community

Mary Ann Middlemiss, Sudha Raj, Bruce Carter,
Luvenia Cowart, Mary Lynne Hensel, Tanya
Horacek, and Carrie Smith

The Human Services and Health Professions non-residential learning
community debuted in the fall of 2002. It is the most interdisciplinary
of SU's communities, bringing together faculty and students from four
related academic areas. A yearlong experience, it draws from both
undergraduate and graduate populations.

THE EVOLUTION OF THE INTERPROFESSIONAL LEARNING COMMUNITY

The Interprofessional Learning Community (IPLC), like many of the other learning communities developed at Syracuse University, evolved in response to the call by Vice Chancellor and Provost Deborah Freund for the development of learning communities in each school and college within the university. Unlike other schools and colleges on campus, the College of Human Services and Health Professions (HSHP) at Syracuse University is an amalgam of three existing academic units with divergent focuses. HSHP is comprised of the formerly independent School of Nursing, School of Social Work, and three departments (nutrition and hospitality management, child and family studies, and marriage and family therapy) from the College for Human Development. Because the planning for the Interprofessional Learning Community occurred during the inaugural year of HSHP, the IPLC represented both a shared project of the diverse groups constituting Syracuse University's newest college and a tangible integration of the fields of study and professional work going on in this college.

The IPLC has a number of elements that make it similar to other learning communities as well as elements that make it quite distinct. Like other learning communities, the IPLC focuses on academic work, primarily through a yearlong, 3-credit-hour course, and shared cultural activities (such as theater) whose focus is germane to the IPLC learning objectives. Unlike many other learning community models, the IPLC includes undergraduate and graduate students as well as faculty from majors within HSHP. Moreover, the IPLC challenges its members to explore their ideas and roles through the lens of interdisciplinary collaboration, and it is this interdisciplinary team approach that distinguishes our Interprofessional Learning Community. Students and faculty from the fields of nursing, social work, nutrition, and child and family studies work together on academic and service learning, seminars, and community action projects, melding their expertise and values and learning both about and from the backgrounds of the other participants.

From the beginning, we recognized the need for faculty involvement, participation, and collaboration from across the disciplines represented in our college. Thus, we launched our planning process with a group of interested faculty, appropriately called the HSHP Learning Community task force. Eighteen faculty originally expressed interest in forming an interprofessional learning community. These individuals attended a series of meetings and faculty forums to discuss the concept of an interprofessional learning community. Both attendance and commitment to the project were mixed. A number of organizing concepts and structures were proposed, discussed, and modified or discarded. After extensive dialogue, the sharing of ideas, and the clarification of expectations about anticipated commitments, time constraints, and other parameters, six faculty and two administrators remained involved and committed to the IPLC. Thus, we cautiously began the process of developing the skeleton of the Interprofessional Learning Community, adding depth and breadth to the project as it grew.

Initially, developing a learning community across academic disciplines seemed both difficult and challenging. However, anxiety and reservations quickly gave way to excitement, energy, and new supportive relationships. The task force began meeting in spring 2002, but most of the constructive work occurred during the summer months of 2002. Throughout this period, faculty met several hours a week to discuss, plan, and develop the program.

The chair of the IPLC task force, appointed by the dean of the college, provided leadership to the group as well as oversight for all administrative functions for the IPLC. These functions included planning focused agendas, scheduling speakers and meeting locations, facilitating meetings, promoting group cohesiveness and team spirit, and developing a public relations plan to keep HSHP and the university informed about the group's progress. The task force chair convened over 20 sessions during a six-month period. Meeting agendas were structured, yet open and flexible enough to encourage faculty dialogue and feedback concerning relevant issues and concerns. Various methodologies were used to facilitate discussions. These included speaker forums and presentations about successful learning communities within the university, personal interviews with the university's learning community faculty coordinator and residence life staff, panel discussions with experts in the field, brainstorming sessions, and directed reviews of both the research literature and data available online.

As suggested by our review of the learning community literature and consistent with the university's plans for learning communities, we focused our initial discussions on identifying a theme for our IPLC. As guest speakers shared their experiences, challenges, successes, and themes, we grew excited, but also anxious because nothing was similar to our emerging vision. Initially, our decision-making focused on exploring various themes. We quickly learned the primary factor for continued faculty commitment was professional interest in a theme and/or relevance to individual faculty's scholarship. After much brainstorming and spirited debate, we identified the theme of interprofessional collaboration, which is consistent with the mission of the College of Human Services and Health Professions. This theme also recognized faculty members' concerns about retaining their academic discipline identity and reflected our collective and individual visions of the nature of this learning community. Thus, we began to solidify as a team and to focus on exploring programmatic and curricular issues. Our emerging vision of the Interprofessional Learning Community called for an integration of a strong academic component for students and a commitment to the professional goals and aspirations of our college. We further agreed to the need for faculty and student interaction in the context of interdisciplinary teams.

Another critical decision for us, as with many learning communities, was to determine whether a residential or nonresidential environment was more appropriate. Most of the learning communities at Syracuse University have been designed as residential learning communities. Time constraints limited our planning to a nonresidential learning community due to the university's scheduling deadline for residence halls. The next steps seemed easier. Key to our organizational makeup was the chair of the IPLC Task Force. The infrastructure for our learning community evolved through her office and through faculty effort and participation. Faculty shared the workload and engaged in decision-making using a small-group structure. Groups of two to three faculty members worked on assigned topics, shared information either during scheduled meetings or electronically, and sought feedback and consensus from the planning group as a whole. Several development and implementation issues, such as our mission statement, objectives, and course syllabus, were discussed within small groups. Other tasks such as credit-bearing status, student population, selection criteria, retreat activities, and programming required large-group dialogue and discussion.

Early in the development process, we recognized that a retreat would facilitate orientation to the learning community experience for both students and faculty. We designed our retreat to provide an opportunity for students and faculty to come together early in the semester in a relaxing, nonthreatening environment, to become acquainted, to have fun, and to feel comfortable with the experience. Retreat activities included group preparation of the dinner meal, exercises designed to facilitate getting acquainted, the development of trust, team building, and learning more about the learning community concept. The collaboration among faculty, administrators, and staff from Syracuse University's Office of Residence Life resulted in a successful retreat, despite a few minor logistical concerns. Ultimately, the retreat provided an opportunity for faculty and students to enter the learning community experience together. The retreat evaluations indicated students were thrilled with the experience and strongly recommended future retreats. When asked whether their expectations for the retreat were met, students were uniformly positive. One student answered, "Yes, and far beyond! What an exceptional experience! I haven't had this much fun in a long time. I truly felt like I sprouted some deep connections with my team members." Following the retreat, students began to spread the word within the college and the university about the Interprofessional Learning Community. They looked forward to a collaborative experience with faculty and began their group activities with excitement and enthusiasm.

During our development process, we focused considerable attention on how we would introduce the learning community to the college and how we would keep the university population informed of our progress. First, we concentrated on developing an information brochure about the learning community. The brochure explained the learning community's background, mission, outcomes, and timeline and included faculty perspectives. These faculty perspectives were important because they helped promote approval and support among non-involved faculty. Here are two examples of faculty perspectives presented in the brochure:

The HSHP Learning Community is very exciting to me. It will give students an opportunity to be part of a creative and exceptional environment where both faculty and students learn and grow with each other. We will be exploring themes and components of self-awareness, diversity, poverty, welfare, global health and politics, utilizing unique venues for this learning process.

Mamie Hensel, Instructor, School of Nursing

I'm excited to work side-by-side with a team of HSHP students in the community. We will improve our understanding and challenge the effectiveness of the interprofessional connections and collaborations between our disciplines. Students in all my classes will benefit from what I learn and how I change as a result of the HSHP Learning Community.

Tanya M. Horacek, Assistant Professor, Department of Nutrition and Hospitality Management

The brochure proved popular and is used by the college enrollment management staff as a recruitment tool for incoming students as well as a means of soliciting participation in the Interprofessional Learning Community.

The College of Human Services and Health Professions provides the primary budget for the Interprofessional Learning Community. The HSHP dean publicly supports the learning community concept and provides resources and monies to ensure its success. In addition, as we have evolved into a more mature learning community, the university has supported our efforts through special resources, monies, and encouragement.

LEARNING OBJECTIVES

An advantage we had in planning our learning community was the generous assistance and guidance from our colleagues in the university community who had already gone through the process of initiating a learning community. In this regard, we were able to build upon their experiences and to envision a new model for our Interprofessional Learning Community. Like other learning communities at SU, well-conceived learning objectives were at the heart of the course planning for the HSHP Interprofessional Learning Community.

The process of developing our specific learning objectives required articulating a shared vision of an interdisciplinary learning experience among the diverse units that make up the College of Human Services and Health Professions. Needless to say, we engaged in numerous robust discussions about the professional core values of each of our disciplines and the academic and developmental needs of our students. Ultimately, we agreed upon a number of concepts and themes that represented consistent threads for the various professions. In addition, we expected our students to acquire particular knowledge, skills, and attitudes about the disciplines within HSHP. The following organizing concepts and themes emerged from our deliberations:

- Self-awareness (communication, values and attitudes, critical thinking, learning styles, teambuilding, and group process)

- Cultural awareness/competence (cultural assessment)

- Global health/social issue (poverty, welfare, health care systems)

- Policy advocacy

- Service learning (interprofessional teams)

- Ethics

Based upon the above organizing concepts, we developed the course objectives for the HSHP IPLC: To create a supportive and interprofessional learning environment in which students:

1. Establish partnerships within the HSHP academic community.

2. Demonstrate purposeful interaction, learning, and participation in the classroom and in the community.

3. Appreciate diverse perceptions of human services, health, and well being.

4. Foster an awareness and understanding of diversity issues.

5. Explore knowledge, skills, values, practice, and ethics relative to global health and social issues.

6. Develop and sustain collaborative partnerships within the community.

Throughout the process of developing the learning objectives, the group reflected on enhancing service learning through interdisciplinary exchanges among the units and fostering the students' appreciation of the interconnectedness of the professions represented. As we completed the task of writing the course objectives, we acknowledged that ours was a work in progress and would be revisited as we learned more about the unique needs of our learning community.

DESCRIPTION OF THE LEARNING COMMUNITY

The Interprofessional Learning Community is a non-residential learning community embedded in a three-credit course. The IPLC is composed of faculty, upper-class, and graduate students from most of the academic departments within the College of Health Services and Human Professions. The IPLC activities extend over the full academic year.

The learning community meets one night each month for three hours. The community always shares a meal together, which is either prepared by the participants, ordered, potluck, or brown bag. The academic component is focused to cover a different theme each month. For the first year, the themes include cultural competence, interprofessional competence, welfare and poverty, policy and advocacy, and health/social issues in a global context. In the second year, we plan to add a leadership theme to our IPLC. First-year activities that complement these themes include a cultural potluck dinner and sharing of cultural artifacts from community members; a welfare-poverty simulation followed by a discussion with a welfare recipient, a welfare advocate, and a social services administrator; a policy advocacy event; and attending cultural events with diversity themes as well as university-wide lectures focused on diversity.

Many activities in the learning community are accomplished by dividing the community into smaller faculty-led interprofessional teams. These teams meet face-to-face or via an online discussion board two times per month and complete 30 hours of community service. Based upon the interprofessional team's interests and in consultation with the Syracuse University Center for Public and Community Service, a community agency was selected for each team's service-learning activities. In collaboration with the selected community members, each team will assess, develop, and implement an interprofessional intervention for an identified community need. This year the teams are engaged in service-learning activities at a senior citizen center, at a local Boys and Girls Club, and at a food pantry. The activities are designed to allow participants to share their developing (in the case of students) and professional (in the case of faculty) perspectives and include ample time for discussion of their experiences.

The course is managed via a grade contract. The syllabus outlines specific requirements and activities that students must complete in order to receive a particular grade. Students decide which assignments they wish to do for the grade they desire to earn. For a C grade, students must participate in large-group and team meetings, the retreat, and the welfare-poverty simulation and complete a learning log of their experiences with the learning community. For a B grade, students add two lectures or plays over the course of the year and are required to provide comments in their learning log and complete the transcultural and interprofessional awareness and competence assessment (which can also be incorporated into their learning log). For the students desiring an A grade (fully 99% of the class), students add two additional lectures and/or plays and make a final presentation analyzing their experiences over the entire year.

RECRUITING STUDENTS

Once the learning community was organized, department chairs and faculty were invited to nominate students who met certain published criteria. All department chairs were provided with the mission, objectives, and summary of events for the learning community. Over the summer, nominated students were sent an invitation letter. A few students decided to join based upon this initial invitation. At the beginning of the fall semester, brochures and flyers were distributed to departments and to HSHP faculty, with the request to refer interested students to one of the learning community faculty. The best recruitment method turned out to be personal contacts that learning community faculty made with students during early fall semester advising and orientation sessions. The learning community purposely started in late September to accommodate these additional recruitment efforts. Our first semester learning community included 14 students, six faculty, and two administrators.

In the future, current learning community students will help recruit students during the spring semester, thus allowing us to start our community at the beginning of the fall semester. This effort will facilitate decision-making about community meeting times and team organization more conducive to individual schedules, professional diversity, and learning goals. Additionally, students need to know the expectation of attendance at the retreat well in advance. Although this requirement was advertised on all materials distributed, a few students missed its significance. As a result, several students who intended to join in late September had a conflict with the retreat date and could not participate in the IPLC, as student participation in the retreat was a minimum requirement.

ASSESSMENT

Initially, success was defined as the intensity of interest, motivation, participation, and enthusiasm demonstrated by the students. However, as faculty involved in a new endeavor, we knew we needed to have clear and public criteria for both students and faculty. The IPLC syllabus clearly described all learning activities, assignments, and grading criteria for each level of the grade contract. Students contracted for the assignments and activities required for their chosen grade. Once the grade contract was complete, students had the option for a lower grade but they could not decide on a higher grade. Grading rubrics were used for all learning activities and assignments. These rubrics provided consistency and clarity for completing and scoring activities and assignments. During orientation, all students completed a self-assessment questionnaire, which asked students to respond to questions about ethnicity, culture, family, communication, knowledge of self, health, professional collaboration, and commonly held beliefs and values. The welfare poverty simulation used pre-and post-assessments to measure students' ethical attitudes toward welfare and poverty.

However, there is no better assessment about our IPLC success than that expressed by the students. In particular, students reported that their expectations for the retreat were met and in most cases exceeded. According to several students, the opportunity to mingle with faculty on a personal level was very rewarding. As one student said: "We've shared experiences that have brought us together, making me feel connected with other students and the faculty." Another student commented: "It's wonderful to break out of the teacher-student roles and to see faculty as multi-faceted people." Faculty also had some strong opinions about the mutual collaboration and emerging relationships. "Getting to know students from other disciplines, knowing the names and the strengths of students made me feel more connected to the students in the IPLC," one faculty participant remarked. "Observing leaders emerging" was rewarding for another faculty member.

Ongoing assessments include journal entries, discussions, focus questions, and scheduled opportunities for faculty and students to share ideas and suggestions about our emerging community. As our first semester ended, students wrote:

> *The learning community has been the best experience in my college career so far. The interprofessional learning is so unique and brought out in a fun and exciting way! I am so glad I decided to be part of this family.*
> Alicia Tural, Junior, School of Nursing

> *The learning community has been an environment where I have experienced issues of diversity in new and innovative ways. It is a community that values comfort and respect, and because*

all issues are approached from this place, together we can discuss issues not normally tackled in regular classes.

Sarah Young, Junior, School of Social Work

It's opened my eyes and helped me reach outside the box. It's much more than a class, which has helped me break stereotypes and accept my classmates in a different way. I'm really glad I started the learning community. It's awesome to interact with my professors on a unique level. I've enjoyed my time. It's been well spent.

Katie Calhoun, Senior, Department of Nutrition

CONCLUSIONS

As this chapter is being written, the Interprofessional Learning Community is completing its very first semester. We have not completed a formal evaluation of the IPLC to date as we are only midway through this full-year learning community. Nonetheless, certain observations and comments by students have allowed us to resolve problems that have arisen and have influenced our plans for the second semester and for our second year.

Our ongoing evaluation of the IPLC has led us to recognize the difficulty of coordinating the activities of students who maintain a rigorous academic schedule and are involved in many extracurricular activities, student internships, and professional training activities (e.g., clinical practice). This recognition dictates that we work assiduously to ensure that IPLC activities form an integral part of student schedules. Similarly, we have recognized the need to coordinate the service-learning experiences of students and integrate them within the broader context of the IPLC experience. These and other issues have been addressed and we anticipate creative solutions to future problems that arise.

In summary, student responses to the Interprofessional Learning Community experience have been overwhelmingly positive. Students and faculty participants alike have noted the valuable insights that have resulted from teams with diverse backgrounds and experiences working together in service-learning contexts (such as work at the food pantry) and discussing the perspectives derived from cultural (e.g., plays), academic (e.g., the welfare poverty simulation), and didactic (e.g., lectures) experiences. Exposure to the differing perspectives, issues, and questions raised by persons with diverse backgrounds (students and faculty, nurses and social workers, etc.) has benefited the participants in many ways. Such benefits include a broader appreciation of the issues pertinent to any given social issue or problem, an increased awareness of the professional skills that colleagues from different backgrounds may bring to bear in addressing a particular issue, and an appreciation of the benefits that interprofessional collaboration may provide for both the service providers and the recipients of service. We expect that students' appreciation of these and other issues will increase over the remainder of this year's learning community and that we will be able to improve student experiences in the subsequent years. The success of our efforts is highlighted by student interest, three months into the project, in the possibility of participating in the IPLC beyond the second semester of this academic year.

The Interprofessional Learning Community offers a different model from most of the other learning communities implemented on our campus. Rather than focusing on one particular topic or issue, our IPLC attempts to integrate the skills, attitudes, and interests of students and faculty from diverse professional and academic backgrounds. We attempt to provide students with a variety of experiences that call upon the various components their professions inculcate in their practitioners. Moreover, we endeavor to give our students the means of integrating their own and other professionals' perspectives in coordinated team-based efforts. Our hope is that the IPLC will provide our students with experiences and values that will serve their needs as human services and health professionals in the future.

Mary Ann Middlemiss, PhD, RN; Sudha Raj, PhD, RD; Bruce Carter, PhD; Mary Lynne Hensel, MS, RN; Tanya Horacek, PhD, RD; Carrie Smith, PhD, MSW are all faculty at the College of Human Services and Health Professions; and Luvenia Cowart, PhD, RN is assistant dean of the College of Human Services and Health Professions, all of Syracuse University.

20

Lessons Learned: A Summary of the Learning Communities' Experiences

Sandra N. Hurd and Ruth Federman Stein

This chapter includes some general observations and key lessons learned as learning communities were established at Syracuse University.

GENERAL OBSERVATIONS

As one reads about learning communities, whether the articles included in the bibliography or the chapters in this book written by the faculty and staff who have designed and implemented learning communities, there are clear themes that rise to the level of general observations about what makes learning communities work and why. We have picked four of the most striking to highlight in this chapter.

Academic Affairs–Student Affairs Partnership

For freshman residential learning communities in particular, the stronger and better the academic affairs–student affairs partnership, the more effective the learning community. Faculty and student affairs professionals bring different sets of knowledge and skills to the table. Faculty are experts in their discipline and the content of the academic courses they teach. Student affairs professionals are experts in student intellectual and moral development, and they understand the culture of the residence halls and how students live their daily lives. They are also more likely to be conversant with popular culture. When they draw on each other's strengths and expertise in creating a learning experience that seamlessly combines in-class and out-of-class elements, the result is a powerful learning environment that is greater than the sum of its parts. The partnership must be an authentic one, however, for it to be effective. If it appears to the students that the faculty and student affairs professionals value in- and out-of-class learning differently or if they act in ways that signal differences in status and power, the students will follow suit and much of the value of the attempted collaboration will be lost. When faculty and student affairs professionals forge collaborations that operate successfully on both the explicit and implicit levels, they create and model for the students the best kinds of learning environments.

Time on Task

Students who live together and take classes together spend more time on academic pursuits—the "time on task" that is so critical to the learning process. Because they are in classes together, they are more likely to be responsible for themselves and each other about attending class regularly. They are also more likely to complete academic tasks. When help is just a door or two away if they get stuck on a problem, don't understand the text, or aren't clear on how to complete an assignment, they are simply less likely to give up and do something else instead. Finally, they are more apt to attend an evening lecture, review session, play, or concert. They are encouraged by faculty and student affairs professionals to attend, it is easy to communicate about such activities, and when they make plans as a group they are less likely to decide not to go at the last minute.

Deeper Learning

Closely related to time on task is the deeper learning achieved by students in residential learning communities. They are more likely to participate in class—asking questions, answering questions, and sharing their insights— request help when they need it, and take intellectual risks. Because of the community they have built, they feel more comfortable with their classmates and their faculty. They also talk more about what they are learning in class as they walk to and from classes, eat together in the dining hall, or spend out-of-class time with faculty and student affairs professionals. Finally, they tend to form natural study groups, collaborative learning environments that are more effective in most cases than studying alone. They are engaged in their learning. In some instances, these benefits extend to nearby students who are not actually part of the learning community but are drawn into academic conversations and join in study groups.

Building Relationships

An important factor contributing to a student's success and satisfaction is building a relationship with a faculty member or student affairs professional early on in her or his academic career. Learning communities can extend dramatically the network of relationships with faculty and student affairs professionals that students develop. Imagine the power of developing multiple such relationships as a first-semester freshman. Even if these particular relationships do not endure, and many of them do, the student has learned much about how to develop other relationships with faculty and student affairs professionals in the future.

COMMON THEMES

Despite the wide variation among the many kinds of learning communities at Syracuse University, the lessons learned from establishing each of these learning communities contain a number of common themes and threads. The faculty and staff involved in creating learning communities inevitably go through similar stages as the learning communities evolve: determining what kind of a learning community they want, creating the academic component(s), establishing learning objectives, recruiting students, assessing the impact of the learning community, and using the assessment to make changes.

Learning Objectives

Each learning community at Syracuse University is expected to develop learning objectives, and each learning community struggles with this task. Trying to clarify exactly what the learning community is attempting to do turns out to be a significant part of the development of the learning community as it forces the faculty and staff to find just the right words to describe, in a way that everyone can agree upon, exactly what the learning community is striving to do for the students participating in it. As people work on the learning objectives, they learn that faculty, administrators, and residence life staff often do have the same goals and concerns; they just use different language. Writing everything down forces people to negotiate the language and goals. The learning community staff also learn that it is important to revisit learning objectives each year as their understanding grows and as different faculty and staff participate in the learning community.

Recruiting Students

Recruiting students for the first iteration of any learning community is difficult. There is no product for students to see when they visit the campus and no history to relate. Students are recruited to participate in a concept that is new and has no track record. To recruit students for the first year of a learning community, letters and personal contact are essential. After the first year, students who were in the learning community become the best recruiters, and the recruiting is much easier the second time around. Because most of the learning communities at Syracuse are residential, careful recruiting is needed so that students don't select the learning community because they want a particular kind of housing; they need to be committed to the community.

Bonding

A learning community is not for all students, and learning communities should not be required. Many students, however, value educational experiences that get them involved, and learning communities provide natural opportunities for engagement and active participation. One of the best ways to jumpstart early bonding for students in the learning community is to hold a retreat. Overnight retreats are especially effective in helping students bond. Many Syracuse University learning communities hold their retreats at a nearby ropes course. Activities on the ropes force students to communicate, to depend on each other for support (mentally and physically), and to bond with each other through this experience. Some learning communities create other ways of bonding. The Online Learning Community students put their bios and pictures online and also do an icebreaker activity. The Interprofessional Learning Community always shares a meal together, either potluck, prepared by the participants, or brown bag. Planning some type of early bonding experience helps the members of the learning community connect with each other more quickly.

Academics

A strong academic component is vital for an effective learning community, and having a required course is imperative for good participation. If the course is an independent study, often it will not count toward graduation for students, and this excludes students who otherwise want to participate. Since the primary goal of learning communities is learning, developing a strong academic component is a major task. Students value the special relationships they develop with faculty when they are in a learning community. They also value educational experiences that get them involved, and learning communities provide those venues. Additionally, one of the benefits of teaching students who live together is that they can work together on projects outside of class or simply help and support each other.

Residential Learning Communities

Residential learning communities have enormous potential because students not only take classes together but also can do other related activities through residence hall programming. Creating residential communities, however, requires close cooperation with housing and residence life offices. First, the type of residence hall and the number of rooms for the learning community must be determined, and enough students have to be recruited for the particular learning community. It is also important to have a serious commitment from the director of the particular residence hall and to have the director involved in the actual planning. The resident advisor (RA) should also be committed to the learning community concept because the RA helps coordinate the residence life activities that tie into the learning community; carefully designed activities are a key component in creating a cohesive community. Also, clear delineation of who has primary responsibility for various community activities is vital.

Assessment

Everyone from administrators, residence life staff, and faculty want to know how the learning community is working, so assessment is expected and essential. It's important not to over assess. Rather, assessment should be embedded in both curriculum and residential experiences so that providing feedback becomes part of the regular academic and social life. For example, keeping reflective journals can be required in a writing course, or students can respond to residence hall activities in a common journal. Group journals not only help to assess the learning community environment, but also help faculty become aware of issues such as students feeling overwhelmed or worried.

One purpose of assessment should be to collect inforr ion for improving the learning community for the following year; faculty and residence life staff should also be included in the assessment effort becaus they, too, will have ideas for improving the community.

Quantitative assessment measures the grade point average and retention data that is important for administrators, but it doesn't capture how students feel about the experience, or what should be kept, and what should be modified for the next iteration of the learning community. It's important to use methods such as focus groups or interviews to collect valuable information from students that can be incorporated into the next year's planning.

Student Voices

Above all, listen to students! Whenever possible, involve students in making change happen. Give students ownership and give them responsibility.

Through ownership and responsibility, they will feel more connected and will learn and gain more from being in a learning community.

Sandra N. Hurd is professor of law and public policy in the Whitman School of Management and director of learning communities for academic affairs, and Ruth Federman Stein is a teaching consultant at the Center for Support of Teaching and Learning, both of Syracuse University.

Bibliography

American Association for Higher Education (AAHE). (1992). *Principles of good practice for assessing student learning.* Washington, DC: American Association for Higher Education.

American Association for Higher Education (AAHE), American College Personnel Association (ACPA), & National Association of Student Personnel Administrators (NASPA). (1998). *Powerful partnerships: A shared responsibility for learning.* Washington, DC: Author.

American College Personnel Association (ACPA). (1994). *The student learning imperative: Implications for student affairs.* Washington, DC: Author. Retrieved February 25, 2003, from http://www.acpa.nche.edu/sli/sli.htm

American College Personnel Association (ACPA), & National Association of Student Personnel Administrators (NASPA). (1997). *Principles of good practice for student affairs.* Washington, DC: Author.

Angelo, T. A. (1993). A "teacher's dozen": Fourteen general, research-based principles for improving higher learning in our classrooms. *AAHE Bulletin, 13,* 3–7.

Angelo, T. A. (1997). The campus as learning community: Seven promising shifts and seven powerful levers. *AAHE Bulletin, 49*(9), 3–6.

Angelo, T. A., & Cross, K. P. (1993). *Classroom assessment techniques: A handbook for college teachers* (2nd ed.). San Francisco, CA: Jossey-Bass.

Arminio, J. (1994). Living-learning centers: Offering students an enhanced college experience. *Journal of College and University Student Housing, 24*(1), 12–17.

Arms, V. M. (1998). A learning community for professionals: The new engineering curriculum. *Metropolitan Universities, 9*(1), 63–72.

Association of American Colleges. (1991). *Liberal learning and the arts and sciences major: The challenges of connected learning* (Vol. 1). Washington, DC: Author.

Astin, A. W. (1984). Student involvement: A developmental theory for higher education. *Journal of College Student Personnel, 25,* 297–308.

Astin, A. W. (1985). *Achieving educational excellence: A critical assessment of priorities and practices in higher education.* San Francisco, CA: Jossey-Bass.

Astin, A. W. (1985). Involvement: The cornerstone of excellence. *Change, 17*(4), 35–39.

Astin, A. W. (1991). *Assessment for excellence: The philosophy and practice of assessment and evaluation in higher education.* New York, NY: American Council on Education/Macmillan.

Astin, A. W. (1997). *What matters in college: Four critical years revisited.* San Francisco, CA: Jossey-Bass.

Avens, C., & Zelley, R. (1992). *QUANTA: An interdisciplinary learning community (four studies).* Daytona Beach, FL.: Daytona Beach Community College. (ERIC Document Reproduction Service No. ED 349 073)

Baker, P. (1999). Creating learning communities: The unfinished agenda. In B. A. Pescosolido & R. Aminzade (Eds.), *The social worlds of higher education* (pp. 95–109). Thousand Oaks, CA: Pine Forge Press.

Banta, T. W., & Kuh, G. D. (1998). A missing link in assessment. *Change, 30*(2), 40–46.

Barefoot, B. O., Fidler, D. S., Gardner, J. N., Moore, P. S., & Roberts, M. R. (1999). A natural linkage—The first-year seminar and the learning community. In J. H. Levine (Ed.), *Learning communities: New structures, new partnerships for learning* (pp. 78–86). Columbia, SC: University of South Carolina, National Resource Center for the First-Year Experience and Students in Transition.

Barr, R. B. (1998). Obstacles to implementing the learning paradigm: What it takes to overcome them. *About Campus, 2*(3), 18–25

Barr, R. B., & Tagg, J. (1995, November/December). From teaching to learning: A new paradigm for undergraduate education. *Change,* 13–25.

Bateman, W. (1990). *Open to question: The art of teaching and learning by inquiry.* San Francisco, CA: Jossey-Bass.

Baxter Magolda, M. B. (1992). *Knowing and reasoning in college: Gender-related patterns in students' intellectual development.* San Francisco, CA: Jossey-Bass.

Bean, J. C. (1996). *Engaging ideas: The professor's guide to integrating writing, critical thinking, and active learning in the classroom.* San Francisco, CA: Jossey-Bass.

Belenky, M., Clinchy, B., Goldberger, N., & Tarule, J. (1986). *Women's ways of knowing: The development of self, voice, and mind.* New York, NY: Basic Books.

Bennett, J. (1999). Learning communities, academic advising, and other support programs. In J. H. Levine (Ed.), *Learning communities: New structures, new partnerships for learning,* Columbia, SC: University of South Carolina, National Resource Center for the First-Year Experience and Students in Transition.

Berlin, J. (1996). *Rhetorics, poetics, and cultures: Refiguring college English studies.* Urbana, IL: National Council of Teachers of English.

Bess, J. L. (2000). *Teaching alone, teaching together: Transforming the structure of teams for teaching.* San Francisco, CA: Jossey-Bass.

Blake, E. S. (1979). Classroom and context: An educational dialectic. *Academe,* 280–292.

Blake, E. S. (1996). The yin and yang of student learning in college. *About Campus, 1*(4), 4–9.

Blimling, G. S. (1993). The influence of college residence halls on students. In J. C. Smart (Ed.), *Higher education: Handbook of Theory and Research* (Volume 9, pp. 248–307). New York, NY: Agathon.

Blimling, G. S., & Hample, D. (1970). Structuring the peer environment in residence halls to increase academic performance in average-ability students. *Journal of College Student Personnel, 20*(4), 310–316.

Blimling, G. S., & Schuh, J. H. (Eds.). (1981). *New directions for student services: No. 13. Increasing the educational role of residence halls.* San Francisco, CA: Jossey-Bass.

Bloland, P. A., Stamatakos, L. C., & Rogers, R. R. (1996). Redirecting the role of student affairs to focus on student learning. *Journal of College Student Development, 37*(2), 217–226.

Bloom, B. (1956). *Taxonomy of educational objectives: The classification of education goals: Handbook I. Cognitive domain.* London, England: Longman, Green.

Board of Regents. (2003). *History of ILS and the Meiklejohn house.* Madison, WI: University of Wisconsin. Retrieved February 26, 2003, from http://www.wisc.edu/ils/history.html

Boettcher, J., & Conrad, R. (1999). *Faculty guide for moving teaching and learning to the web.* Mission Viejo, CA: League for Innovation in the Community College.

Borden, V., & Rooney P. M. (1998). Evaluating and assessing learning communities. In J. H. Levine (Guest Ed.), *Metropolitan Universities* [Special Issue: Learning Communities], *9*(1), 73–88.

Boyer Commission on Educating Undergraduates in the Research University. (1998). *Reinventing undergraduate education: A blueprint for America's research universities.* Stanford, CA: Carnegie Foundation for the Advancement of Teaching.

Boyer, E. L. (1987). *College: The undergraduate experience in America.* New York, NY: Harper & Row.

Boyer, E. L. (1990). *Scholarship reconsidered: Priorities of the professoriate.* Princeton, NJ: The Carnegie Foundation for the Advancement of Teaching.

Brady, S. (1999). Students at the center of education: A collaborative effort. *Liberal Education, 85*(1), 14–21.

Brookfield, S. D. (1995). *Becoming a critically reflective teacher.* San Francisco, CA: Jossey-Bass.

Brookfield, S. D., & Preskill, S. (1999). *Discussion as a way of teaching: Tools and techniques for democratic classrooms.* San Francisco, CA: Jossey-Bass.

Brown, J. (1997). On becoming learning organizations. *About Campus, 1*(6), 5–13.

Brown, R. D. (1974). Student development and residence education: Should it be social engineering? In D. DeCoster & P. Mable (Eds.), *Student development and education in college residence halls.* Cincinnati, OH: American College Personnel Association.

Brown, R. D., Knoll, R. E., Donaldson, C., & Ensz, G. (1975). Making a living unit work: One student, one professor, and an idea. *Journal of College Student Personnel, 16,* 24–29.

Bruffee, K. A. (1984). Collaborative learning and the "Conversation of Mankind." *College English, 46*(7), 635–652.

Bruffee, K. A. (1985). *A short course in writing: Practical rhetoric for teaching composition through collaborative learning.* Boston, MA: Little Brown & Company.

Bruffee, K. A. (1987). The art of collaborative learning. *Change, 3,* 42–47.

Bruffee, K. A. (1999). *Collaborative learning: Higher education, interdependence and the authority of knowledge* (2nd ed.). Baltimore, MD: The Johns Hopkins University Press.

Burns, J. S. (1995). Leadership studies: A new partnership between academic departments and student affairs. *NASPA Journal, 32,* 242–250.

Bystrom, V. A. (1997). Getting it together: Learning communities. In W. E. Campbell & K. A. Smith (Eds.), *New paradigms for college teaching* (pp. 243–267). Minneapolis, MN: Interaction Book Company.

Bystrom, V. A. (1999). Learning communities in the community college. In J. H. Levine (Ed.), *Learning communities: New structures, new partnerships for learning* (pp. 87–95). Columbia, SC: University of South Carolina, National Resource Center for the First-Year Experience and Students in Transition.

Cabral, A. C. (1995). Evaluation of transferable academic skills. *Integrating community service and academics: A manual for faculty.* Rochester, NY: Nazareth College.

Campbell, W. E., & Smith, K. A. (Eds.). (1997). *New paradigms for college teaching.* Minneapolis, MN: Interaction Book Company.

Centra, J. A. (1968). Student perceptions of residence hall environments: Living-learning versus conventional units. *Journal of College Student Personnel, 4,* 266–272.

Chamberlain, P. C. (1979). Evaluating a living-learning program. In G. Kuh (Ed.), *Evaluation in student affairs.* Cincinnati, OH: American College Personnel Association.

Chickering, A. W., & Gamson, Z. F. (1987). Seven principles of good practice in higher education. *AAHE Bulletin, 39*(7), 3–6.

Chickering, A. W., & Gamson, Z. F. (Eds.). (1991). *New directions for teaching and learning: No. 47. Applying the seven principles of good practice in higher education*. San Francisco, CA: Jossey-Bass.

Christensen, C. R., Garvin, D. A., & Sweet, A. (1991). *Education for judgment: The artistry of discussion leadership*. Boston, MA: Harvard Business School Press.

Clifford, J. (1991). The subject in discourse. In P. Harkin & J. Schilb (Eds.), *Contending with words: Composition and rhetoric in a postmodern age* (pp. 38–51). New York, NY: Modern Language Association.

College of Literature, Science, and the Arts, University of Michigan. (1995, March). *Restructuring the first-year experience: Final report*. Ann Arbor, MI: Author.

Coplin, W. D. (2000). *How you can help: An easy guide to doing good deeds in your everyday life*. New York, NY: Routledge.

Cornwell, G. H., & Stoddard, E. (1997). Residential colleges: Laboratories for teaching through difference. In R. Guarasci & G. Cornwell (Eds.), *Democratic education in an age of difference: Redefining citizenship in higher education* (pp. 73–106). San Francisco, CA: Jossey-Bass.

Council of Writing Program Administrators. (1999). The WPA outcomes statement for first-year composition. *WPA: Writing Program Administration, 23*(1/2), 59–66. Retrieved December 24, 2003, from http://www.english.ilstu.edu/Hesse/outcomes.html

Creed, T. (1997a). A virtual communal space. *The National Teaching and Learning Forum, 6*(5), 5–6.

Creed, T. (1997b). Choosing a virtual communal space for your course. *The National Teaching and Learning Forum, 7*(1), 3–5.

Creeden, J. (1998). Student affairs biases as a barrier to collaboration: A point of view. *NASPA Journal, 26,* 60–63.

Cross, K. P. (1998). Why learning communities? Why now? *About Campus, 3*(3), 4–11.

Cross, K. P. (1999). *Learning is about making connections*. Phoenix, AZ: League for Innovation in the Community College.

Cross, K. P. (2000). *Collaborative learning 101*. Phoenix, AZ: League for Innovation in the Community College.

Cross, K. P., & Steadman, M. H. (1996). *Classroom research: Implementing the scholarship of teaching.* San Francisco, CA: Jossey-Bass.

Crowley, S. (1998). *Composition in the university: Historical and polemical essays.* Pittsburgh, PA: University of Pittsburgh Press.

Cullen, R. J. (1985, Spring). Writing across the curriculum: Adjunct courses. *ADE Bulletin, 80,* 15–17.

Cuseo, J. S. (1991). *The freshman orientation seminar: A research-based rationale for its value, delivery, and content* (The First-Year Experience Monograph Series No. 4). Columbia, SC: University of South Carolina, National Resource Center for the First-Year Experience and Students in Transition.

Davis, B. G. (1993). *Tools for teaching.* San Francisco, CA: Jossey-Bass.

Davis, J. R. (1995). *Interdisciplinary courses and team teaching: New arrangements for learning.* Phoenix, AZ: ACE/Oryx.

DeCoster, D. A., & Mable, P. (1974). Residence education: Purpose and process. In D. A. DeCoster, & P. Mable (Eds.), *Student development and education in college residence halls.* Cincinnati, OH: American College Personnel Association.

Deppe, M. J., & Davenport, F. G. (1996). Expanding the first-year experience: A report for Hamline University. *About Campus, 1*(4), 27–30.

Dewey, J. (1916). *Democracy and education.* New York, NY: Macmillan.

Diamond, R. (1998). *Designing and assessing courses and curricula.* San Francisco, CA: Jossey-Bass.

Draves, W. (2000). *Teaching online.* River Falls, WI: LERN Books.

Duke, A. (1996). *Importing Oxbridge: English residential colleges and American universities.* New Haven, CT: Yale University Press.

Duncan, C. M., & Stoner, K. L. (1976). The academic achievement of residents living in a scholar residence hall. *Journal of College and University Housing, 6*(2), 7–10.

Ebert, D. (1999). Learning communities and collaborative teaching: An interdisciplinary approach for increasing student success and retention. *International Journal of Innovative Higher Education, 13,* 22–26.

Eby, K. K., & Gilbert, P. R. (2000). Implementing new pedagogical models: Using undergraduate teaching assistants in a violence and gender learning community. *Innovative Higher Education, 25*(2), 127–142.

Education. (2000, November/December). *Brown Alumni Magazine, 101.* Retrieved December 12, 2002, from http://www.brown.edu/Administration/Brown_Alumni_Magazine/01/11-00/features/education.html

Elliot, J., & Decker, E. (1999). People, structure, funding and context: Resources for learning communities. In J. H. Levine (Ed.), *Learning communities: New partnerships for learning.* Columbia, SC: University of South Carolina, National Resource Center for the First-Year Experience and Students in Transition.

Ely, D. (1990, Winter). Conditions that facilitate the implementation of education technology innovations. *Journal of Research on Computing in Education, 23*(2), 298–305.

Ender, S. C., Newton, F. B., & Caple, R. B. (Eds.). (1996). *New directions for student services: No. 75. Contributing to learning: The role of student affairs.* San Francisco, CA: Jossey-Bass.

Engstrom, C. M., & Tinto, V. (2000). Developing partnerships with academic affairs to enhance student learning. In M. J. Barr & M. K. Desler (Eds.), *The handbook of student affairs administration* (2nd ed., pp. 425–452). San Francisco, CA: Jossey-Bass.

Erickson, B. L., & Strommer, D. W. (1991). *Teaching college freshmen.* San Francisco, CA: Jossey-Bass.

Evenbeck, S. E., & Foster, M. C. (1996). *The urban university first-year experience: Building community benefits faculty and other university professionals and serves students well.* Washington, DC: ERIC Clearinghouse on Higher Education. (ERIC Document Reproduction Service No. ED 418 608)

Evenbeck, S. E., Jackson, B., & McGrew, J. (1999). Faculty development in learning communities: The role of reflection and reframing. In J. H. Levine (Ed.), *Learning communities: New structures, new partnerships for learning* (pp. 51–58). Columbia, SC: University of South Carolina, National Resource Center for the First-Year Experience and Students in Transition.

Evenbeck, S. E., & Williams, G. (1998). Learning communities: An instructional team approach. In J. H. Levine (Guest Ed.), *Metropolitan Universities* [Special Issue: Learning Communities], *9*(1), 35–46.

The Evergreen State University. (n.d.). *Learning community commons.* Olympia, WA: Author. Retrieved December 29, 2003, from http://learningcommons.evergreen.edu

Ewell, P. T., & Jones D. P. (1993). Actions matter: The case for indirect measures in assessing higher education's progress on the National Education Goals. *Journal of General Education, 42,* 123–148.

Fiechtner, S. B., & Davis, E. A. (1984/1985). Why some groups fail: A survey of students' experiences with learning groups. *The Organizational Behavior Teaching Review, 9*(4), 58–71.

Finkel, D. L. (2000). *Teaching with your mouth shut.* Portsmouth, NH: Boynton/Cook.

Finley, N. J. (1990). Meeting expectations by making new connections: Curriculum reform at Seattle Central. *Educational Record, 71*(4), 50–53.

Finley, N. J. (1995). Psychology in context: Making connections to other disciplines. *Teaching of Psychology, 22*(2), 105–108.

Fried, J. (1995). Border crossing in higher education: Faculty/student affairs collaboration. In J. Fried & Associates (Eds.), *Shifting paradigms in student affairs: Culture, context, teaching, and learning.* Landam, MD: American College Personnel Association.

Fulwiler, T. (1987). *Teaching with writing.* Portsmouth, NH: Boynton/Cook.

Gabelnick, F. (1997). Educating a committed citizenry. *Change, 29*(1), 30–35.

Gabelnick, F., Howarth, J., & Pearl, N. (1983). *Facilitating intellectual development in university honors students.* College Park, MD: University of Maryland Honors Program.

Gabelnick, F., MacGregor, J., Matthews, R. S., & Smith, B. L. (1990). *New directions for teaching and learning: No. 41. Learning communities: Creating connections among students, faculty, and disciplines.* San Francisco, CA: Jossey-Bass.

Gabelnick, F., MacGregor, J., Matthews, R. S., & Smith. B. L. (1992). Learning communities and general education. *Perspectives, 22*(1), 104–121.

Gaff, J. G. (1999). *General education: The changing agenda.* Washington, DC: Association of American Colleges and Universities.

Gamson, Z. F. (2000). The origins of contemporary learning communities: Residential colleges, experimental colleges, and living-learning communities. In D. DeZure (Ed.), *Learning from Change* (pp. 113–116). Sterling, VA: Stylus.

Gamson, Z. F., & Associates. (1984). *Liberating education.* San Francisco, CA: Jossey-Bass.

Gardiner, L. F. (2000). *Redesigning higher education: Producing dramatic gains in student learning.* San Francisco, CA: Jossey-Bass.

Gardiner, L. F. (1998). Why we must change: The research evidence. *Thought and Action, 16,* 71–88.

Gay, P. (1991). A portfolio approach to teaching a biology-linked basic writing course. In P. Belanoff & M. Dickson (Eds.), *Portfolios: Process and product* (pp. 182–193). Portsmouth, NH: Boynton/Cook.

Gillette, J., & McCollom, M. (Eds.). (1995). *Groups in context: A new perspective on group dynamics.* Reading, MA: Addison-Wesley.

Gilligan, C. (1982). *In a different voice: Psychological theory and women's development.* Cambridge, MA: Harvard University Press.

Golde, C. M., & Pribbenow, D. A. (2000). Understanding faculty involvement in residential learning communities. *Journal of College Student Development, 41*(1), 27–40.

Goodsell, A. S. (1993). *Freshman interest groups: Linking social and academic experiences of first-year students.* Unpublished doctoral dissertation, Syracuse University.

Goodsell, A. S., Maher, M., & Tinto, V. (Eds.). (1992). *Collaborative learning: A source book for higher education.* University Park, PA: National Center on Postsecondary Teaching, Learning and Assessment.

Goodsell, A. S., Russo, P., & Tinto, V. (1994). Building community among new college students. *Liberal Education, 79*(4), 16–21.

Goodsell, A. S., & Tinto, V. (1994). Freshman interest groups and the first-year experience: Constructing student communities in a large university. *The Journal of the Freshman Year Experience, 6*(1), 7–28.

Goodsell Love, A. (1999). What are learning communities? In J. H. Levine (Ed.), *Learning communities: New structures, new partnerships for learning.* Columbia, SC: University of South Carolina, National Resource Center for the First-Year Experience and Students in Transition.

Goodsell Love, A., & Tokuno, K. A. (1999). Learning community models. In J. H. Levine (Ed.), *Learning communities: New structures, new partnerships for learning* (pp. 9–17). Columbia, SC: University of South Carolina, National Resource Center for the First-Year Experience and Students in Transition.

Gordon, S. S. (1973). Living and learning in college. *Journal of General Education, 25,* 235–245.

Graff, G. (1992). *Beyond the culture wars: How teaching the conflicts can revitalize American education.* New York, NY: W. W. Norton.

Grass, R. (1974). The struggle for a living/learning community. *Change, 6*(8), 51–54.

Griffith, C. W. (1985). Programs for writing across the curriculum: A report. *College Composition and Communication, 36*(4), 398–403.

Guarasci, R., & Cornwell, G. H. (1997*). Democratic education in an age of difference.* San Francisco, CA: Jossey-Bass.

Halliburton, D. (1997). John Dewey: A voice that still speaks to us. *Change, 29*(1), 24–29.

Halpern, D. J. (1994). *Changing college classrooms.* San Francisco, CA: Jossey-Bass.

Heller, R. (1998). Learning communities: What does the research show? *AAC&U Peer Review, 1*(1), 11.

Henry, K. B., & Stein, H. K. (1998). Academic community in residence halls: What differentiates a hall with a living/learning program? *The Journal of College and University Student Housing, 27*(2), 9–13.

Herrington, A., & Moran, C. (1992). *Writing, teaching, and learning in the disciplines.* New York, NY: Modern Language Association.

Higher Education Research Institute, University of California–Los Angeles. (1996). *Social change model of leadership development* (Guidebook Version III). Los Angeles, CA: Author.

Hill, P. J. (1975). The incomplete revolution: A reassessment of recent reforms in higher education. *Cross Currents, 24,* 424–445.

Hill, P. J. (1985). Communities of learners: Curriculum as the infrastructure of academic communities. In L. W. Hall, & B. L. Kevles (Eds.), *In opposition to the core curriculum: Alternative models of undergraduate education* (pp. 107–134). Westport, CT: Greenwood.

Hill, P. J. (1985). *The rationale for learning communities.* Paper presented at the Inaugural Conference of the Washington Center for Improving the Quality of Undergraduate Education, Olympia, WA.

Horner, B. (2001). "Students' right," English only, and re-imagining the politics of language. *College English, 63*(6), 741–758.

Howard, R. M. (2001). Collaborative pedagogy. In G. Tate, A. Rupiper, & K. Schick (Eds.), *A guide to composition pedagogies* (pp. 54–71). New York, NY: Oxford University Press.

Hurd, S. N., Peckskamp, T. L., & Yonai, B. A. (2002). *Assessing learning communities: Student affairs/academic affairs collaboration.* Paper presented at The Ohio State University Conference on Living-Learning Programs, Columbus, OH.

Hurtado, S. L., Milem, J. F., Clayton-Pederson, A. R., & Allen, W. R. (1998). *Enacting diverse learning environments* (ASHE-ERIC Higher Education Report Series 26[8]). Washington, DC: George Washington University.

Hutchings, P. (1996). *Making teaching community property: A menu for peer collaboration and peer review.* Washington, DC: American Association for Higher Education.

Hutchings, P. (1998). *The course portfolio: How faculty can examine their teaching to advance practice and improve student learning.* Washington, DC: American Association for Higher Education.

Jackson, B., Levine, J., & Patton, J. (Eds.). (2000). *Restructuring for urban student success: Essay collection.* Washington, DC: ERIC Clearinghouse on Higher Education. (ERIC Document Reproduction Service No. ED 442 922)

Jackson, J. F. L., & Ebbers, L. H. (1999). Bridging the academic-social divide: Academic and student affairs collaboration. *College Student Journal, 33*(3), 380–384.

Jerome, J. (1971). The living-learning community. *Change, 3*(5), 46–55.

Johnson, D. W., Johnson, R. T., & Smith, K. A. (1998). *Active learning: Cooperation in the college classroom.* Edina, MN: Interaction Book Company.

Johnson, D. W., Johnson, R. T., & Smith, K. A. (1998). Cooperative learning returns to college: What evidence is there that it works? *Change, 30*(4), 27–35.

Johnson, J. L., & Romanoff, S. J. (1999). Higher education residential learning communities: What are the implications for student success? *College Student Journal, 33,* 385–399.

Jones, J. L. (1998). Master learners: Faculty development & the enhancement of undergraduate education. *Liberal Education, 84,* 42–47.

Jones, R. M. (1981). *Experiment at Evergreen.* Cambridge, MA: Schenkman.

Jones, R. M., & Smith, B. L (Eds.). (1984). *Against the current.* Cambridge, MA: Schenkman.

Jundt, M., Etzkorn, K., & Johnson, J. (1999). Planning the production: Scheduling, recruiting, and registering students in learning communities. In J. H. Levine (Ed.), *Learning communities: New structures, new partnerships for learning* (pp. 29–37). Columbia, SC: University of South Carolina, National Resource Center for the First-Year Experience and Students in Transition.

Kadel, S., & Keehner, J. A. (1994). *Collaborative learning: A sourcebook for higher education* (Vol. II). University Park, PA: National Center on Postsecondary Teaching, Learning and Assessment.

Kadel, S., Russo, P., & Tinto, V. (1995). Learning communities and student involvement in the community college. In J. Gardner & J. Hankin (Eds.), *Promoting new student success in community colleges.* Columbia, SC: University of South Carolina, National Resource Center for the First-Year Experience and Students in Transition.

Kanoy, K. W., & Bruhn, J. W. (1996). Effects of a first-year living and learning residence hall on retention and academic performance. *Journal of the Freshman Year Experience & Students in Transition, 51,* 201–211.

Kendall, J. (Ed.). (1990). *Combining service and learning: A resource book for community and public service* (Vol. 1). Raleigh, NC: National Society for Internships and Experiential Education.

Kerr, N. H., & Picciotto, M. (1992). Linked composition courses: Effects on student performance. *Journal of Teaching Writing, 11*(1), 105–118.

Ketcheson, K., & Levine, J. H. (1999). Evaluating and assessing learning communities. In J. Levine (Ed.), *Learning communities: New structures, new partnerships for learning.* Columbia, SC: University of South Carolina, National Resource Center for the First-Year Experience and. Students in Transition.

Kezar, A., & Rhoads, R. (2001). The dynamic tensions of service-learning in higher education: A philosophical perspective. *The Journal of Higher Education, 72,* 148–171.

King, P. M. (1978). William Perry's theory of intellectual and ethical development. In L. Knefelkamp, C. Widick, & C. A. Parker (Eds.), *New directions for student services: No. 4. Applying new developmental findings* (pp. 35–41). San Francisco, CA: Jossey-Bass.

King, P. M., & Kitchener, K. S. (1994). *Developing reflective judgment.* San Francisco, CA: Jossey-Bass.

Kirsch, G. (1988). Writing across the curriculum: The program at Third College, University of California, San Diego. *WPA: Writing Program Administration, 12*(1/2), 47–55.

Klein, T. (2000). From classroom to learning community: One professor's reflections. *About Campus, 5*(3), 12–19.

Knefelkamp, L. L. (1991). *The seamless curriculum. CIC Deans Institute: Is this good for our students?* Washington, DC: Council for Independent Colleges. (ERIC Document Reproduction Service No. ED 356 720)

Knoblauch, C. H., & Brannon, L. (1983). Writing as learning through the curriculum. *College English, 45*(5), 465–474.

Kolb, D. A. (1984). *Experiential learning: Experience as the source of learning and development.* Englewood Cliffs, NJ: Prentice Hall.

Komives, S. R., Lucas, N., & McMahon, T. R. (1998). *Exploring leadership: For college students who want to make a difference.* San Francisco, CA: Jossey-Bass.

Koolsbergen, W. (2001, Summer/Fall). Approaching diversity: Some classroom strategies for learning communities. *Peer Review,* 25–27.

Kouzes, J. M., & Posner, B. Z. (2003). *The leadership challenge* (3rd ed.). San Francisco, CA: Jossey-Bass.

Kuh, G. D. (1995). The other curriculum: Out-of-class experiences associated with student learning and personal development. *Journal of Higher Education, 66,* 123–155.

Kuh, G. D. (1996). Guiding principles for creating seamless learning environments for undergraduates. *Journal of College Student Development, 37*(2), 135–148.

Kuh, G. D., Pace, C. R., & Vesper, N. (1997). The development of process indicators to estimate student gains associated with good practices in undergraduate education. *Research in Higher Education, 38,* 435–454.

Kuh, G. D., Schuh, J. H., Whitt, E. J., & Associates. (1991). *Involving colleges: Successful approaches to fostering student development and learning outside the classroom.* San Francisco, CA: Jossey-Bass.

Kusnic, E., & Finley, M. L. (1993). Student self-evaluation: An introduction and rationale. In J. MacGregor (Ed.), *Student self-evaluation: Fostering reflective learning* (pp. 5–14). San Francisco, CA: Jossey-Bass.

Laib, C. J. (2002, March). Increasing our cultural competence. *The Diversity Campus Report,* 1.

Laing, J., Swayer, R., & Noble, J. (1989). Accuracy of self-reported activities and accomplishments of college-bound seniors. *Journal of College Student Development, 29,* 362–368.

Landa, A. (1981a). *Is there life after federated learning communities?* Stony Brook, NY: State University of New York at Stony Brook, Federal Learning Community Program.

Landa, A. (1981b). *Significant changes: Analysis and discussion of fifty-seven responses to the invitation, "Describe the Most Significant Changes You See in Yourself as a Result of the Federated Learning Communities Experience."* Stony Brook, NY: State University of New York at Stony Brook, Federated Learning Community Program.

Laughlin, J. S. (1997). WAC revisited: An overlooked model for transformative faculty development. *To Improve the Academy, 16,* 165–178.

Leean, C., & Miller, P. (1981). A university living-learning program: Factors that enhance or impede it. *Journal of College and University Student Housing, 11,* 18–22.

Lemonns, J., Carter, J., Grumbling, O., Morgan, P., & Sabowski, E. (1992). An integrated learning community to increase environmental awareness. *Environmental History Review, 16*(1), 64–76.

Lenning, O., & Ebbers, L. (1999). *The powerful potential of learning communities: Improving education for the future* [ASHE-ERIC Higher Education Report Series 26[6]). Washington, DC: George Washington University.

Levine, A. (1994). Guerilla education in residential life. In C. Schroeder & P. Mable (Eds.), *Realizing the educational potential of residence halls.* San Francisco, CA: Jossey-Bass.

Levine, A. L., & Cureton, J. S. (1998). *When hope and fear collide: A portrait of today's college student.* San Francisco, CA: Jossey Bass.

Levine, J. H. (1998). Building learning communities for faculty. *About Campus, 2*(6), 22–24.

Levine, J. H. (Ed.). (1999). *Learning communities: New structures, new partnerships for learning.* Columbia, SC: University of South Carolina, National Resource Center for the First-Year Experience and Students in Transition.

Levine, J. H., & Shapiro, N. S. (2000). Curricular learning communities. In B. Jacoby (Ed.), *New directions for higher education: No. 109. Involving commuter students in learning.* San Francisco, CA: Jossey-Bass.

Levine, J. H., & Shapiro, N. S. (2000). Hogwarts: The learning community. *About Campus, 5*(4), 8–13.

Levine, J. H., & Tompkins, D. (1996). Making learning communities work. *AAHE Bulletin, 48*(10), 3–6.

Light, R. J. (1992). *The Harvard assessment seminars: Explorations with students and faculty about teaching, learning, and student life* (second report). Cambridge, MA: Harvard University.

Lindblas, J. L. H. (1995). *Restructuring the learning environment: A cross-case study of three collaborative learning communities in American undergraduate education.* Unpublished doctoral dissertation, The Pennsylvania State University, College Park.

Love, A. G. (1999). What are learning communities? In J. H. Levine (Ed.), *Learning communities: New structures, new partnerships for learning*. Columbia, SC: University of South Carolina, National Resource Center for the First-Year Experience and Students in Transition.

Love, A. G., Russo, P., & Tinto, V. (1995). Assessment of collaborative learning programs: The promise of collaborative research. In Washington Center Evaluation Committee (Eds.), *Assessment in and of collaborative learning: A handbook of strategies*. Olympia, WA: Washington Center for Improving the Quality of Undergraduate Education.

Love, P. G., & Goodsell Love, A. (1995). *Enhancing student learning: Intellectual. social and emotional intention* (ASHE-ERIC Higher Education Report No. 4). Washington, DC: George Washington University.

Love, P. G., & Guthrie, V. L. (1999, Winter). *New directions for student services: No. 88. Understanding and applying cognitive development theory*. San Francisco, CA: Jossey-Bass.

Love, P. G., Kuh, G. D., MacKay, K. A., & Hardy, C. M. (1993). Side by side: Faculty and student affairs cultures. In G. D. Kuh (Ed.), *Cultural perspectives in student affairs work*. Washington, DC: American College Personnel Association.

Love, P. G., & Tinto, V. (1995). Academic advising through learning communities: Bridging the academic and social divide. In M. L. Upcraft & G. L. Kramer (Eds.), *First-year academic advising: Patterns in the present, pathways to the future*. Columbia, SC: University of South Carolina, National Resource Center for the First-Year Experience and Students in Transition.

Lunsford, A. A., & Ede, L. (1990). *Singular texts/plural authors: Perspectives on collaborative writing*. Carbondale, IL: Southern Illinois University Press.

MacGregor, J. (1987). Intellectual development of students in learning community programs, 1986–1987 (Washington Center Occasional Paper No. 1). Olympia, WA: The Evergreen State College.

MacGregor, J. (1990). Collaborative learning: Shared inquiry as a process of reform. In M. Svinicki (Ed.), *New directions for teaching and learning: No. 42. The changing face of college teaching* (pp. 9–30). San Francisco, CA: Jossey-Bass.

MacGregor, J. (1991). What differences do learning communities make? *Washington Center News, 6*(1), 4–9. Olympia, WA: Washington Center for Improving the Quality of Undergraduate Education.

MacGregor, J. (1992). Collaborative learning: Reframing the classroom. In A. Goodsell, M. Mahar, & V. Tinto (Eds.), *Collaborative learning: A sourcebook for higher education* (pp. 37–40). University Park, PA: National Center on Postsecondary Teaching, Learning and Assessment.

MacGregor, J. (Ed.). (1993). *New directions in teaching and learning: No. 56. Student self-evaluation: Fostering reflective learning.* San Francisco, CA: Jossey-Bass.

MacGregor, J. (1995). Going public: How collaborative learning and learning communities invite new assessment approaches. In Washington Center Evaluation Committee (Eds.), *Assessment in and of collaborative learning: A handbook of strategies.* Olympia, WA: Washington Center for Improving the Quality of Undergraduate Education.

MacGregor, J. (Ed.). (1999). *Strengthening learning communities: Case studies from the National Learning Communities Dissemination Project (FIPSE).* Olympia, WA: Washington Center for Improving the Quality of Undergraduate Education.

MacGregor, J. (2000, Spring). Teaching communities within learning communities. *Washington Center News, 9.*

MacGregor, J., Cooper, J. L., Smith, C. A., & Robinson, P. (2000). *New directions in teaching and learning: No. 81. Strategies for energizing large classes: From small groups to learning communities.* San Francisco, CA: Jossey-Bass.

MacGregor, J., Smith, B. L., Matthews, R. S., & Gabelnick, F. (1999). *Creating learning communities.* San Francisco, CA: Jossey-Bass.

Magnarella, P. J. (1979). The continuing evaluation of a living-learning center. *Journal of College Student Personnel, 20*(1), 4–9.

Magnotto, J. (1990). Prince George's Community College. In T. Fulwiler & A. Young (Eds.), *Programs that work: Models and methods for writing across the curriculum* (pp. 65–82). Portsmouth, NH: Boynton/Cook.

Malinowitz, H. (1998). A feminist critique of writing in the disciplines. In S. C. Jarratt & L. Worsham (Eds.), *Feminism and composition studies: In other words* (pp. 291–312). New York, NY: Modern Language Association.

Matthews, R. S. (1986). Learning communities in the community college. *Community College Technical and Junior College Journal, 57*(2), 44–47.

Matthews, R. S. (1994). Enriching teaching and learning through learning communities. In T. O'Banion (Ed.), *Teaching and learning in the community college* (pp. 179–200). Washington, DC: American Association of Community College.

Matthews, R. S., Cooper, J. L., Davidson, N., & Hawkes, P. (1995). Building bridges between cooperative and collaborative learning. *Change, 27*(4), 34–40.

Matthews, R. S., Smith, B. L., MacGregor, J., & Gabelnick, F. (1996). Learning communities: A structure for educational coherence. *Liberal Education, 82*(3), 4–9.

McCarthy, L. P. (1987). A stranger in strange lands: A college student writing across the curriculum. *Research in the Teaching of English, 21*(3), 233–265.

Meiklejohn, A. (1923). *Freedom and the college.* New York, NY: The Century Company.

Meiklejohn, A. (1932). *The experimental college.* New York, NY: Harper & Row.

Meyers, C., & Jones, T. B. (1993). *Promoting active learning: Strategies for the college classroom.* San Francisco, CA: Jossey-Bass.

Miller, M. (1982). On making connections. *Liberal Education, 69*(2), 101–107.

Millis, B. J., & Cottell, P. G., Jr. (1998). *Cooperative learning for higher education faculty.* Phoenix, AZ: ACE/Oryx.

Moore, D. M., & Kerlin, S. P. (1994). *Research report: Examining the effectiveness of coordinated studies:1990–1994.* Seattle, WA: North Seattle Community College.

Moore, W. (1990). *The measure of intellectual development (MID): An instrument manual.* Olympia, WA: Center for the Study of Intellectual Development.

Nelson, A. R. (2002). *Education and democracy.* Madison, WI: University of Wisconsin Press.

Newcomb, T. (1962). Student peer-group influences. In N. Sanford (Ed.), *The American college: A psychological and social interpretation of the higher learning* (pp. 469–488). New York, NY: John Wiley and Sons.

O'Banion, T. (1997). *A learning college for the 21st century.* Phoenix, AZ: Oryx.

Office of Learning Communities. (2000). *Mission statement.* Syracuse, NY: Syracuse University.

Pace, C. R. (1984). *Measuring the quality of college student experiences.* Los Angeles, CA: University of California–Los Angles, Higher Education Research Institute.

Pace, C. R., & Kuh, G. D. (1998). *College student experiences questionnaire* [survey instrument]. Bloomington, IN: Indiana University.

Palloff, R., & Pratt, K. (1999). *Building learning communities in cyberspace: Effective strategies for the online classroom.* San Francisco, CA: Jossey-Bass.

Palmer, P. (1987). Community, conflict, and ways of knowing. *Change, 19*(5), 20–25.

Palmer, P. (1998). *The courage to teach: Exploring the inner landscape of a teacher's life.* San Francisco, CA: Jossey-Bass.

Palmer, P. (2000, Spring). Learning communities: Reweaving the culture of disconnection. *Washington Center News,* 3–5.

Parks, G. (1992). *Food for thought—Did it help or not?: A comparative study of the effects of learning communities for pre-transfer composition.* Seattle, WA: Shoreline Community College.

Pascarella, E. T. (1996). Is differential exposure to college linked to the development of critical thinking? *Research in Higher Education, 37*(2), 159–174.

Pascarella, E. T., & Terenzini, P. T. (1991). *How college affects students.* San Francisco, CA: Jossey-Bass.

Pascarella, E. T., Terenzini, P. T., & Blimling, G. S. (1994). The impact of residential life on students. In C. L. Schroeder & P. Mable (Eds.), *Realizing the educational potential of residence halls* (pp. 22–52). San Francisco, CA: Jossey-Bass.

Pascarella, E. T., Whitt, E. J., Nora, A., Edison, M., Hagedorn, L. S., & Terenzini, P. T. (1996). What have we learned from the first year of the national study of student learning? *Journal of College Student Development, 37*(2), 182–92.

Peer Review. (2001, Summer/Fall). Washington, DC: Association of American Colleges and Universities. Retrieved December 30, 2003, from http://www.aacu-edu.org/peerreview/index.cfm

Perry, W. G. (1999). *Forms of intellectual and ethical development in the college years: A scheme.* San Francisco, CA: Jossey-Bass.

Pike, G. R. (1989). Background, college experiences, and The ACT-COMP exam: Using construct validity to evaluate assessment instruments. *Review of Higher Education, 13,* 91–117.

Pike, G. R. (1995). The relationships between self reports of college experiences and achievement test scores. *Research in Higher Education, 36,* 1–22.

Pike, G. R. (1999). The effects of residential learning communities and traditional residence living arrangements on educational gains during the first year of college. *Journal of College Student Development, 40*(3), 269–284.

Pike, G. R., Schroeder, C. C., & Berry, T. R. (1997). Enhancing the educational impact of residence halls: The relationship between residential learning communities and first-year college experiences and persistence. *Journal of College Student Development, 38*(6), 609–621.

Pope, R. L., & Reynolds, A. L. (1997). Student affairs core competencies: Integrating multicultural awareness, knowledge, and skills. *Journal of College Student Development, 38,* 266–277.

Potter, D. L. (1999). Where powerful partnerships begin. *About Campus, 4*(2), 11–16.

Reed, H. (1991). *Mathematics assessment project, 1990–1991.* Olympia, WA: The Evergreen State College.

Reumann-Moore, R., El-Haj, A., & Gold, E. (1997). *Friends for school purposes: Learning communities and their role in building community at a large urban university.* Philadelphia, PA: Temple University.

Rhoads, R. A., & Black, M. A. (1995). Student affairs practitioners as transformative educators. Advancing a critical cultural perspective. *Journal of College Student Development, 36,* 413–421.

Rong, Y. (1998). A literature review of the history and perspectives of college student classroom and residence hall learning. *Journal of College and University Student Housing, 27*(2), 3–8.

Russell, D. (1995). Activity theory and its implications for writing instruction. In J. Petraglia (Ed.), *Reconceiving writing, rethinking writing instruction* (pp. 51–78). Mahwah, NJ: Lawrence Erlbaum.

Ryan, M. B. (1992). Residential colleges: A legacy of living and learning together. *Change, 24*(5), 26–35.

Schein, H. K., & Bowers, P. M. (1992). Using living/learning centers to provide integrated campus services for freshmen. *Journal of the Freshman Year Experience, 4*(1), 59–77.

Schilling, K. M., & Schilling, K. L. (1999). Increasing expectations for student effort. *About Campus, 4*(2), 4–10.

Schneider, C. G., & Schoenberg, R. (1998). *The academy in transition: Contemporary understandings of liberal education.* Washington, DC: Association of American Colleges and Universities.

Schneider, C. G., & Schoenberg, R. (1999). Habits hard to break: How persistent features of campus life frustrate curricular reform. *Change, 31*(2), 30–35.

Schoem, D., Frankel, L., Zúñiga, X., & Lewis, E. A. (1993). *Multicultural teaching in the university.* Westport, CT: Praeger.

Schroeder, C. C. (1998). *Developing collaborative partnerships that enhance student learning and educational attainment.* Washington, DC: American College Personnel Association. Retrieved December 24, 2003, from http://www.acpa.nche.edu/srsch/charles_schroeder.html

Schroeder, C. C. (1999). Forging educational partnerships that advance student learning. In G. S. Blimling & E. J. Whitt (Eds.), *Good practice in student affairs: Principles to foster student learning* (pp. 133–156). San Francisco, CA: Jossey-Bass.

Schroeder, C. C., & Hurst, J. (1996). Designing learning environments that integrate curricular and cocurricular experiences. *Journal of College Student Development, 37*(2), 174–181.

Schroeder, C. C., & Maple, P. (1994). *Realizing the educational potential of residence halls.* San Francisco, CA: Jossey-Bass.

Schroeder, C. C., Minor, F., & Tarkow, T. (1999). Learning communities: Partnerships between academic and student affairs. In J. H. Levine (Ed.), *Learning communities: New structures, new partnerships for learning* (pp. 56–69). Columbia, SC: University of South Carolina, National Resource Center for the First-Year Experience and Students in Transition.

Schuh, J. H. (1999). Guiding principles for evaluating student and academic affairs partnerships. In J. Schuh & E. J. Whitt (Eds.), *New directions for student services: No. 87. Creating successful partnerships between academic and student affairs* (pp. 85–92). San Francisco, CA: Jossey-Bass.

Schuh, J. H. (Ed.). (1999). *Educational programming and student learning in college and university residence halls* (ACUHO-I monograph). Columbus, OH: The Ohio State University.

Schuh, J. H., & Whitt, E. J. (1999). *New directions for student services: No. 87. Creating successful partnerships between academic and student affairs.* San Francisco, CA: Jossey-Bass.

Senge, P. M. (1990). *The fifth discipline: The art and practice of the learning organization.* New York, NY: Doubleday.

Seymour, D. (1995). *Once upon a campus: Lessons for improving quality and productivity in higher education.* Phoenix, AZ: American Council on Education.

Shapiro, N. S., & Levine, J. H. (1999). *Creating learning communities: A practical guide to winning support, organizing for change, and implementing programs.* San Francisco, CA: Jossey-Bass.

Shapiro, N. S., & Levine, J. H. (1999). Introducing learning communities to your campus. *About Campus, 4*(5), 2–10.

Sharan, Y., & Sharan, S. (1992). *Expanding cooperative learning through group investigation.* New York, NY: Teachers College Press.

Silverman, A., & Schneider, L. (1997, May). *Report on learning communities for entering freshmen.* Garden City, NY: Nassau Community College.

Singleton, R. A., Jr., Garvey, R. H., & Phillips, G. A. (1998). Connecting the academic and social lives of students: The Holy Cross first-year program. *Change, 30*(3), 18–25.

Smith, B. L. (1991). Taking structure seriously: The learning community model. *Liberal Education, 77*(2), 42–48.

Smith, B. L. (1993). Creating learning communities. *Liberal Education, 79*(4), 32–39.

Smith, B. L. (1994). Team teaching methods. In K. Prichard & B. Mclarn Sawyer (Eds.), *Handbook of college teaching.* Westport, CT: Greenwood.

Smith, B. L. (2001). *The challenge of learning communities as a growing national movement.* Prepared for the Association of American Colleges and Universities Conference on Learning Communities, Providence, RI. Retrieved December 12, 2002, from http://www.cgc.maricopa.edu/learning/communities/pdf/lc_conf_2001.pdf

Smith, B. L. (2002, October 10). *The challenges of learning communities as a growing national movement.* Paper presented at the Making of Learning Communities on the Occasion of the 75th Anniversary of Alexander Meiklejohn's Experimental College, Madison, WI.

Smith, B. L., & Hunter, R. (1988). Learning communities: A paradigm for educational revitalization. *Community College Review, 15*(4), 45–51.

Smith, B. L., & Jones, R. M. (Eds.). (1984). *Against the current: Reform and experimentation in higher education.* Cambridge, MA: Schenkman.

Smith, B. L., & MacGregor, J. (1991). Reflective interviews with learning community teaching teams: Strengthening dialogue about teaching and learning. *Washington Center News, 6*(1), 26–28.

Smith, B. L., & McCann, J. (Eds.). (2001). *Reinventing ourselves: Interdisciplinary education, collaborative learning, and experimentation in higher education.* Bolton, MA: Anker.

Smith, K. A., & MacGregor, J. (2000). Making small-group learning and learning communities a widespread reality. In J. MacGregor, J. L. Cooper, K. A. Smith, & P. Robinson (Eds.), *Strategies for energizing large classes: From small groups to learning communities* (pp. 77–88). San Francisco, CA: Jossey-Bass.

Smith, T. B. (Ed.). (1993). *Gateways: Residential colleges and the first-year experience.* Columbia, SC: University of South Carolina, National Resource Center for the First-Year Experience and Students in Transition.

Smith, T. B. (1994). Integrating living and learning in residential colleges. In C. L. Schroeder & P. Mable (Eds.), *Realizing the educational potential of residence halls* (pp. 241–265). San Francisco, CA: Jossey-Bass.

Springer, L., Terenzini, P., Pascarella, E., & Nora, A. (1995). Influences on college students' orientations toward learning for self-understanding. *Journal of College Student Development, 36*(1), 5–18.

Sorensen, J. (1991, September 10). *Learning communities: A study of types of learning, retention and perceptions of students and faculty in linked and coordinated courses at Skagit Valley College.* Prepared for the Skagit Valley College Assessment Steering Committee.

Stage, F. K., Muller, P. A., & Kinzie, J. (1998). Creating learning centered classrooms: What does learning theory have to say? (ASHE-ERIC Higher Education Report No. 26). Washington, DC: George Washington University.

Stein, R. F. (1997). *Conditions that facilitate the implementation of innovative freshman experience courses: A comparative analysis of three courses.* Unpublished doctoral dissertation, Syracuse University.

Stein, R. F. (1999). *Gateway student forum report.* Syracuse, NY: Syracuse University, Center for Support of Teaching and Learning.

Stein, R. F. (2000). *Gateway student forum report.* Syracuse, NY: Syracuse University, Center for Support of Teaching and Learning.

Stein, R. F., & Hurd, S. N. (2000). *Using student teams in the classroom: A faculty guide.* Bolton, MA: Anker.

Student retention and success programs at Eastern Washington University: An overview. (1993). Cheney, WA: Eastern Washington University.

Study Group on the Condition of Excellence in Higher Education. (1984). *Involvement in learning: Realizing the potential of higher education.* Washington, DC: National Institute of Education.

Sullivan, C. (1991). *Supportive communication: An investigation of the effects of the freshman interest group program on perceptions of support and college adjustment.* Unpublished doctoral dissertation, University of Washington.

Sutton, M. (1978). The writing adjunct program at the Small College of California State College. In J. P. Neel (Ed.), *Options for the teaching of English: Freshman composition* (pp. 104–109). New York, NY: Modern Language Association.

Syracuse University. (2002, July 16). *Learning outcomes for WRT 105: Academic writing.* Retrieved December 24, 2003, from http://wrt.syr.edu/pub/handbook/105outcomes.html

Tatum, B. D. (1997). *"Why are all the black kids sitting together in the cafeteria?" and other conversations about race.* New York, NY: Basic Books.

Terenzini, P. T. (1994). The case for unobtrusive measures. In B. Townsend (Series Ed.), J. S. Stark, & A. Thomas (Eds.), *Assessment and Evaluation* (pp. 619–628). Needham Heights, MA: Simon and Schuster.

Terenzini, P. T., & Pascarella, E. T. (1994, January/February). Living with myths: Undergraduate education in America. *Change, 26*(1), 28–32.

Terenzini, P. T., Pascarella, E. T., & Blimling, G. (1996). Students' out-of-class experiences and their influence on learning and cognitive development: A literature review. *Journal of College Student Development, 37*(2), 149–162.

Theophilides, C., & Terenzini, P. T. (1981). The relation between non-classroom contact with faculty and students' perception of instructional quality. *Research in Higher Education, 15,* 225–270.

Thompkins, J. (1996). *A life in school: What the teacher learned.* Reading, MA: Addison-Wesley.

Thompson, K. (1991). *Learning at Evergreen: An assessment of cognitive development.* Olympia, WA: The Evergreen State College.

Tiberius, R. G. (1990). *Small group teaching: A trouble-shooting guide.* Toronto, Ontario: Ontario Institute for Studies in Education.

Tierney, W. G. (1993). *Building communities of difference: Higher education in the twenty-first century.* Westport, CT: Bergen and Garvey.

Tinto, V. (1993). *Leaving college: Rethinking the causes and cures of student attrition* (2nd ed.). Chicago, IL: University of Chicago Press.

Tinto, V. (1994). *Building learning communities for new college students.* University Park, PA: National Center on Postsecondary Teaching, Learning and Assessment.

Tinto, V. (1994). *Learning communities, collaborative learning, and the pedagogy of educational citizenship.* Chicago, IL: National Association of State Universities and Land-Grant Colleges.

Tinto, V. (1996). Reconstructing the first year of college. *Planning for Higher Education, 25*(1), 1–6.

Tinto, V. (1997, November/December). Classrooms as communities: Exploring the educational character of student persistence. *Journal of Higher Education, 68*(6), 599–623.

Tinto, V. (1998). Colleges as communities: Taking research on student persistence seriously. *Review of Higher Education, 21*(2), 167–177.

Tinto, V. (2000). What have we learned about the impact of learning communities on students? *Assessment Update, 12*(2), 1–2.

Tinto, V., & Goodsell, A. (1993). *A longitudinal study of freshman interest groups at the University of Washington.* A Study by the National Center for Postsecondary Teaching, Learning and Assessment. University Park, PA: The Pennsylvania State University.

Tinto, V., Goodsell, A., & Russo, P. (1993). Building community among new college students. *Liberal Education, 79*(4), 16–21.

Tinto, V., & Goodsell Love, A. (1993). Freshman interest groups and the first-year experience: Constructing student communities in a large university. *Journal of the Freshman Year Experience, 6*(1), 7–28.

Tinto, V., Goodsell Love, A., & Russo, P. (1994). *Building learning communities for new college students: A summary of research findings of the collaborative learning project.* University Park, PA: National Center on Postsecondary Teaching, Learning and Assessment.

Tinto, V., & Russo, P. (1993). *A longitudinal study of the coordinated studies program at Seattle Central Community College.* A Study by the National Center for Postsecondary Teaching, Learning and Assessment University Park, PA: The Pennsylvania State University.

Tinto, V., & Russo, P. (1994). Coordinated studies programs: Their effect on student involvement at a community college. *Community College Review, 22*(2), 16–25.

Tinto, V., Russo, P., & Kadel, S. (1994). Constructive educational communities: Increasing retention in challenging circumstances. *Community College Journal, 64,* 26–29.

Tinto, V., Russo, P., & Kadel-Taras, S. (1996). Learning communities and student involvement in the community college: Creating environments of inclusion and success. In J. N. Hankin (Ed.), *The community college: Opportunity and access for America's first-year students* (Monograph No. 19, pp. 135–141). Columbia, SC: University of South Carolina, National Resource Center for the First-Year Experience and Students in Transition.

Tokuno, K. (1993). Long-term and recent student outcomes of the freshman interest groups. *Journal of the Freshman Year Experience, 5*(2), 7–28.

Tokuno, K., & Campbell, F. (1992). Freshman interest groups at the University of Washington: Effects on retention and scholarship. *Journal of the Freshman Year Experience, 4*(1), 7–22.

Tollefson, G. (1990). *Collaborative learning communities in Washington community colleges.* Unpublished doctoral dissertation, Seattle University.

Tollefson, G. (1991). An outside-inside view: Faculty views of collaborative learning communities in Washington community colleges. *Washington Center News, 6*(10), 10.

Tompkins, U. P., & Mader, R. (1998). Creating learning communities among teachers: Faculty development in learning communities. *Metropolitan Universities, 9*(1), 17–24.

Tussman, J. (1969). *Experiment at Berkeley.* London, England: Oxford University Press.

Tussman, J. (1997). *The beleaguered college: Essays on educational reform.* Berkeley, CA: University of California, Institute of Government Studies Press.

University of Missouri–Columbia. (1996, Fall). A student success story: Freshmen interest groups at the University of Missouri–Columbia. *Student Life Studies Abstracts, 1,* 1–4.

University of Wisconsin–Oshkosh. (1994). *University learning community: Program evaluation, 1987–1994.* Oshkosh, WI: Author.

Waluconis, C. J. (1993). Self-evaluation: Settings and uses. In J. MacGregor (Ed.), *Student self-evaluation: Fostering reflective learning.* San Francisco, CA: Jossey-Bass.

Warren, R. G. (1997). Engaging students in active learning. *About Campus, 2*(1), 16–20.

Washington Center for Improving the Quality of Undergraduate Education. (1994). *The Washington Center casebook on collaborative teaching and learning.* Olympia, WA: The Evergreen State College.

Washington Center for Improving the Quality of Undergraduate Education. (1995). *Assessment in and of collaborative learning.* Olympia, WA: The Evergreen State College.

Washington Center for Improving the Quality of Undergraduate Education. (1998). *Seminars: A collection of materials on seminar approaches and evaluation strategies.* Olympia, WA: The Evergreen State College.

Wenger, E. (1999). *Communities of practice: Learning, meaning, and identity.* Cambridge, England: Cambridge University Press.

White, C. R. (1998). Placing community building at the center of the curriculum. In J. H. Levine (Guest Ed.), *Metropolitan Universities* [Special Issue: Learning Communities], *9*(1), 55–62.

White, K. (1990). *An application of Gadamer's hermeneutics through an empirical description of communication in a collaborative learning community.* Unpublished doctoral dissertation, University of Washington.

White, K., & Weight, B. (2000). *The online teaching guide: A handbook of attitudes, strategies, and techniques for the virtual classroom.* Boston, MA: Allyn and Bacon.

Wilkie, G. (1990). *Learning communities enrollment study, 1986–1990 at North Seattle Community College.* Seattle, WA: North Seattle Community College.

Wingspread Group on Higher Education. (1993). *An American imperative: Higher expectations for higher education.* Racine, WI: The Johnson Foundation.

Wlodkowski, R. J., & Ginsberg, M. B. (1995). *Diversity and motivation: Culturally responsive teaching.* San Francisco, CA: Jossey-Bass.

Woods, D. R. (1994). *Problem based learning: How to gain the most from PBL.* Hamilton, Ontario: McMaster University.

Youtz, B. (1984). The Evergreen State College: An experiment maturing. In R. M. Jones & B. L. Smith (Eds.), *Against the current.* Cambridge, MA: Schenkman.

Zawacki, T. M., & Williams, A. T. (2001). Is it still WAC? Writing within interdisciplinary learning communities. In S. H. McLeod, E. Miraglia, M. Soven, & C. Thaiss (Eds.), *WAC for the new millennium: Strategies for continuing writing-across the-curriculum-programs* (pp. 109–140). Urbana, IL: National Council of Teachers of English.

Zlotkowski, E. (Ed.). (1998). *Successful service-learning programs: New models of excellence in higher education.* Bolton, MA: Anker.

Index